T0364633

Quarter Century of Liberalisation in India

Quarter Century of Liberalisation in India

Essays from
Economic & Political Weekly

OXFORD
UNIVERSITY PRESS

Oxford University Press is a department of the University of Oxford.
It furthers the University's objective of excellence in research, scholarship,
and education by publishing worldwide. Oxford is a registered trademark of
Oxford University Press in the UK and in certain other countries.

Published in India by
Oxford University Press
2/11 Ground Floor, Ansari Road, Daryaganj, New Delhi 110 002, India

First Edition published in 2018

ISBN-13: 978-0-19-948107-1
ISBN-10: 0-19-948107-5

Typeset in Arno Pro 10.5/15
by The Graphics Solution, New Delhi 110 092
Printed in India by Replika Press Pvt. Ltd

Contents

III   Reforms, State Intervention and the Market

Preface

The narrative of India's economic "reforms" and liberalisation starts, in popular perception, from 1991. The debate over Nehruvian Socialism and its "ruination" of India's enterprise, however, predates this narrative by nearly four decades. The formation of the Swatantra Party in 1959 by proponents of the free market was one of the milestones. Indeed, the sharp exchange of opposing opinions continued through the 1960s. The piecemeal efforts towards liberalisation of the economy intensified in the late 1970s and mid-1980s, and found fruition in 1991 under the Congress government with Manmohan Singh as the Finance Minister. It is this year that marks a sharp turn towards the scrapping of industrial licensing, relaxing restrictions on foreign direct investment and imports. It marked the absolute belief in market forces and the virtues of competition. The events leading up to this have been reiterated often: the sharp rise in international oil prices, the mortgaging of India's gold stocks in the face of the dwindling foreign exchange reserves and eventually, the seeking of assistance from the International Monetary Fund. The pages of the *Economic Weekly* and later, the *Economic & Political Weekly* (*EPW*) are faithful witnesses to the opinions, insights and comments by the finest minds and boldest thinkers that spanned these decades.

To be sure, the course of the economy's turn away from the "old" was marked by criticism and opposition in 1991 and later. To a large extent the mainstream press reflected this and the behind-the-scenes political manoeuvring and jostling. The English press, however, particularly failed to critique and analyse these "reforms" in the context of the complexities of economic growth and development. The *EPW* carried on this singular task, among others.

This book is a collection of 13 articles that take a long and discerning look at the 1991 "reforms" and their impact over the past 25 years. These articles first appeared in *EPW* between July 2016 and March 2017. Among the authors are economists, educators and writers who were involved in the 1991 reform process, have studied and tracked its implications widely, and written on it extensively.

The shift of 1991 has generated tremendous changes, while pressing economic concerns and acute disparities remain. The articles reproduced in this book look back at this period of immense transition to explore the changes and continuity in the State's interaction with capital. These articles examine varied aspects of the Indian economy and society that are affected by liberalisation, and comment on the roadmap for the future. The debate over the effects of liberalisation will continue, and this volume undoubtedly offers valuable insights over the processes that liberalisation meant, a quarter century after its pronounced initiation in 1991.

We at the *EPW* are grateful for the patience and encouragement of the team at Oxford University Press India. We also acknowledge with thanks the contributions of the authors of the articles published herein and the erudite insights they bring to the pages of the *EPW*.

I

THE CASE OF 1991

The 1991 Reforms

How Home-grown Were They?

Montek S. Ahluwalia

Refuting the allegation that the 1991 reforms were thrust upon an unwilling government by the International Monetary Fund and the World Bank in return for financial assistance, it is argued instead that 1991 was the logical culmination of internal rethinking that took place well before the 1990 crisis. The reforms would have stopped within two years had they been only undertaken because of the need for the IMF's assistance. Though admittedly slowly, their continuation has been evident over successive governments.

೪⊷⊷ई

The 25th anniversary of the 1991 reforms is an important occasion for reflection. There were reforms before 1991, but they were at best incremental, adding flexibility to the system without changing the system itself. 1991 was the first time an effort was made to change the system of economic management, which was devised in the 1950s and early sixties, and had become quite unsuitable for the time.

The story of how the reforms were conceived and implemented, what went right and what did not, deserves to be told in full detail and I am currently working on a book that hopes to do precisely that. This article deals with only one aspect of the story and that is whether the reforms were home grown or were pushed by the IMF onto a helpless government, as a price for financial assistance. I argue that there was a home-grown process of rethinking on economic policy which had been underway, and pointed to the need to make many changes in policy. These changes were part of the adjustment programme submitted to the IMF to obtain assistance and in that sense they were part of the conditionality of IMF assistance, but that is not the same thing as saying that the IMF dictated the contents.

The Evolution of Thinking on Economic Policy

The domestic pedigree of the 1991 reforms is best assessed by looking at the evolution of thinking in the pre reforms period. It is useful in this context to distinguish between the period upto 1980, and the next decade.

The Period up to 1980

The period up to 1980 was a period of uncritical acceptance of the strategy for industrialization, fashioned in the fifties and early sixties. The strategy was conceptualized by P.C. Mahalanobis and drew heavily from the Feldman closed economy model in which faster growth needed higher investment, which required availability of capital goods. In a closed economy this was only possible if there was sufficient domestic production of capital goods. This led to the policy conclusion that investment should not only be increased, but most of it should be directed towards expanding capacity in the capital goods sector rather than consumer goods, as that would facilitate a rapid increase in the rate of investment over time. This was the rationale for pushing the public sector into these capital intensive areas, and also for controlling private investment through industrial licensing to ensure that scarce resources were not diverted to non-priority use. Critics at the time (e.g., Hannan Ezekiel) did point out that capital goods could needed to realize investment could have been imported and paid for by exports provided investment were directed towards export industries. This option was ruled out by the closed economy assumption, which was justified by export pessimism which was popular at the time.[1]

Comprehensive import licensing was introduced in 1956–57, initially to deal with balance of payments problems, but it became a permanent feature of the system with damaging consequences. Control over imports was seen as the only way of managing the balance of payments, and allocating scarce imports to so called priority uses. This gave the bureaucracy enormous discretionary power since imports were allowed only after clearance from the "indigenous angle", i.e., there was no domestic substitute available and also the "essentiality angle," i.e., the imported item was "really needed". Both decisions were taken by groups of officials and domestic producers typically lobbied strongly to deny imports.

The economy performed reasonably well under this strategy in the 1950s, when the growth rate averaged 3.6% and even the first half of the 1960s when it averaged 4.9%. This was lower than the 5% target, but it was much better that in the half century prior to independence when growth of GDP averaged only 1%. However, performance deteriorated sharply in the 1970s averaging only 3% per year, at a time when population was expanding by about 2.2%. This was a period when South East Asian countries grew much more rapidly, driven by strong export performance tapping expanding markets in industrialised countries.

India's heavy industry dominated industrial sector was ill suited to exploit export prospects in simple consumer goods. The private sector could have exploited these possibilities, but restrictions placed on private sector investment getting into "non priority areas", including the reservation of many of the items for small scale industry, made this difficult. In any case, pervasive domestic protection raised the cost of production in India, making Indian producers hopelessly uncompetitive.

These weaknesses were clearly brought out by Bhagwati and Desai (1970), but this did not lead to any reconsideration of policy. In fact, policy in the mid-seventies seemed to accept lower growth as unavoidable, and called for greater emphasis on programs aimed at directly benefiting the poor. The Fifth Five Year Plan for the period 1974–75 to 1978–79 stipulated a lower growth target of 4.4% and emphasized self-reliance to deal with balance of payments problems.

A natural opportunity to restructure policies arose when Indira Gandhi ended the Emergency in 1977, and called a general election. She was roundly defeated and a Janata party government, under Prime Minister Morarji Desai, took office in 1977. Morarji Desai was generally regarded as pro-business and it might have been thought that he could have tilted policies to make them a little more market friendly, with a greater role for the private sector, operating in a competitive environment. The government did set up the Committee on Controls and Subsidies under Vadilal Dagli, then editor of the well-known business weekly Commerce but its report was submitted in 1979, which was too late for any action since Morarji resigned in July 1979 to be replaced by Chaudhary Charan Singh, who resigned six months later in January 1980.

Debroy (2004) has called the Dagli Committee a forerunner of the 1991 reforms, but in my view it is a profoundly disappointing document. This is because it fully recognised the dysfunctionality of the control system, but failed to make specific recommendations for change. The Committee noted that the control system had become dysfunctional. Controls had proliferated, vesting considerable discretionary powers on the control authorities and generated corruption and delays.[2] However, when it came to recommendations, pronounced that each set of controls—industrial licensing control, Monopolies and Restrictive Trade Practices (MRTP) control, import control, price control, capital issues control etc—were all justifiable but they needed to be reviewed by the Ministries concerned to be sure they were indeed serving the purpose intended, and were exercised with transparency and that multiple points of control were avoided, etc., etc. Referring these issues to be decided by the Ministries administering the system was a guarantee that only marginal improvements would emerge.

Policy Rethinking after 1980

The Janata experiment ended in 1980 when a general election was called and was convincingly won by Mrs Indira Gandhi, who once again became Prime Minister in 1980. The new government initiated some important changes. One change was qualitative-controls under industrial licensing and MRTP remained in place, but they were administered more flexibly. The earlier bias against the private sector was greatly moderated and it was recognized that Indian industry needed to modernize and upgrade technology. 1982 was declared the year of productivity and some steps were taken to introduce flexibility. Automatic expansion of licensed capacity was allowed upto 25% over a five year period. The concept of "broad banding" was introduced which allowed automobile producers of four wheeled vehicles to switch from producing cars to producing any other four wheeled vehicle.

By the mid-1980s it was clear that deeper policy changes would be needed. Isher Ahluwalia (1984) examined the many different arguments advanced to explain the slow growth of Indian industry including the slowdown in agricultural growth or in import substitution, or public investment. She found that although lower investment in infrastructure did matter, the slowdown in industrial growth could not be explained by these factors. The main explanatory factor was a slowdown in total factor productivity growth. This suggested that the policy framework, including especially controls on investment and open ended protection, needed to be reviewed.

The first official recognition of the need to rethink the system of controls can be seen in the report of the Committee to Examine "The Principles of a Possible Shift from Physical to Financial Controls". The Committee, under the Chairmanship of M. Narasimham, was appointed in 1984 and submitted its report in 1985 (GoI 1985). The Committee acknowledged that while the system of controls had produced a diversified industrial sector, it was a high cost structure with insufficient attention to quality, and this was due to the way the strategy of import substitution was implemented, and internal competition discouraged by controls on investment and production. As a result, "the rate of industrial growth has been adversely affected and employment opportunities in the industrial sector have not expanded sufficiently. India could not also take advantage of the tremendous expansion in world trade which took place in the Sixties."

Unlike the Dagli Committee, the Narasimham Committee suggested specific changes including (a) delicensing of industries on the basis of certain criteria, although subject to existing controls on Foreign Direct

Investment (FDI) and MRTP; (b) shifting controls on import of capital goods from quantitative controls via licensing to tariffs, along with an outline plan on how to do it (c) raising the limit for MRTP controls from Rs 20 crores in terms of total investment to Rs 75 crores, and (d) establishing a quasi-statutory Securities and Exchange Board to oversee the functioning of the stock exchanges (although regulatory control was to be retained in the Finance Ministry). Unfortunately, the Narasimham Committee made no recommendations regarding the extensive import control on items other than capital goods.

Several steps were taken to liberalise the economy in the second half of the 1980s under the Prime Ministership of Rajiv Gandhi. A number of industries were freed from industrial licensing, and by 1990 30 industries had been delicensed. The MRTP limit was raised from Rs 20 crores to Rs 100 crores. Capital goods imports were liberalized, along with an increase in duty as recommended by the Narasimham Committee. The OGL window, which had begun with 79 capital goods items in 1976, had been widened to cover 1170 capital goods items and 949 items of raw materials and other intermediates by 1988.[3] It is worth noting however that these were mainly items not produced in India. Items produced in India remained subject to import licensing, although the system was administered more liberally, with greater recognition that imports were often justifiable to ensure the quality of domestic production.

The Securities and Exchange Board of India was established as a non-statutory body to begin with, to work on the outlines of a regulatory system for both the stock exchanges and capital issues, but with the intention of transferring these functions out of the Finance Ministry in due course.

India's economic performance improved in the 1980s with GDP growth averaging 5.6% over the decade, much higher than in the preceding period. There are different views on how much of the acceleration can be attributed to actual liberalisation, and how much to the more pro-business attitude of the government in operating the control system, Bradford deLong (2001) has argued that the latter was the dominant factor, but a good case can be made that the reforms, incremental though they were, did make a difference (see, for example, Panagariya 2004).

1990: The M Document

The next step documenting the internal rethinking on policy was a paper written by me in June 1990. This may seem to be an unseemly exercise in self projection, for which I apologise to readers, but as will become clear, it is relevant to the issue of how much of the thinking behind the reforms was home grown.

I had served as the Special Secretary to the Prime Minister, when Rajiv Gandhi was the Prime Minister, and I remained in that position when V.P. Singh took over. In the course of a conversation in May 1990, in which V.P. Singh commented on the performance of South East Asian countries, he asked me why these countries had done so much better than India. I responded that it was because they had been much bolder in undertaking structural reforms. He asked me to prepare a paper on what we should do and I prepared a note on "Restructuring India's Industrial and Trade Policies". The note put together ideas we had planned to submit to Rajiv Gandhi if he was reelected. V.P. Singh instructed that it should be discussed in the Committee of Secretaries chaired by the Cabinet Secretary.

The note was discussed in two meetings of the Committee of Secretaries. The Press soon got hold of a copy and it was printed in the Financial Express. Although the authorship of the paper was never acknowledged, it was widely known that it was authored by me, and it came to be referred to in the Press as the "M Document". The specific proposals in the M Document were never approved as government policy, but the fact that it was sent by the Prime Minister to the Committee of Secretaries for discussion establishes that the proposals were being considered internally. This was well before any IMF arrangement was contemplated, and indeed even before the crisis exploded.

The specific points made in the M Document[4] are summarized below.

Broad Approach

The M Document argued that the process of liberalization that had been underway needed to be taken further. It noted that most developing countries had already gone further than we had, and even the Eastern European countries were replacing state and bureaucratic controls with market economy mechanisms. India's competitive ability would suffer if our industry continued to operate in a restricted environment. It then went on to identify a reform programme in five inter related areas discussed briefly below. It explicitly excluded two important sectors—agriculture and infrastructure—which needed to be considered separately.

Macroeconomic Balance

The M Document emphasized the need to bring the fiscal deficit under control over a two year period. The measures suggested were to restrain defence expenditure, reduce subsidies and address the problem of over-staffing of Ministries. It suggested that a group under the Cabinet Secretary should advise on abolition of certain departments and mergers of other departments.

Public Sector Reform

It noted the enthusiasm for privatization in the world but did not endorse it. Instead, it took the view that India needed a strong public sector, and made some recommendations to strengthen it. (a) The system of price and purchase preferences, whereby public sector units gave preference to other public sector units in purchases, should be given up (b) Public sector units that are demonstrably unviable have to be closed down and while it may not be practical to close down all of them, we should make a start with closing down some and (c) It also recommended partial privatization to bring in new capital and inject a new management culture. ITDC and Air India were specifically mentioned in this context.

Industrial Licensing

The recommendations on industrial licensing in the M document were conditioned by the fact that the government had only a few days earlier, announced a new (and somewhat limited) liberalization of policy whereby projects below Rs 25 crore, (Rs 75 crore in backward areas) in a defined list of industries (to be announced later) would be exempted from industrial licensing subject to the conditions that imported capital goods were not more than 30% of the value of the investment and imports of raw materials and components were below 30% of the value of production. Some steps were proposed to increase the scope of delicensing within the framework of the policy recently announced, viz (a) the list of industries to be delicensed should be extensive (b) the list once announced should be expanded over time, (c) the value limit of the investment exempted from licensing should be progressively increased and (d) the import limits should also be pro- gressively relaxed.

MRTP Act

The M Document argued against subjecting proposals from MRTP houses to separate scrutiny, in order to prevent monopoly or avoid concentration of economic power. Prevention of monopoly was better achieved by increas- ing competition by delicensing investment in the area and also by freeing imports. It also pointed out that preventing the emergence of large Indian companies would hurt our ability to compete internationally, since world markets were dominated by large companies. It did not suggest an aboli- tion of the MRTP Act, but it suggested (a) that the asset limit for MRTP which was fixed in 1985 at Rs 100 crore, should be raised to "say Rs 300 or Rs 500 crores" and (b) various other flexibilities should be introduced for companies covered.

Reducing the Level of Protection

The proposals for reducing protection were in some ways the most important proposals in the M document. It emphasized that high levels of protection made the protected domestic market much more attractive than the highly competitive export market and it also raised the domestic cost structure making our exports uncompetitive. The higher cost structure could be offset to some extent through various export incentive schemes, these could never offset the full impact. It therefore recommend reducing duty protection to 30 to 40% by 1994–95, i.e., by more than 50 to 60% from their existing levels. Earlier reports had talked in general terms about reducing duties, but had not suggested a specific target for reduction.

It also recommended a shift from import licensing to tariff based protection. Consumer goods imports could continue to be banned, but all capital goods, intermediates, raw materials etc. should be freely importable subject only to duty protection.[5] Replacing licensing with tariffs would call for some increases in tariffs initially, but these tariffs would come down over time as part of phased duty reduction. It was emphasised that duties on imported of inputs should also be reduced, so that negative protection is avoided.

Recognising that reduced tariffs would be a shock to producers, the M Document argued that this could be cushioned by a depreciation of the rupee. Earlier Committees which recommended a phased reduction in duties over time, had not drawn attention to the need for parallel action on the exchange rate. For modest duty reduction productivity increases could be expected to offset the shock, but when duties are to be reduced from around 100% to say 30 or 40%, the productivity increase needed would be very large. The M Document argued that a real depreciation of 20% over a five year period would enable a substantial duty reduction to take place over the same period without shocking the system.

The M Document acknowledged that reduction in duties would have also have an adverse effect on revenue, and it argued that this needed to be offset by an increase in domestic tax revenues. Earlier recommendations favouring a phased reduction in tariffs, had ignored the revenue impact, although this would be a major concern of the Finance Ministry.

Finally, the M document recognized that there may be hesitation in embarking on import liberalization for fear of the consequences for the Balance of Payments. It therefore suggested a transitional mechanism of keeping import licensing in place, but liberalizing imports linked to tradeable replenishment licenses given to exporters. The existing system included replenishment licenses given to exporters at different rates to meet their need for imported inputs. It was suggested that the rates at which tradeable replenishment licenses were issued could be increased to 30% of export value for all products over a two year period, and any one wishing to import any restricted item that would otherwise require a license could do so against a replenishment license purchased from exporters. Since the volume of imports resulting from this particular liberalisation would be linked to export earnings, they would not destabilize the balance of payments. Excess demand for imports would lead to a higher premium on the licenses, which would incentivize exports and also serve as a guide to how far the exchange rate was out of line. One year later, the trade reforms in mid 1991 adopted precisely this approach, with the replenishment licenses renamed "Eximscrips".

Foreign Direct Investment

The M Document also proposed that the prevailing restrictive approach to foreign direct investment needed to be liberalised. It suggested a positive list of industries where foreign investment up to 40% should be "welcomed" with another high priority list where investment up to 51% would be allowed. This had been allowed recently for hotels, and it was proposed that it should be extended to manufacturing also. It also proposed a pro active approach towards good quality foreign investors by encouraging some of our large public sector organisations and private corporations, to seek out foreign investors as partners.

The reaction within government when the M Document was discussed in the Committee of Secretaries was mixed. Secretary Industrial Development Amarnath Verma, who later played a critical role in steering the reforms in 1991 as the Principal Secretary to the Prime Minister, was strongly supportive. He had only a month earlier succeeded in persuading the Industry Minister, Ajit Singh, to push a more aggressive industrial policy through the Cabinet, but it was opposed by the Finance Ministry and as a result only a weak initiative was cleared. The Planning Commission was especially critical because they had just prepared an approach paper for the Eighth Plan to be circulated to the National Development Council, which took a very different approach, emphasizing traditional labour intensive industries rather than modernization of industry. The Press had a field day reporting that some parts of the government were thinking differently from others. Several articles appeared in newspapers commenting on the proposals. Many were broadly supportive, although some demurred.

The Crisis of 1990: A Brief Recap

The internal rethinking summarized above pre dated the crisis. However, the reforms when they were actually introduced were against the backdrop of a balance of payments crisis of exceptional severity. A brief recap of the crisis itself is appropriate to give a sense of the urgency of implementing the reforms.

It is frequently said that the crisis of 1990 was triggered by the sharp increase in oil prices in August 1990 because of the Gulf War following Saddam Hussein's invasion of Kuwait. However, the oil price was not the only cause: if it had been, normalcy would have returned very quickly because oil prices fell back to normal by February 1991. There were two other factors that were important.

One was the macro economic imbalance in the form of high fiscal deficits which built up in the late 1980s. This generated excess aggregate demand, which spilt over into a large current account deficit, which in turn was financed by an increase in external borrowing, mainly in the form of

NRI deposits, and a steady erosion of foreign exchange reserves. This was clearly not a sustainable external situation and corrective action should have been taken in 1989. The need for such action was discussed internally, but an election was due towards the end of 1989, and it was felt that the adjustment programme, could be postponed until after the election.

As it happened, Rajiv Gandhi lost the election of 1989 and a new government was formed under Prime Minister of V.P. Singh. The V.P. Singh government lasted only eleven months, but this was time enough to take corrective action. V.P. Singh was also made aware of the problem, but it was ignored because political preoccupations took centre stage.

V.P. Singh had campaigned on the promise of empowering the backward classes by implementing the Mandal Commission recommendations extending reservation of seats in educational institutions and government jobs to the Other Backward Classes. This was announced in early August 1990 and it triggered an explosion of student protests, especially in North India. This was just about the time when the invasion of Kuwait sent oil prices sky rocketing, creating uncertainty about our exports to the region as well as remittances from it.

Domestic political instability made the crisis worse than it might otherwise might have been and the situation unravelled very quickly. The BJP withdrew support from the government and V.P. Singh was replaced by a minority government led by Chandrashekhar, supported from the outside by the Congress Party. This was an inherently unstable situation and no one believed that the government would last or could take tough decisions. There was an entirely predictable loss of market confidence. Foreign banks withdrew lines of credit and NRI deposits, which had become a substantial source of financing for the balance of payments, turned negative from October 1990 onwards. As expected, the Chandrashekhar government lasted only a few months—the Congress party withdrew its support in early March, triggering a general election.

Rajiv Gandhi campaigned vigorously for the may election in the hope of forming a Congress government. Tragically, in the last stage of the campaign, he was assassinated by a female Tamil terrorist who blew herself up as she bent to touch his feet. When the votes were counted, the Congress Party was in a position to form a government. Mrs Sonia Gandhi was invited to lead the party but declined and P.V. Narasimha Rao was elected the leader.

Manmohan Singh's Convocation Address at IIM Bangalore

Before moving to what was done by the new government it is important to note that just before the election, in April 1991, Dr Manmohan Singh, who had just returned from Geneva at the end of his term as Secretary General of the South Commission, delivered the Convocation address at the IIM Bengaluru. He knew at the time that the country was facing a crisis, and his remarks were therefore made in the context of a crisis. The address outlined a course of action outlined by Dr Singh in his capacity as a technocrat and it is important because it is a reflection of what he thought was the professionally correct thing to do. What he did not know at the time was that two months later, he would be directly in charge of handling the crisis.

The address called for action on both the fiscal deficit and on structural reforms to improve efficiency and growth. On the fiscal deficit, the address was conventional, focusing on the need to contain current expenditure and reduce subsidies. The difficulty in reducing subsidies, especially food subsidies, was recognized but it was suggested that in other cases the ends envisaged could be better met by other means. Export subsidies could be replaced by a more aggressive use of the exchange rate, which is exactly what happened. Fertiliser subsidies could be reduced by raising fertiliser prices, without affecting fertiliser use, provided procurement prices were also raised. The address also dealt with tax reforms to generate the revenue needed for rural infrastructure and universalizing access to basic social services like health and education. It called for "a broad based, moderately progressive and elastic tax system so that tax revenue can increase faster than national income even without frequent revision of tax rates". The tax structure should also have "built in incentives to promote savings, and reward risk-bearing activities" (Singh 1991).

On structural reforms, the address recommended a number of innovative approaches.

(a) On the role of the public sector, it boldly called for a reconsideration of the Industrial Policy Resolution of 1956, which reserved certain industries exclusively for the public sector. Public enterprises operating in competition with private sector enterprises would have greater incentives to perform well and it would also be easier to judge their performance.

(b) Privatisation was ruled out, but the address urged that we should think of ways to increase autonomy and accountability. Loss making PSUs that are patently unviable needed to be closed, but in a manner which protected the interest of labour, including through provision a social safety net so that the cost of adjustment is not borne exclusively by labour.

(c) On industrial licensing and MRTP control the address was crystal clear. It said firms must be free to expand and diversify in the light of their perception of market opportunities. The objective of discouraging investment flowing to "low priority activities", was better met by having a short negative list of industries where capacity creation is discouraged.

(d) On foreign trade control, it said that the acute balance of payments difficulties meant that import restrictions could not be dispensed with immediately, but this should not become an excuse to perpetuate the regime of quantitative import controls. Full participation in the emerging global economy necessitated progressive liberalization of import controls and exchange controls. He called for a well thought out plan to make the rupee a convertible currency in a reasonable period of time, in any case before the end of the decade.

The 1991 Reforms

The new Congress Government, headed by P.V. Narasimha Rao, was sworn in on June 21 and it was clear that it faced a desperate situation. Foreign exchange reserves had dropped continuously to reach a low of $1.1 billion in April, only enough for two weeks' imports. There was speculation that a default on payments might be imminent. Prime Minister Rao was advised that he should get a technocrat as Finance Minister, and preferably one who was well regarded in international financial circles, and Manmohan Singh fit the bill perfectly.

Manmohan Singh had very little time to send out signals that would restore confidence. Within a few days of the government taking office, he devalued the rupee by about 20% in a two step operation. A depreciation of the exchange rate was an essential aspect of any serious adjustment programme, but it was also highly sensitive politically. There is no doubt that the government's willingness to act firmly on this matter helped create credibility in markets. Shortly thereafter, an unprecedented series of reforms in many different areas, were rolled out and the rationale for the reforms was outlined in Dr Manmohan Singh's Budget speech of July 24.

The reforms could be broadly described as proceeding on two tracks (a) stabilization by reducing the fiscal deficit with a view to containing excess aggregate demand, and thereby containing the balance of payments deficit and (b) structural reforms, aimed at improving efficiency and thereby stimulating growth. There was general agreement that stabilization through belt tightening was necessary, though of course there were different views on exactly how the belt should be tightened, and who should feel the greatest pinch. The real controversies however related to the structural reform component which was designed to put the economy on a higher growth path in which benefits would flow to all segments.

The structural reforms represented a significant departure from the past, giving much greater play for market forces, reducing the role of the public sector, and opening the economy to foreign trade and foreign investment. To many, they seemed completely contrary to long held perceptions on India's economic strategy, and it was perhaps natural for opponents to claim that they were forced upon the government by the IMF. However, a comparison of what was actually done, with the proposals that were being considered in the course of internal policy rethinking as documented above, demonstrates that the reforms had a strong domestic pedigree.

A key feature of the reforms was the delicensing of all except 18 industries, where licensing control was retained for security and environmental reasons. This was in the direction proposed by the Narasimham Committee and also the M document, though the action taken was much bolder, and fully in line with the Convocation address at Bangalore.

The reforms also abolished the separate approval under the MRTP Act that was required for so called large houses. This was again in the direction proposed earlier, but much bolder in line with the Bangalore convocation address.

The list of items reserved exclusively for the public sector was reduced from 17 to 8, consisting of industries with a security aspect. This was entirely in line with the Convocation address in Bangalore. Instead of privatization, there was to be partial "disinvestment" of government equity to financial institutions and mutual funds in order to raise non inflationary finance for the government and to create a culture of working which would encourage efficiency. It was also announced that the Sick Industrial Companies Act would be amended to bring PSUs under its purview, so that sick public sector units could be subjected to the same discipline regarding closure as the private sector. Both steps were in line with what had been said in the M Document and later in the Convocation address.

The extent of import licensing was drastically cut by making imports earlier allowed on OGL or on import licenses freely importable against Eximscrips issued to exporters at 30% of the value of exports (or 40% in some cases). This was fully in line with the transitional arrangement recommended in the M Document.

At the time the Eximscrip idea was announced, it was also announced that government would move to full convertibility of the rupee on the current account in three to five years which was a much shorter time span than the decade suggested in the Convocation address. As it happened, we moved even more rapidly by replacing the Eximscrips with a dual exchange rate in March 1992 whereby exporters of goods and services

(Eximscrips did not apply to services) would surrender 40% of their earnings at the official rate and retain 60% of their earnings to be sold freely in the open market to be used for imports and service payments. Within one year, i.e., on March 1, 1993, the exchange rate was unified and became a floating rate.

The entire planning for the introduction of the Eximscrip and the transition to a unified floating rate was homegrown and not even pushed by the IMF though they supported it after it was announced. The pace of the transition was also much faster than the IMF imagined was possible.

The rules regarding foreign investment were liberalised in several ways. Foreign equity, which hitherto had been restricted to 40% and not necessarily on an automatic basis, was automatically allowed up to 51% in a range of priority industries. Equity above 51% was permitted subject to clearance by a newly established Foreign Investment Promotion Board, which was expected to adopt a pro active approach in attracting investment. Equity beyond 51% was initially subjected to the condition that foreign exchange outflow on dividend payments on the additional equity above 40% be balanced by export earnings. These proposals were broadly in line with what was suggested in the M Document and also the Convocation address. The condition regarding balancing dividend payments with export earnings was unduly restrictive and was removed within a year.

The Convocation address had spoken of tax reforms. A Committee under Raja Chelliah was appointed to recommend reforms in taxation (both direct and indirect taxes) and the recommendations of this Committee guided tax policy reforms for the next several years. A similar Committee under M. Narasimham guided reforms in the financial sector.

The Reforms and After

The 1991 reform were generally well received by the Press as signaling a resolve to deal with the crisis, but there were reservations from several quarters. The Left were profoundly suspicious of the scaling down of the role of the public sector, the weakening of control over large houses, greater reliance upon market forces and especially external liberalisation. This was despite the fact that Deng Tsiao Peng's industrial reforms in China had been pressing in this direction since 1983, giving China a headstart of more than a decade over India. The Left was also unaffected by the collapse of statist models in East Europe, soon to be followed by the collapse of the Soviet Union itself, less than six months after the 1991 reforms.

Indian industry had a mixed reaction. They welcomed the removal of controls on domestic investment, but they were ambivalent about the external competition via imports and especially the liberalization for FDI. A group of industrialists, christened by the Press as the Bombay Club, argued that Indian industry needed time before they could make themselves ready to face competition. We know in retrospect that these fears were overdone. Indian industry did get a lot of time. Large parts of the industrial sector, such as the entire consumer goods range, were not opened to imports until 2002, eleven years after the reforms began. FDI also did not flow in very quickly, although many foreign companies began to express interest. On the whole, those domestic companies that adapted to the new environment and opportunities came out stronger.

An assessment of the full impact of the reforms is well beyond the scope of this article, but one aspect of the post reforms performance is worth mentioning. The performance of the economy in the years after the reforms certainly belied the fears of those who had warned of a negative impact on growth. However, it is also true that the growth rate in first ten years or so after the reforms was not markedly higher than the growth rate in the 1980s. This led Dani Rodrik and Arvind Subramaniam (2004) to argue that the shift to a more pro business attitude in the 1980s was perhaps more important in raising growth than the deeper reforms of the 1990s, including external liberalisation, which were otherwise much applauded.

This is an important point and I would like to list the reasons why I disagree. First, the high growth of the 1980s was partly due to the expansionary fiscal policy that was followed in the second half of the 1980s, and to that extent part of the growth in the 1980s could be called unsustainable.

Second, retaining a restrictive set of controls but operating them liberally is not the best way of building a strong private sector, and could even become a recipe for cronyism. It was important to move to a system that would transparently provide flexibility for all, which is what the reforms of 1991 did. Third, opening the economy was critical for the longer term health of the economy. There can be little doubt that we would not have seen the explosion in the IT services and soft ware sector if the external reforms had not been undertaken. Rodrick and Subramaniam do not deny this.

Perhaps the most important point about the post reforms performance is that because of gradualism, the impact of the deeper reforms of the 1990s took time to materialize. On this view, the effect of the cumulative reforms which started in 1991 but continued over subsequent years is best reflected in the fact that the growth rate of the economy in the thirteen years 2003–04 to 2015–16 averaged 7.7%, much higher than achieved in the pre reform period. Furthermore, contrary to the fears that opening the economy would increase our vulnerability, we have not needed to go to the IMF in this period, despite two external shocks—the financial crisis in 2008 and the Eurozone crisis in 2011. This is also a period when poverty fell much faster in period 2004–05 to 2011–12, which is the latest period for which data are available, than in the earlier periods.

Conclusions

The limited purpose of this article was to show that what was done in 1991, was a logical culmination of a home grown process of rethinking. In fact, the policy response in the area of both trade and exchange rate policy went well beyond what the IMF and the World Bank had thought possible. Equally, the conscious exclusion of privatisation made the reform programme very different from what the IMF and the World Bank would have liked.

Two other points are relevant to establish that the reforms were not imposed from outside. First, the IMF programme ended within two years, and we did not need to make subsequent drawings under the ESAF, which we were considering. Nevertheless, the reforms continued, at a slower pace admittedly, but they did continue. Had the government only been forced to undertake the reforms because of the need for IMF funding, it could have reversed course from 1994 onwards. It did not.

Second, the "working consensus" in favour of the reforms went beyond the Congress Government. The left leaning United Front Government that followed, under Prime Ministers Deve Gowda and Inder Gujral, supported by the Left parties, continued down the same track. So did the subsequent NDA Government under Prime Minister Vajpayee. Politicians in each party criticized the policy initiatives when they were in the opposition, but this did not prevent them from continuing the very same policies in office, and on many occasions even strengthening them.

There are important lessons here. Democracy is not a consensual form of government. It is an adversarial form in which it is the business of the opposition to oppose. Claiming a consensus on reforms when they are introduced runs the risk of an immediate denial by the political opposition, whose function is to oppose. This often worries investors, but they need to separate the noise from the signal, and in a democracy the noise to signal ratio is typically high. What is really important is that there should be no sudden disruptive reversals in policy just because governments change. Indian policy making since 1991 has survived that test thus far. That said, it is fair to say that the economy would have been better off if the reforms had been implemented faster and with greater clarity about intent.

Notes

1. The fact that the models actually used in the Planning Commission allowed for both exports and imports does not negate this criticism, since exports in these models were typically fixed exogenously and served only to determine the maximum value of imports the economy could sustain.

2. Delays are integrally connected with corruption since they become the instrument for extracting bribes.

3. See Pursell (1992) and Panagariya (2004).

4. The "M Document" can be found at: http://www.epw.in/system/files/The%20M%20Document%201990%20%281%29.pdf

5. Conceding continuation of a ban on consumer goods imports was primarily on political grounds. These items were typically produced by smaller producers and it was logical to first get the prices of basic intermediates, produced by much larger producers in line with world prices before opening this sector to competition.

References

Ahluwalia, Isher Judge (1985): *Industrial Growth in India: Stagnation since the Mid-sixties*, Delhi: Oxford University Press.

Bhagwati, Jagdish and Padma Desai (1970): *India: Planning for Industrialization, Industrialization and Trade Policies since 1951*, Delhi: Oxford University Press.

DeLong, J Bradford (2001): "India since Independence: An Analytical Growth Narrative," *Modern Economic Growth: Analytical Country Studies*, Dani Rodrik (ed), Princeton, NJ: Princeton University Press.

Debroy, Bibek (2004): *India: Redeeming the Economic Pledge*, New Delhi: Academic Foundation.

GoI (1985): "Report of the Committee to Examine Principles of a Possible Shift From Physical to Financial Controls," January, Government of India, New Delhi.

Panagariya, Arvind (2004): "India in the 1980s and 1990s: A Triumph of Reforms," IMF Working Paper No WP/04/43, March, International Monetary Fund, Washington DC.

Pursell, Garry (1992): "Trade Policy in India," *National Trade Policies*, Dominick Salvatore (ed), New York: Greenwood Press, pp 423–58.

Rodrik, Dani and Arvind Subramanian (2004): "From Hindu Growth to Productivity Surge: The Mystery of the Indian Growth Transition," IMF Working Paper No WP/04/77, May, Washington DC.

Singh, Manmohan (1991): "Challenges on the Economic Front Today," excerpts from the 16th Annual Convocation Address at IIM Bangalore, Indian Institute of Management Bangalore, 15 April, viewed on 7 July 2016, http://www.iimb.ernet.in/node/264.

Economic Liberalisation in India

Then and Now*

Deepak Nayyar

Even if adjustment and reform in 1991 were driven by economic compulsions, it was the political process that made these possible. However, liberalisation was shaped largely by the economic problems of the government rather than by the economic priorities of the people or by long-term development objectives. Thus, there were limitations in conception and design, which have been subsequently validated by experience. Jobless growth, persistent poverty and rising inequality have mounted as problems since economic liberalisation began. And, 25 years later, four quiet crises confront the economy, in agriculture, infrastructure, industrialisation and education as constraints on the country's future prospects. These problems must be resolved if economic growth has to be sustained and transformed into meaningful development. In this quest, India needs a developmental state for its market economy to improve the living conditions of her people.

కోల

For the economy of independent India, 1991 was a tumultuous and momentous year that witnessed radical departures from the past. Over the past six months, it has been the focus of much discussion not only in the media, but also among scholars in economics and politics. This is no

*This is the second part of *EPW*'s special issue "25 Years of Economic Liberalisation". Part 1 was published in the issue dated 16 July 2016.

surprise. It is 25 years since July 1991, when economic liberalisation began life in India. For those who lived through the times as adults, it is etched in memories as a watershed. For those who were young, or at school, or not yet born, it is essentially folklore.

The object of this article is to analyse economic liberalisation in India during the past quarter century. In doing so, it traces its origins and examines its limitations, to discuss the implications of outcomes that have unfolded, and problems that have surfaced for economic development in India. The article is divided into three parts. The first part outlines the story of 1991 to focus on how liberalisation began life, to consider not only the economics but also the politics of the process. The second part sets out the economic rationale of reforms and changes introduced then to examine the limitations that were discernible at the time and have been subsequently validated by experience. The third part shifts attention to the present to highlight some outcomes and some problems, visible now, that might constrain future development prospects, and suggests what needs to be done. In conclusion, the article argues that it is absolutely essential to rethink and redefine the economic role of the state in the quest for development.

The Story of 1991

At the outset, before starting my narrative of those times, there is a disclosure to be made. I lived through that era as Chief Economic Adviser to three successive governments in a span of two years marked by economic crises and political uncertainties. As a witness to, and participant in, the process, there are three propositions I wish to stress here. First, the story of July 1991 began much earlier although it surfaced in late 1990. Second, there were many actors, in leading or supporting roles, in this drama. Third, it was the largely ignored political process, driven by the economic compulsions of the time, which made liberalisation possible.

It is essential to trace the origins of what transpired then, simply because history fosters our understanding of reality. During the 1980s, the competitive politics of populism reinforced by the cynical politics of soft options led governments into a spending spree. But it was not possible for the government, or the economy, to live beyond its means year after year. Government finances became progressively unsustainable. The inevitable crunch did come in the form of an acute economic crisis that was waiting to happen (Nayyar 1996). It was triggered by an increase in world crude oil prices, following Iraq's invasion of Kuwait in August 1990. This minor oil shock was the proverbial last straw that broke the camel's back (Bhaduri and Nayyar 1996). The balance of payments situation became almost unmanageable. The fear of acceleration in the rate of inflation loomed large. The underlying fiscal crisis was acute. The uncertain political situation, which was superimposed on an economy already under severe strain, exacerbated problems.

The V.P. Singh government that assumed office in December 1989 inherited the problem as legacy. But it did not act soon enough, probably lulled into false comfort by the same advisers who had assured Rajiv Gandhi that the situation could be managed. However, the minor oil shock did strengthen a growing cognition of the impending crisis. Alas, the political situation became more complicated. There were mounting strains in the coalition supported by the Bharatiya Janata Party (BJP) and the left from outside but not in government. Growing agitations on reservations for Other Backward Classes compounded problems. Even so, in early October 1990, Singh authorised initiating negotiations with the International Monetary Fund (IMF). This was in sharp contrast with Rajiv Gandhi's decision, in September 1989, to reject a proposal that suggested approaching the IMF.

In November 1990, Singh lost the vote of confidence in Parliament and was succeeded by Chandra Shekhar as Prime Minister. To begin with, the then Prime Minister was hostile to the IMF. A cabinet minister, who promised to bring $2 billion from the Sultan of Brunei and superrich non-resident Indians (NRIs), was given two weeks' time. It was no surprise that he failed to deliver. A fortnight later, as it became clear that there was no such miracle on the horizon, Shekhar authorised a resumption of negotiations with the IMF. The resistance was transformed into an acceptance based on the realisation that India was close to defaulting on its international payments obligations and an understanding that the IMF was needed not simply as a lender of the last resort but also for its imprimatur essential to restore international confidence.

Achilles Heel of Economy

The external debt crisis and payments situation was the Achilles heel of the economy. It was particularly vulnerable for three reasons: short-term debt was about $6 billion, of which $2 billion was rolled-over every 24 hours with overnight borrowing in international capital markets; outstanding NRI deposits, more than $10 billion, were prone to capital flight, while foreign exchange reserves were a mere $1 billion that were not enough to finance imports even for a fortnight, let alone debt service payments (Nayyar 1996). The prospect of default hung over our heads like the sword of Damocles.

The negotiations with the IMF, which I led, had the complete support of Yashwant Sinha, then Finance Minister, and Shekhar. The use of the first credit tranche and the Compensatory and Contingency Financing Facility (to help meet the increased cost of petroleum imports) at the IMF helped raise $1.8 billion in January 1991 after tough bargaining almost without conditions. The Union Budget exercise began in right earnest and was completed. The broad contours of this budget, which could not be presented to Parliament by Sinha as scheduled in February 1991 because the Congress party withdrew support, were broadly the same as what was ultimately presented in July 1991.

The accentuated political uncertainties that surfaced were juxtaposed with an already formidable macroeconomic crisis. The challenge was to manage the crisis in the short term and return the economy to a path of sustained growth with price stability in the medium term. It was fire-fighting day-by-day, surviving month-by-month, while working at solutions, and strategising for what needed to be done when a government was in place. This was an exercise in multitasking. The IMF loan provided some breathing time, but not for long, as the relentless pressure of the liquidity crunch persisted. Cash margins on imports were raised from a substantial 50% to a whopping 200% in March 1991. Some debt service payments, on earlier defence purchases, were deferred through discussion and mutual agreement. As events unfolded, it seemed that all these efforts might not be enough.

There was a caretaker government and a general election to come. The assassination of Rajiv Gandhi in May 1991 in the midst of the elections prolonged the interregnum. Foreign exchange reserves were perilously low. There was capital flight from non-resident deposits. In April 1991, the caretaker government decided to ship 20 tonnes of gold, confiscated from smugglers, to raise $200 million from the Union Bank of Switzerland through a sale with a repurchase option. In a society where only a bankrupt household would mortgage its gold, and Shekhar said so in chaste Hindi when he approved, it was a brave decision that was also high risk.

These events do highlight the resilience of the political process despite all its flaws and warts. Two short-lived governments that inherited an economic crisis made tough decisions instead of postponing the day of reckoning. The governmental system and its institutions did everything possible to avert default even when there was no elected government that could make policy decisions.

P.V. Narasimha Rao assumed office as Prime Minister on 21 June 1991, and appointed his Cabinet, with Manmohan Singh as Finance Minister, three days later. Critical decisions were made within one month. Exchange rate adjustments, which were announced in two steps on 1 and 3 July, led to a depreciation of the rupee by 23.3% vis-à-vis the US dollar. Gold from the reserve assets of the Reserve Bank of India (RBI), 47 tonnes, was shipped out soon thereafter to raise $405 million from the Bank of England and the Bank of Japan. On 24 July 1991, the Statement on Industrial Policy announced dramatic changes in the morning, while the union budget presented to Parliament announced far-reaching decisions, way beyond the remit of conventional budgets, in the evening. Around then, I was also tasked to negotiate a Stand-By Arrangement with the IMF and a Structural

Adjustment Loan with the World Bank, both of which were concluded in September 1991. It must be said that any government that had come to power in mid-1991 would have done roughly the same. The blueprints existed. There was little choice. And the room for manoeuvre was negligible. However, it was possible only for a government elected by the people to make these decisions.

Even so, there is a political question that arises. How were such far-reaching changes introduced by what was then a minority government (some of which were announced even before it had established its majority in Parliament), while Rajiv Gandhi with an overwhelming majority was unable to do so despite stated intentions to liberalise?

The answer is provided by reality in the national context and conjuncture in the international context (Bhaduri and Nayyar 1996). For one, the changes were dictated by the immediate economic compulsions of crisis management, combined with a political realisation that the outside world was no longer willing to lend to India and that governments can become insolvent even if countries do not go bankrupt. For another, the collapse of communism and the break-up of the erstwhile Union of Soviet Socialist Republics (USSR) removed the countervailing force that had always been a prop for India, to replace competing ideologies with a dominant ideology.

There were three other supportive factors. The emerging concerns about efficiency and productivity had led to rethinking about the economic policies, through the late 1980s, so that the manifesto of every political party for the 1991 elections, across the ideological spectrum, talked about the need for restructuring the economy. There was also a consciousness among politicians across parties, which did not necessarily mean an understanding, about the crisis in the economy. Above all, the political system was somewhat tired of conflict, so that opposition parties were simply not willing to bring down the government and force another round of elections.

Obviously, there is nothing better than a crisis to focus minds. Yet, debates might have continued and laws of inertia—characteristic of the economy and the polity in India—might have prevailed. It was a minority government that had not yet won its vote of confidence, which acted promptly and decisively. There can be little doubt that its actions were largely crisis-driven, which would simply not have been possible to conceive or design, in the short span of one month, without plans-in-place put together by many individuals and institutions in the governmental system over the preceding six months, if not longer. Yet, it would be reasonable to ask who the decisive factor among the dramatis personae was at the time. Until not so long ago, the common perception was that Manmohan Singh, the then Finance Minister, and Prime Minister later for a decade, was the architect of economic liberalisation. This was not so. In fact, recent reportage, interviews and analyses have corrected that popular belief. And, Rao, Prime Minister then, has received some recognition and credit, even though the Congress party has sought to minimise, if not erase, his role from memories. These correctives have also been made explicit in two recently published books (Sitapati 2016; Baru 2016).

It was Rao, the consummate politician, who made a difference. In sharp contrast with his own political past, he was most decisive in this incarnation, particularly on the economy. The decisions about the exchange rate adjustments, the shipping of gold from RBI vaults, the tough measures incorporated in the union budget designed to sharply reduce the fiscal deficit, including the substantial increase in the prices of petroleum products, the slashing of subsidies on fertilisers and food, turned out to be possible essentially because Rao was so decisive, whether in the cabinet committees or in discussions with concerned ministers and officers. He could indeed have kept a plaque on his table that read "the buck stops here".

Prime Minister Narasimha Rao was just as deft in political management. He saw that political support for economic reforms was minimal. There was no consensus even in the ruling party, let alone across the political spectrum, about what needed to be done. But he recognised the political value of the reality in the national context and the conjuncture in the international context. And he exploited to the fullest the three other supportive factors mentioned above. Even if silence did not mean consent he treated it as acceptance. There were a few trade-offs, or compromises, but he did not waver.

Rationale and Limitations

Beyond the narrative, it is necessary to set out the rationale for the changes introduced in mid-1991, in the wider context of the economy. This would help highlight the striking differences with the past, which would also help examine the limitations in conception and design that were discernible at the time, and have been subsequently validated by experience.

There were earlier episodes of liberalisation in the late 1970s and the mid-1980s, which were perceived as correctives for an industrialising economy, but did not contemplate any fundamental changes in the objectives or strategy of development (Nayyar 1994). The changes in 1991 were significant enough to be characterised as a shift of paradigm. It is worth highlighting three dimensions (Nayyar 1996). First, the essential objective was economic growth combined with economic efficiency. The earlier concerns about equity were subsumed in the pursuit of growth on the premise that it would reduce poverty. Second, there was a conscious decision to substantively reduce the role of the state in the process of development and rely far more on the market. In doing so, the large share of the public sector in investment and output would be reduced, while the government would no longer guide the allocation of scarce investible resources in the private sector. Third, the degree of openness of the economy in trade, investment and technology was sought to be increased significantly and rapidly. The idea was to enforce a cost-discipline on the supply side, and the hope was that foreign investment and foreign technology would perform a strategic role in industrialisation.

The economic reforms introduced in July 1991 had two components: macroeconomic stabilisation and structural reform. The object of the former was to manage the fragile balance of payments situation by reducing the current account deficit and curb inflationary expectations by reducing the rate of inflation. The focus was on the demand side. The time horizon was the short-run. Once the economy in crisis had stabilised, this adjustment at the macro level was expected to return the economy to a path of sustained growth. The object of the latter was to raise the rate of growth of output. The focus was on the supply side. The time-horizon was the medium-term and beyond. Structural reform was meant to shift resources from the non-traded goods sector to the traded goods sector (within it from import-competing activities to export activities) and from the government sector to the private sector, to improve resource allocation. It was also meant to improve resource utilisation by increasing the degree of openness of the economy and by changing the structure of incentives which would reduce the role of the government to rely more on the market, dismantle controls to rely more on prices, and wind down the public sector to rely more on the private sector.

Prudent Macroeconomic Management

For an economy in crisis, a return to prudent macro-management of the economy was both necessary and desirable. The fiscal adjustment in the union budget for 1991–92 was sorely needed. The exchange rate adjustment was necessary to stem destabilising expectations, dampen imports and stimulate exports. Even the sale and pledge of gold was an important symbolic gesture that helped restore confidence in international capital markets. There was no default on international payments obligations. The economy in crisis was stabilised. In the short-run, the contraction in demand led to a sharp slowdown in growth. But the current account deficit was reduced to manageable proportions within three years. It took a little longer for the rate of inflation to drop below double-digit levels. Growth in gross domestic product (GDP) returned to pre-crisis levels in five years (Nayyar 2001). In this transition from crisis to stabilisation, India did far better than most developing countries.

The limitation was that the idea of prudent macro-management was reduced to a fetishism about the gross fiscal deficit of the government (Nayyar 1996). The size of the fiscal deficit, or the amount of government borrowing is the symptom and not the disease. And there is nothing in macroeconomics which stipulates an optimum level to which the fiscal deficit must be reduced as a proportion of GDP. Indeed, it is possible that a fiscal deficit at 6% of GDP is sustainable in one situation, while a fiscal deficit at 3% of GDP is unsustainable in another situation. The real issue is the use to which government borrowing is put in relation to the cost of borrowing by the government. Thus, government borrowing is always sustainable if it is used to finance investment and if the rate of return on such investment is higher than the interest rate payable (Bhaduri and Nayyar 1996). The misplaced emphasis on the gross fiscal deficit led to a neglect of the revenue deficit (revenue receipts plus non-tax revenues minus consumption expenditure) which shows whether the fiscal situation is sustainable, or the primary deficit (gross fiscal deficit minus interest payments) which shows whether the fiscal situation is getting better or worse.

The focus of structural reforms was on the industrial sector, the trade regime, foreign investment, foreign technology, the public sector and the financial sector.

Industrial policy reform removed barriers-to-entry for new firms and limits on growth in the size of existing firms. The dismantling of the complex regime of controls on investment decisions embedded in the licence–permit raj was both necessary and desirable. But there was no symmetrical removal of barriers-to-exit. And no anti-trust legislation was put in place (Nayyar 1996). The competition law came more than a decade later. It is a watchdog mostly without teeth, so that it does not effectively regulate the market to ensure necessary competition among domestic firms.

Trade policy reform abolished the complex import-licensing system, slashed import tariffs and eliminated export subsidies. Some of this was much needed. But import liberalisation hurt the manufacturing sector and the problem was exacerbated by the absence of effective anti-dumping laws. Exposure to international competition was meant to force domestic firms to become more efficient but the pace of change could have enforced closures rather than efficiency at a micro level. In terms of speed and sequence, increased openness in trade should have been compatible with initial conditions and consistent with each other (Nayyar 1996, 2004).

Similarly, the policy regime for foreign investment and foreign technology was liberalised at a rapid pace, in the hope of stimulating non-debt-creating capital inflows and enhancing international competitiveness. There was nothing selective or strategic about this approach, which was necessary to foster industrialisation. It also failed to recognise that imports of technology cannot substitute for domestic technological capabilities. There was a clear and present danger that such non-discriminatory openness could simply replace domestic firms by foreign firms, instead of making domestic firms more competitive with foreign firms, in the manufacturing sector.

Public sector reform sought to reduce the activities of the public sector, facilitate the closure of loss-making units and ease the burden on the exchequer on account of the public sector. It was long on words and short on substance. In fact, it was mostly about asset-sales or closures, which meant selling the flagships and keeping the tramp-ships, or sending a few white elephants to the slaughter house. The dire need to restructure public sector firms or increase their efficiency was simply neglected (Nayyar 1996, 2004).

Financial sector reform sought to improve the profitability of government-owned commercial banks and the functioning of the domestic capital market, assuming that the discipline of market forces alone will achieve both objectives. Reform dispensed with over-regulation but did nothing to address the problem of under-governance by creating institutional structures and legal frameworks for governance. The short-term outcome was that scams proliferated (Bhaduri and Nayyar 1996). The deregulation and liberalisation of the financial sector also carried the risk of changing incentives and rewards in its favour at the expense of the real sector of the economy.

Apart from these specific limitations in each sphere, there are some general analytical limitations in the economic logic underlying structural reforms. First, resources are neither as mobile nor as substitutable in use across sectors as orthodoxy believes. In fact, economies are characterised by structural rigidities rather than structural flexibilities. Second, the belief that getting-prices-right makes an elementary but common-place error in the design of policies. It confuses *comparison* (of equilibrium positions) with *change* (from one equilibrium position to another). In the real world, economic policy must be concerned not only with comparison but how to direct the process of change. Third, the presumption that policy regimes that are necessary are also sufficient is wrong. Policy regimes can allow things to happen but cannot cause things to happen. And there is nothing automatic about competition. The creation of competitive markets that enforce efficiency may, in fact, require strategic interventions through policies, just as it may require the creation of institutions.

It is clear enough that both macroeconomic adjustment and structural reforms were driven by economic problems confronting the government in mid-1991. The immediate short-term compulsions were managing the critical balance of payments situation, manifest in the external debt crisis, and controlling inflation to restrain inflationary expectations. The medium-term needs were finding a sustainable solution to the fiscal crisis, through fiscal adjustment, and returning the economy to a path of sustained growth, through structural reforms that would increase in the productivity of investment and make the economy more efficient in its use of resources. The economic priorities of the people and long-run national development objectives were not part of either the conception or the design of economic liberalisation at the time.

The problems of management of the economy are largely the concern of the government and, with the exception of inflation, do not concern the people of India. Economic priorities, however, are a different matter, for these are determined by the needs and aspirations of people. Those who live in absolute poverty do not have the incomes to meet their basic human needs in terms of food, clothing and shelter, leave alone healthcare and education. For the poor, who do not have any assets and have nothing to sell but their labour, employment is the only means of improving their living conditions and eradicating their poverty. Yet, poverty and employment were simply not part of the discourse on economic liberalisation. There was an unstated presumption that economic growth would reduce poverty and create employment.

Similarly, the debate on economic liberalisation proceeded as if the agricultural sector or rural India does not exist or, if it exists, it does not matter. This was incredible for an economy in which two-thirds of the workforce was directly or indirectly employed in agriculture, while rural India was home to a larger proportion of the total population and to more than three-fourths of the poor. Obviously, no sensible restructuring of the economy is even thinkable without a clear perspective on agriculture. For ordinary people in India, their well-being is also shaped by the infrastructural facilities, whether physical infrastructure such as roads, electricity, public transport and railways, or social infrastructure such as drinking water, sanitation facilities, health services and schools. The high-priests of economic liberalisation were more concerned with expenditure cuts for fiscal adjustment and believed that, the private sector would provide what the government could not.

The focus of economic liberalisation, then, was so much on the short-run or the medium-term, that national development objectives in the long-run were largely neglected. It is ironical that so little was said or done about social sectors—education and health—in an economy where improving the quality of human resources was the only means of mobilising our most abundant resource, people, for development. There was a similar neglect of managerial and technological capabilities among firms and technological development in the economy at the macro level (Nayyar 2011).

Outcomes and Problems

It is not possible to provide a systematic assessment of economic liberalisation over the past 25 years. This would need another article. However, it is possible to highlight some outcomes that have unfolded and some problems that have surfaced, particularly those which have implications for the future.

The rapid economic growth in India is often attributed to economic liberalisation but this is not quite correct. If we consider the 20th century in its entirety, the turning point in economic performance, or the structural break in economic growth, is 1951–52. If we consider the period 1950–51 to 2000–01, the turning point in economic growth is

1980–81 (Nayyar 2006). During the 20th century, the most significant structural break, or departure from the long-term trend in economic growth, was 1951–52, followed by 1980–81. In either case, 1991 was not a turning point (Nayyar 2006; Rodrik and Subramanian 2005). And even if we consider period 1980–81 to 2010–11 (since growth slowed down starting 2011–12), the turning point is 2003–04. Therefore, it is not possible to attribute the significant jump in India's growth performance to economic liberalisation even on a post hoc, ergo propter hoc basis. Of course, it is likely that economic liberalisation contributed to sustaining rapid growth rates from the mid-1990s, just as the boom in the world economy contributed to the further acceleration in growth rates during 2003–04 to 2007–08.

It is just as important to recognise that India has met with more success than most developing countries and transition economies following economic liberalisation. This success is, to a significant extent, attributable to institutional capacities which existed at the time that the reforms were introduced. And the essential foundations were provided by the preceding four decades of economic development in India. The entrepreneurial abilities were created. A system of higher education was developed. The social institutions and the legal frameworks necessary for a market economy were in place. In this milieu, it was possible to create new institutional capacities with relative ease. Given the importance of initial conditions, it must also be recognised that economic reforms in India yielded benefits in significant part because of the essential foundations that were laid in the preceding four decades. The politics of democracy was the other critical factor that sustained the process in India.

This performance is impressive in aggregates but conceals as much as it reveals, for growth is necessary but not sufficient. It is important to remember that per capita income is an arithmetic mean. Social indicators of development are also statistical averages. Neither captures the well-being of the poor or the common man, because the distribution is so unequal. And it is not as if all is well with the economy as a whole. There are three persistent, yet mounting, crises manifest in jobless growth, persisting poverty and rising inequality. A long-term view reveals the quiet, almost silent, crises in agriculture, infrastructure, industrialisation and education. The persistent crises, which could worsen in the future, are discernible in retrospect through the era of economic liberalisation.

Jobless Growth, Persistent Poverty, Rising Inequality

The first persistent crisis is the phenomenon of jobless growth. The biggest failure of the past 25 years is that, despite such rapid economic growth, employment creation has simply not been commensurate. In fact, the employment elasticity of output declined steadily from reasonably high levels during 1972–73 to 1983 (0.60) through modest levels during 1983 to 1993–94 (0.41), to low levels during 1993–94 to 2004–05 (0.17) and 2004–05 to 2011–12 (0.04). In fact, between 2004–05 and 2011–12, employment elasticity of output in agriculture (−0.42) and in manufacturing (0.13) plummeted, as compared to the 1983 to 1993–94 period when it was much higher in both agriculture (0.49) and manufacturing (0.47) (IHD 2014).

The second persistent crisis is that poverty persists on a large scale even after three decades of the most rapid economic growth, faster than anywhere in the developing world, as also in history, except for China. Of course, growth has helped bring about a significant reduction in absolute poverty. Yet, its incidence remains high. In 2011–12, at least 25%, possibly 30%, of 1.2 billion people live in absolute poverty below the critical minimum in terms of food and clothing. These are the perennial poor. If we were to use a higher poverty line that allows for other basic needs such as appropriate shelter, adequate healthcare and education, it is estimated that about 75% of the population lives in absolute poverty. These are the vulnerable poor. The population between the two poverty lines, more than 40% of the total is vulnerable to any shock such as a bad harvest, high inflation, or an illness in the family which could push them deeper into poverty. In fact, in 2011, of the total number of poor in the world (below each of the two poverty lines), around one-third lived in India (Nayyar 2017).

The third persistent crisis, which has worsened in the era of economic liberalisation, is rising inequality. In fact, but for this, rapid growth in GDP would have reduced poverty far more. The evidence on trends in inequality is fragmented and incomplete. Even so, it is clear. Between 1990 and 2010, the Gini coefficient of consumption inequality in India (estimated from the National Sample Survey Office [NSSO] data) rose from 29.6 to 36.8 (Nayyar 2017). The increase in income inequality is bound to have been significantly greater because the poor save little or dis-save, while it is the rich who save. Atkinson (2015) estimates that the Gini coefficient of income inequality in India in 2010 was almost 50. The share of the super-rich, the top 1%, in national income rose from 5% in 1980 to 12% in 2000, while the share of the ultra-rich, the top 0.1%, in national income rose even more from 1% in 1980 to 5% in 2000 (Atkinson and Piketty 2012).

The four quiet, almost silent, crises in the economy, which loom large as potential constraints on future prospects, are at least in part a consequence of what was done and what was not done in the era of economic liberalisation.

The first is the almost silent crisis in agriculture that runs deep, perhaps much worse than it was in the mid-1960s. But there is little discernible cognition. Its near absence from the discourse on the economy, and the radar screen of the public domain, suggests that agriculture's long neglect has worsened in the era of economic liberalisation. Farmers' suicides are reported in the newspapers. Maoist movements are considered law and order problems. But neither of these are recognised as symptomatic of deeper crises in rural India. Between 1993–94 and 2011–12, the share of the agricultural sector in GDP dropped from 25% to 15%, while its share in total employment dropped from two-thirds to less than one-half. Thus, GDP per capita in the agricultural sector has been only one-tenth of GDP per capita in the non-agricultural sector for the past 25 years. Yet, its political significance shaped by its share of votes in a democracy is directly proportional to its share in the population. Its potential economic significance is also considerable since incomes from agriculture could drive economic growth from the demand side. Agriculture needs serious attention across a wide range. There is need to revive extension facilities, including credit for inputs that had been provided by state governments but were wound up progressively during the 1990s in the hope that markets would do it better. There is need to revive public investment in irrigation as private tube wells are rapidly depleting the groundwater potential. There is need to develop technologies for dry land farming. There is need to create transportation, storage and processing facilities for fruits and vegetables that perish without reaching consumers. There is need to develop rural infrastructure, whether roads or power, which would help promote non-agricultural rural employment.

The second quiet crisis is in infrastructure. The physical infrastructure—power, roads, transport, ports, and communications—is grossly inadequate. Some of it is creaking at the seams. Some of it is on the verge of collapse. The story is much the same for the social infrastructure—education and health-care, or even sanitation facilities and safe drinking water. In this milieu, human development is at risk and economic growth is unsustainable. The ideological belief in the magic of markets has led to a premature withdrawal of the state from public investment in infrastructure, but private investment, whether domestic or foreign, has simply not been forthcoming. Faith in the much touted public–private–partnership model represents a triumph of hope over experience. It is almost a non-starter. Even where it has materialised, in a few places, there is a socialisation of costs and privatisation of benefits. The role of the state, and the importance of public action, in creating a physical and social infrastructure cannot be stressed enough. Without it, growth cannot be sustained, let alone be transformed into development.

The third quiet crisis in the economy, just about discernible, is its industrialisation that is not at par with emerging economies in the developing world. This suggests regress as compared with the past, as there was progress until 1990. Independent India created the initial conditions and laid the essential foundations for industrialisation during the period from the late-1940s to the mid-1960s. Its enormous industrial potential was unlocked by developing infrastructure and a capital goods sector, emphasising higher education, science and technology, designing intervention and support from the government, formulating industrial and trade policies, and nurturing managerial and technological capabilities. India did learn to industrialise (Lall 1987), although necessary changes in strategy or policies were not introduced in the 1970s to enhance competitiveness in price and quality. Even so, by the mid-1980s, some success was visible in pharmaceuticals, two-wheelers, auto components, and clothing, when the information technology sector was also born. The share of manufacturing in GDP reached its peak level of 17.3% in 1979–80 and fluctuated in the range of 16% until 1995–96 when it was 17.3% once again, to hover in the range of 15–16% until 2007–08 but declined thereafter to 12.9% in 2013–14 (Nayyar 2017a). India's share in manufacturing value added in, and manufactured exports from, the developing world declined steadily in the two decades from 1990 to 2010 (Nayyar 2013). This was in sharp contrast with the steadily rising shares not only of China but also of Indonesia, Malaysia and Thailand (Nayyar 2013; ADB 2013).

Beginnings of De-industrialisation?

Between 1995–96 and 2013–14, the share of manufacturing in India's GDP dropped by more than four percentage points, to a level less than one-half of that in the aforesaid Asian countries. This does suggest the beginnings of de-industrialisation. In fact, during the past 25 years, India's progress in terms of industrialisation has been most disappointing. This outcome contradicts the claims of those who argued that economic liberalisation would increase efficiency and foster growth of the manufacturing sector. India needs to industrialise for obvious reasons. Manufacturing can utilise its most abundant resource, labour, through employment creation; drive productivity increase through linkages, spillovers or externalities in other sectors; and unleash India's enormous industrial potential embedded in its pool of entrepreneurs, just as it can mobilise its managerial and technological capabilities so much in evidence among migrants in industrialised countries. The revival of industrialisation in India, inter alia, requires radical changes in monetary policy, correctives in exchange rate policy, calibration of trade policy, and a rebirth of industrial finance. Strategic coordination of these policies in a long-term perspective, often described as industrial policy, was at the foundations of success at industrialisation elsewhere in Asia. Without such a coordinated policy mix, "Make in India" will be no more than a fond hope.

The fourth quiet, almost silent, crisis is in education. But for those who know this world, it stares us in the face. The educational opportunities for our people are simply not enough and what exists is not good enough. This is true across the entire spectrum from primary education and secondary education, through vocational education, to higher education, and professional or technical education. Learning outcomes are often poor. The excellence in a few islands in each of these domains is deceptive. It is created by the enormous reservoir of talent and a Darwinian selection process. Institutions and individuals possibly excel despite the system, which is just not conducive to learning and does little for those with average abilities or without social opportunities. The comparative advantage that India had in a few segments of higher education is being slowly, yet surely, squandered. It would seem that the education sector is caught in a pincer movement.

At one level, there is a belief that markets can solve the problem through private players, which is leading to treating education as business, shutting the door on large numbers who do not have the means to finance themselves. At another level, governments that believe in the magic of markets are virtual control freaks with respect to public educational institutions. This is motivated by the desire to exercise political influence in education for patronage, rents and vested interests, as politicians are also in the business of education. It strangles autonomy and stifles creativity without creating any accountability. The quality of education is collateral damage. There is a desperate need for reform and change in education. It is not rocket science. And there are blueprints galore. It needs political will. This can only come from recognition that the spread of education in society is at the foundations of development everywhere, in which primary education is the base and higher education is the cutting edge.

In Conclusion

It would seem that economic liberalisation introduced in 1991 was shaped largely by the economic problems of the government rather than by economic priorities of the people and long-term development objectives of the nation. This needs correction. It is essential to attach the highest priority to the economic aspirations of ordinary people, the common man, so that liberalisation improves their well-being. This is not possible unless the role of the state in India's market economy is redefined with clarity. The real shortcoming, if not failure, is that this has not even been attempted over the past 25 years. It is now an imperative if we think of the next 25 years.

The second half of the 20th century witnessed a complete swing of the pendulum in thinking about the role of the state in economic development. We moved from a widespread belief, prevalent in the 1950s, that the state could do nothing wrong, to a gathering conviction, fashionable in the 1990s, that the state could do nothing right. The dramatic change in thinking was attributable to past experience (inappropriate or excessive intervention) and the conjuncture in time (collapse of communism), reinforced by the dominant political ideology of the times (markets and capitalism). This ideology is now subject to question everywhere, in the wake of the market-driven financial crisis and the persistent recession in the world economy. It is no longer dominant in the world outside. In India, however, the belief in markets remains strong among the literati and the influential, because of rapid economic growth and because of little faith in governments. Even if failures or limitations of markets are recognised, concerns about inept or corrupt governments are larger than life.

More-of-the-same or business-as-usual is obviously neither acceptable nor desirable. In India, it is time to rethink and redefine the role of the state in a market economy in a very different national context, 70 years after independence, and a profoundly changed international context. Such rethinking can be set out in terms of two simple propositions (Bhaduri and Nayyar 1996). First, the state and the market are, by and large, not substitutes; instead they must complement one another in many spheres.

Second, the relationship between the state and the market cannot be speci-fied once-and-for-all in any dogmatic manner; instead the two institutions must adapt to one another through cooperation, rather than conflict, as the economy develops. Given that the entrepreneurial talents of the private sector and the capabilities of the government sector, as also the needs of the economy, change over time, this relationship must be flexible and adap-tive. In such a milieu, the state and the market can provide mutual checks and balances that function as institutionalised self-correcting mechanisms when things go wrong. Indeed, the history of capitalism suggests that success at economic development is observed mostly in countries where governments and markets complement one another and adapt to one another as circumstances and times change.

In the earlier stages of industrialisation, state intervention alone can create the initial conditions by building a physical infrastructure with government investment in energy, transport and communication, and by developing human resources through education and healthcare. These tasks remain unfinished in India. Clearly, the state must not only continue to perform this role in the economy but also do so much better than it has so far. In the later stages of industrialisation, both the degree and nature of state intervention in the economy must change to incorporate functional, institutional and strategic roles. Functional intervention is necessary to correct for market failures, both specific and general, as economic deci-sions are shaped more and more by the market. Institutional intervention is needed to govern the market by setting rules of the game for players in the market, to create frameworks for regulating markets and establish insti-tutions to monitor its functioning, since a market economy requires rules of the game to ensure a level-playing field and to pre-empt a free-for-all. Strategic intervention is desirable to guide the market, interlinked across activities or sectors, to attain broader long-term objectives of development.

Those who emphasise the costs of state intervention in the past must also recognise the costs of state inaction in the present and its implications for the future of India's economic development and the well-being of our people. They would also do well to remember that a government which fails in intervention is also bound to fail in liberalisation. For the same reason, a state that cannot provide governance or run enterprises cannot regulate, let alone guide or govern, markets. Indeed, efficient markets need effective governments. In sum, India needs a developmental state for its market economy to improve the living conditions of her people.

The respective roles of the government or the public sector and the market or the private sector are bound to change over time at different stages of development. Even so, at every stage, there are many things that only markets can and should do. These are best left to markets and the private sector. However, at every stage, there are other things that only governments can and must do. If governments perform these tasks badly, it is not possible to dispense with governments and replace them with markets. Government must be made to perform better. This is easier said than done. Yet, it is feasible, for the government is accountable to people. In India's vibrant democracy, there is a growing political consciousness among citizens. The accountability of governments to their people is clearly visible at election time. Performance is rewarded when incumbent governments are re-elected. Non-performance is penalised when incumbent governments are kicked out. Even if democracy works slowly—and with time lags—the implicit incentives and disincentives for political leaders and political parties do provide checks and balances. A better world is possible, if only we can activate and realise the enormous potential of our political democracy.

References

ADB (2013): *Asia's Economic Transformation: Where to, How and How Fast?* Key Indicators for Asia and the Pacific 2013, Special Chapter, Manila: Asian Development Bank.

Atkinson, Anthony B. (2015): *Inequality: What Can Be Done?* Cambridge, Massachusetts: Harvard University Press.

Atkinson, A.B. and T. Piketty (eds) (2012): *Top Incomes: A Global Perspective*, Oxford: Oxford University Press.

Baru, Sanjaya (2016): *1991: How P V Narasimha Rao Made History*, Delhi: Aleph.

Bhaduri, Amit and Deepak Nayyar (1996): *The Intelligent Person's Guide to Liberalization*, New Delhi: Penguin Books.

IHD (2014): *India Labour and Employment Report,* Institute for Human Development, New Delhi: Academic Press.

Lall, Sanjaya (1987): *Learning to Industrialize: The Acquisition of Technological Capability in India*, Basingstoke: Macmillan.

Nayyar, Deepak (1994): "The Foreign Trade Sector, Planning and Industrialization in India," *The State and Development Planning in India*, T.J. Byres (ed), Delhi: Oxford University Press.

——— (1996): *Economic Liberalization in India: Analytics, Experience and Lessons,* R C Dutt Lectures on Political Economy, Calcutta: Orient Longman.

——— (2001): "Macroeconomic Reforms in India: Short-term Effects and Long-term Implications," *Adjustment and Beyond: The Reform Experience in South Asia*, W. Mahmud (ed), London: Palgrave.

——— (2004): "Economic Reforms in India: Understanding the Process and Learning from Experience," *International Journal of Development Issues*, Vol 3, pp 31–55.

——— (2006): "India's Unfinished Journey: Transforming Growth into Development," *Modern Asian Studies*, Vol 40, pp 797–832.

——— (2011): "Economic Growth and Technological Capabilities in Emerging Economies," *Innovation and Development*, Vol 1, pp 245–58.

——— (2013): *Catch Up: Developing Countries in the World Economy*, Oxford: Oxford University Press.

——— (2017): "Can Catch Up Reduce Inequality?," *Sustainable Development Goals and Income Inequality*, Peter van Bergeijk and Rolph van der Hoeven (eds), London: Edward Elgar, forthcoming.

——— (2017a): "India's Path to Structural Transformation: An Exception and the Rule," *The Oxford Handbook of Structural Transformation,* Justin Lin and Celestin Monga (eds), Oxford: Oxford University Press, forthcoming.

Rodrik, D. and A. Subramanian (2005): "From Hindu Growth to Productivity Surge: The Mystery of the Indian Growth Transition," IMF Staff Papers, Vol 52, pp 193–228.

Sitapati, Vinay (2016): *Half-Lion: How P V Narasimha Rao Transformed India*, New Delhi: Penguin Books.

II

TRANSITION AND REFORMS

Economic Liberalisation and the Working Poor

Prabhat Patnaik

Economic liberalisation is usually taken to mean a general "retreat of the state". This is erroneous. The state in a "liberalised regime" acts almost exclusively in the interests of globalised capital and the domestic corporate–financial oligarchy that gets integrated with it, which means inter alia a withdrawal of state support from traditional petty production, including peasant agriculture. This is what underlies the phenomenon of absolute impoverishment of the working people, notably in the form of growing nutritional deprivation, which "liberalisation" has unleashed in India over the last 25 years, and which, notwithstanding assiduous denials by its votaries, is quite indubitable.

Economic liberalisation is often seen either as just a set of administrative measures for "rationalising" the economic regime (older government economists tend to see it this way), or as a move towards "Walrasian equilibrium," where demand and supply are equal at ruling prices in all markets and where the allocation of resources is "optimal" (some academic economists tend to see it this way). These are obviously flawed perceptions. Economic liberalisation entails the introduction of an altogether new economic regime which has nothing to do with any Walrasian equilibrium, in the place of the old *dirigiste regime* that had more or less been in place since the 1950s, with a different political economy, a different class basis and a different dynamics.

State and Economic Liberalisation

Central to economic liberalisation is the opening up of the economy to the vortex of globalised capital flows. In India we still do not have complete currency convertibility, but the economy is substantially open to capital flows, including especially financial flows, which has a decisive impact on state policy.

Any economy open to global financial flows is vulnerable to sudden capital flight, which forces the state to ensure that it retains at all times the confidence of international financiers. It is constrained therefore to pursue policies that finance capital demands, such as fiscal responsibility, tax concessions to the rich and the corporates, and eschewing direct state activism for promoting the level of activity and people's welfare. The state does not retreat as is often claimed; it intervenes by way of providing incentives to globalised capital, with which the domestic corporate-financial oligarchy gets closely integrated; in fact the so-called retreat itself becomes a euphemism for the promotion of corporate interests.

This has an obvious implication for democracy. No matter which political formation comes to power, it pursues the same economic policies as long as the economy remains within the vortex of global capital flows, not because these policies are optimal in any sense but because not pursuing them would bring financial crisis and hence transitional suffering even for the poor. This makes the electoral choice between alternative political formations a meaningless exercise, at least as far as people's economic destinies are concerned. But since I have discussed this matter elsewhere (Patnaik 2014), I shall not pursue it here.

There are, however, three economic characteristics of a liberalised regime, all of which have manifested themselves in India and which shape its overall dynamics. I shall discuss these seriatim.

The first is the withdrawal of support of the state from traditional petty production including peasant agriculture. The anti-colonial struggle in India had taken off in the 1930s with the support of the peasantry that had seen acute distress because of the Great Depression, and it had held out the promise that such distress would never again visit the peasantry in independent India. The *dirigiste regime*, seeing itself as a legatee of the anti-colonial struggle, had accordingly adopted an array of policies for protecting and promoting not just peasant agriculture but traditional petty production in general, that is, not just the peasantry but craftsmen, fishermen, handloom weavers and other such producers. Not that all sections among them were equal beneficiaries of such measures, but notwithstanding internal differentiation within this segment (within peasant agriculture, for instance), the encroachment by corporate capital from outside upon this segment, was kept in check, as was the vulnerability of this segment to world market price fluctuations.

In agriculture, not only was there tariff protection and quantitative restriction for insulating the sector from world price fluctuations, but also "remunerative prices" and public procurement, including for a number of cash crops where commodity boards were entrusted with the task of market intervention. There was a substantial step up in public investment, Research and Development in public sector organisations (which were responsible for the high-yielding variety seeds), subsidised inputs including credit (the provision of which was an objective of bank nationalisation), and a network of public extension services. Similar measures were instituted for other traditional petty production sectors. All these not only directly aided traditional petty production, but also ensured that big corporate capital whether domestic or foreign had no direct access to this sector and hence could not subjugate it.

Liberalisation changed this. The neo-liberal state, with a changed focus towards the exclusive promotion of the interests of globalised capital, marked a departure from the earlier bourgeois state which appeared to stand above society and to intervene benevolently in favour of all classes including the traditional petty producers, and even, on occasions, the working class.

The state under neo-liberalism withdraws substantially from its earlier role of protecting and promoting the interests of traditional petty producers, which is evident in the case of agriculture with the drying up of institutional credit, a rise in input prices including of credit, a dismantling of the public extension network, a removal of the marketing function of commodity boards, trade liberalisation that makes domestic prices mirror world price fluctuations, a cutback in public investment, and the direct access of corporate capital and agribusiness to the peasantry. Procurement, on the verge of being abandoned some years ago, got a fresh lease of life because of the inflationary upsurge that began around that time. But its continuation remains uncertain, even according to this year's budget speech.

The reduced profitability of agriculture, the spate of peasant suicides, and the broader agrarian crisis, reflected in the fact of peasants abandoning agriculture to flock to cities in search of non-existent jobs, and also in the fact that the number of labourers in agriculture now exceeds that of cultivators for the first time in the county's history; are all consequences of the state's withdrawal from its role of defending and promoting petty production. This has meant leaving traditional petty production to encroachment and subjugation by corporate capital and agribusiness, and indeed being complicit in the process (which facilitates what Marx had called "primitive accumulation of capital").

It is noteworthy that between 1990–91 and 2013–14 (a peak year) per capita foodgrain output in the country remained virtually stagnant. What is even more striking is that per capita foodgrain availability actually declined over this period. This decline in availability has been sought to be explained in several ways, but there can be little doubt that it is the result of a squeeze in purchasing power in the hands of the bulk of the working people, an instance of "income deflation". Underlying it is not only the rise in prices of a host of essential services like education and healthcare owing to privatisation (a rise that cannot be captured by the standard price indices), but also the lack of growth of proper employment despite supposedly impressive gross domestic product (GDP) growth (on this more later).

This decline in per capita foodgrain availability in the period of liberalisation should be seen in its historical context. At the beginning of the 20th century in "British India," average annual per capita foodgrain availability was 199 kilograms (for the quinquennium 1897–1902); it decreased to 148.5 for the quinquennium 1939–44 (and to 136.8 for the individual year 1945–46) (Blyn 1966). During the *dirigiste* period it increased to 177 kilograms for India as a whole for the triennium ending 1991–92. The period of liberalisation has seen a decline in this figure: for the triennium centred on 2011–12 (a good agricultural year), the figure was 163 kilograms. The per capita annual foodgrain absorption in India today according to Food and Agricultural Organization (FAO) data is lower than in sub–Saharan Africa and in the Least Developed Economies.

This decline also manifests itself in the data on calorie intake. The percentage of the urban population accessing less than 2,100 calories per person per day, which is the official benchmark for defining poverty, declined marginally from 60 in 1973–74 to 57 in 1993–94; it increased to 65 in 2011–12. Likewise the percentage of rural population unable to access 2,200 calories per person per day, which is the benchmark for defining poverty, had stood at 56.4 in 1973–74 and 58.5 in 1993–94; it increased to 68 in 2011–12.[1]

Two questions are immediately raised by these figures. The first relates to the sharp contrast between the apparently impressive GDP growth rate in the period of liberalisation and the growing mass hunger. While this issue is discussed below, it is obvious that GDP growth is an entirely inappropriate index of the performance of a regime. This is so not only because of the conceptual and statistical pitfalls associated with the GDP growth rate itself, but also because such a measure, even if accurate, privileges the "nation" above the people, which is a throwback to the days of mercantilism that needs emphatically to be rejected. The opposite position was articulated long ago by John Stuart Mill (1849: 315), who had said apropos the "stationary state" (whose prospect loomed large in his time) that he did not mind a "stationary state" if the workers were better off under it. In India during the period of liberalisation the working population has become distinctly worse off by the most elemental standard of judging welfare, viz, hunger, notwithstanding impressive GDP growth rates.

The second issue is the sharp contrast between growing hunger and the supposed reduction in poverty in this period. It is not just the official poverty estimates that claim such a reduction; even those who question official poverty estimates for understating its level, do not disagree with such estimates with regard to its trend. How do we explain the contrasting trends with regard to nutrition and such estimates of poverty? The simple answer is that all poverty estimate trends based on the use of price indices (such as for instance, those which update a "poverty line") are seriously flawed.

The use of any such index presupposes that the same goods which were available in the base period are also in the terminal period, and that if a different bundle is nonetheless chosen in the terminal period even though the base period bundle lies within the budget constraint, then the reason must be that this different bundle makes one better off. But the goods of the base period, such as for instance public education and healthcare facilities, are simply not available in the terminal year because such facilities have been run down and the tasks have been privatised, even though the private service providers charge exorbitantly for what they provide. Estimates of poverty trends therefore, whether by the government or by private researchers, are highly questionable,[2] while nutrition estimates, being firmer, throw a better light on changes in the state of well-being.

A Vicious Cycle

The crucial factor contributing to the income deflation that underlay the growth in hunger over the period of liberalisation was the absence of proper employment. And here a second characteristic of liberalisation becomes relevant, namely, the lifting of restrictions on the pace of structural-cum-technological change, which set up a vicious cycle that needs to be understood.

Consider an economy with substantial labour reserves which keep the vector of real wages down to the neighbourhood of some subsistence level, in the manner highlighted by the renowned development economist W. Arthur Lewis in his celebrated model. Unless these labour reserves start diminishing as a proportion of the total labour force, the vector of real wages is unlikely to show any upward trend. Such an economy, however, continues to experience increases in labour productivity. The increase in labour productivity depends of course, upon the rate of growth of total output itself, a point emphasised in separate empirical analyses by the Cambridge economist Nicholas Kaldor and the Dutch econometrician Petrus Johannes Verdoorn (and often referred to as the Kaldor–Verdoorn Law). But it also depends on the level of, and the change in, the share of surplus (that is, output minus wage bill) in total output.

The latter set of effects can be understood as follows. The surplus accrues largely to persons with higher incomes, and they are influenced in their pattern of consumption by the lifestyles prevailing in the advanced countries. Advanced country lifestyles however entail consuming a bundle of commodities which on average are less employment-intensive than the commodities consumed by the working people in India. Hence any increase in the share of surplus has the effect of raising the rate of growth of labour productivity under a neo-liberal dispensation, as production adjusts to changes in the pattern of demand.

There is another factor to consider. The commodities which surplus earners consume, precisely because they represent metropolitan lifestyles, also entail rapid product innovation and hence rapid technological change involving increases in labour productivity. Hence the larger the level of the share of surplus the greater ceteris paribus will be the rate of growth of labour productivity.

Denoting the output growth rate by g, the growth rate of labour productivity by g_p the share of surplus by a, and the rate of change in the share of surplus by da/dt, we can therefore say:

$$g_p = F\ (g,\ a,\ da/dt),\ \text{with}\ F'(.) > 0\ \text{for all arguments} \qquad \ldots(A)$$

For simplicity we shall ignore da/dt in the discussion that follows. Let n denote the rate of growth of the supply of labour consisting of both the natural increase in size of the workforce and the displaced (or migrant) petty producers of the traditional activities including of peasant agriculture seeking employment. (We assume for simplicity that their migration itself does not affect output in the sectors where they had been employed earlier.) Now, suppose, to start with, that the rate of growth of employment falls short of the rate of growth of labour supply, that is,

$$(g - g_p) < n \qquad\qquad …(B)$$

then the initial size of the labour reserves increases relative to the work-force, which means that real wages do not rise. But since labour productivity is rising, that is, $g_p > 0$, the share of surplus rises, which means from (A) that g_p rises still further. Hence if $(g - g_p) < n$ to start with, then for any given g, the rate of growth of labour productivity keeps increasing, the rate of growth of employment keeps falling, and the relative size of the labour reserves keeps increasing, thus setting up a vicious cycle of growing inequality (because of the rise in the share of surplus), and growing relative labour reserves.

It may be thought that as the share of surplus rises the investment ratio must also rise and hence the rate of growth of output must also rise. This was the premise of David Ricardo, the classical economist who was a believer in Say's law that "supply creates its own demand" (that is, that there can never be any deficiency in aggregate demand and hence any question of investment being determined by anything other than full capacity savings). He had used this premise in arguing that the introduction of machinery, though harmful for employment in the short-run, could never be harmful in the long-run since the rate of growth of output and hence employment became higher because of the introduction of machinery. But since the Ricardo–Say view that "supply creates its own demand" is invalid, there is no reason why a rise in the share of surplus should raise the growth rate of output (in fact it is more likely to reduce the growth rate owing to the shrinking value of the Keynesian multiplier).

It follows therefore that unless the output growth rate is such that the employment growth rate associated with it exceeds the rate of growth of labour supply to start with (which itself is a necessary not a sufficient condition), the economy will fall into a vicious cycle of growing inequality and growing relative labour reserves. If fiscal policy is simultaneously moving towards "sound finance" (so that the purchasing power put into the hands of the working population from budgetary sources is cut) and privatisation of public services is also occurring, then there can even be growing hunger accompanying such a growth process.

This, as mentioned earlier, is what has been occurring in the Indian economy, with only one difference. The growing relative labour reserves do not appear as such, but only in a camouflaged form as casual employment, intermittent employment, and disguised unemployment that underlies the upsurge of petty entrepreneurship. Work-rationing in other words does not take the form of some workers being fully employed and others unemployed, but of all, or almost all, being partially employed. This however only modifies our argument without negating it.

Disguised unemployment in the form of an upsurge of petty entrepreneurship may give the misleading impression that what we are witnessing is not growing labour reserves but burgeoning entrepreneurship from below. But just as it would have been erroneous to interpret the growth of "shoeshine boys" in Britain during the Great Depression of the 1930s as a pronounced boom in the shoeshine industry rather than as an increase in disguised unemployment, it would likewise be erroneous to interpret the observed growth of employment in India under heads like petty entrepreneurship as anything other than a growth in relative labour reserves.

This growth in labour reserves, to recapitulate, even in the midst of apparently impressive output growth, arises because of the removal of constraints on the pace of technological-cum-structural change, which is a feature of economic liberalisation. The coexistence of rapidly growing GDP and increasing inequality and even poverty which has been a characteristic of the Indian economy in the period of liberalisation can be explained as above.

It is noteworthy in this context that both Gandhi and Mao in different ways had seen the imposition of constraints on the pace of structural-cum-technological change as the means to overcome poverty in the large economies they came from, and that the Soviet Union, precisely through such imposition inter alia, became the first economy in modern times to witness systemic labour-shortage as opposed to perennial unemployment.[3] Neo-liberalism pursues the very opposite goal, and, not surprisingly, lands in a vicious cycle of growing relative labour reserves.

Capitalism as a Demand-constrained System

The third feature of neo-liberalism which we are witnessing now is its depriving capitalism of any exogenous stimulus for growth,[4] and hence making growth dependent almost exclusively on the formation of property price "bubbles". In the specific world context in which we are placed, this means property price bubbles in the most powerful economy of the world, the United States (US).

Let me elaborate. Once we abandon Say's law, hence the presumption that all economies are at all times at full capacity output, and see capitalism as a "demand-constrained system," growth of the system must be perceived necessarily to depend upon the operation of a set of exogenous stimuli which are outside of the multiplier-accelerator or other similar mechanisms (which explain growth endogenously, that is, by virtue of the fact that it occurs because it has been occurring). The most common exogenous stimulus that has traditionally been adduced to explain growth under capitalism is innovations, but it is doubtful if innovations can be considered genuinely exogenous, that is, whether their adoption is an autonomous factor expanding the market or whether they themselves get introduced only when the market is expanding anyway. The work of economists like Arthur Lewis (1978) who see the Great Depression of the 1930s as having delayed the introduction of innovations (rather than itself being overcome through such introduction), would certainly suggest that innovations do not constitute a genuinely exogenous stimulus.

In that case, however, the only genuinely exogenous stimuli that capitalism has experienced are encroachments into "outlying regions" (which

Rosa Luxemburg had emphasised) and state expenditure (which Keynes had recommended and post-war capitalism had adopted). While the scope for the first of these is more or less exhausted, and the second of these, as already seen, is constricted by the prevalence of the policy of "sound finance" which globalised finance capital imposes on nation states, the neo-liberal regime is left without any exogenous stimuli. (The US which in principle can escape thraldom to "sound finance" is not too keen on enlarging its fiscal deficit to boost activity within a neo-liberal setting, that is, in the absence of protection, because that would entail creating jobs elsewhere while pushing the US itself into deeper external indebtedness.) Finance can no doubt act as an exogenous stimulus, via generating debt-financed demand, but this can only be transitory.

This therefore leaves "bubbles" as the sole remaining stimulus for growth, and indeed the "dotcom bubble" in the US in the 1990s (which had produced what Stiglitz calls the "roaring nineties"), followed by the "housing bubble," sustained the boom in the world economy for almost two decades and accounted for the high growth rates experienced by the so-called "newly-emerging economies" that cashed in on it.

That phase is now over, and not only is the world economy gripped by a protracted crisis, but economies like India are also starting to experience its fall-out. Until a new "bubble" arises, of which there are no signs, the world economy, and with it the economies of countries like India, will remain trapped in crisis unless they change their economic regimes away from export-orientation within a framework of neo-liberalism.

The tendency among many countries in the world at present is to attempt to overcome the crisis they face through exchange rate depreciations vis-à-vis the US dollar. This, except at the expense of the US (which is likely to go more protectionist), entails a "beggar-my-neighbour" policy, which is self-defeating by its very nature: when each tries to grab more of a stagnant world market at the expense of others, all of them collectively remain more or less where they were. If anything, the world market shrinks further, because the risks associated with investment increase in a situation of competitive exchange rate depreciations.

Since a coordinated fiscal stimulus by several governments acting together is nowhere on the horizon (and even if the logistical problems associated with such an effort could be overcome, the opposition of globalised finance to any such move would scuttle it), the only way out of the current stagnation, at least for large countries, is by each country undertaking state-led expansion to increase its output for the home market, even as it prevents others, through protectionist measures, from running away with the additional demand so generated. This at least would make all countries Pareto-wise better off (in the sense of having a larger output vector) compared to the state of crisis, or to the state that "beggar-my-neighbour" policies would reduce them to.

Any nation state that embarks on such a course, since it would face opposition from globalised finance, would have to expand mass consumption through state expenditure for mobilising people behind such a course.

Neo-liberalism in short has reached the end of its tether. As long as countries do not break away from it, they would continue to be mired in crisis. And from the fact, discussed earlier, that the period of boom in India was also one of growing hunger, one cannot obviously conclude the opposite, namely, that a period of crisis would be one of growing plenitude for the people. If they suffered during the boom, they would suffer even more during the crisis, until a new regime (which will have to start by imposing capital controls), involving an activist state engaged in promoting mass consumption and people's welfare, comes into being.

Notes

1. Figures for earlier years are based on Utsa Patnaik (2013) and for 2011–12 on an unpublished paper by her.
2. This theoretical argument is developed at greater length in Prabhat Patnaik (2013).
3. Janos Kornai (1982) had drawn attention to this difference between the capitalist and the erstwhile socialist economies. See also Kalecki (1972).

4.   The argument which follows has been developed at length in Prabhat Patnaik (2016).

References

Blyn, George (1966): *Agricultural Trends in India 1891–1946*, Philadelphia: University of Pennsylvania Press.

Kalecki, M. (1972): *Selected Essays in the Growth of the Socialist and the Mixed Economy*, Cambridge: Cambridge University Press.

Kornai, J. (1982): *Growth, Shortage and Efficiency*, Oxford: Blackwell.

Lewis, W.A. (1978): *Growth and Fluctuations 1870–1913*, London: Allen and Unwin.

Mill, John Stuart (1849): *Principles of Political Economy*, Vol II, Second Edition, London: John William Parker.

Patnaik, Prabhat (2013): "A Critique of the Welfare-Theoretic Basis of the Measurement of Poverty," *Economic & Political Weekly*, Vol 48, No 14, pp 16–19.

———— (2014): "Neo-liberalism and Democracy," *Economic & Political Weekly*, Vol 49, No 15, pp 39–44.

———— (2016): "Capitalism and Its Current Crisis," *Monthly Review*, New York, January.

Patnaik, Utsa (2013): "Poverty Trends in India 2004–05 to 2009–10," *Economic & Political Weekly*, Vol 48, No 40, pp 43–58.

Indian Economy in Transition

The New Order of Things

Anjan Chakrabarti

Taking cognisance of India's long-run economic transition in the post-planning era, it is argued that the triad of neo-liberal globalisation, global capitalism and inclusive development has come to constitute the new order of things of Indian economy. This article explores the appearance of each, and the roles they played in reshaping the Indian economic map, and in displacing the rationale and practice of Indian state. This triad in turn has become the site of reference and departure for a novel set of contradictions–crises–resistance in contemporary India.

I have argued elsewhere that Indian economic transition encapsulates both change and no change (Chakrabarti, Dhar and Dasgupta 2015). Here, I focus only on the changes. What is new about India's economic transition in the last 25 years? Roughly and broadly, the movement from self-reliance based on planned economy to neo-liberal globalisation, capitalism transiting from national to global, and development going inclusive are shown to be forming a novel triad—the new order of things—within which the Indian economy has been relocated. Sometimes, this triad in totality is referred to as "Development". These components reinforce, compensate and intersect one another, forming in the process, a mutually constitutive relation through which the Indian economy not only functions, but its contradictions and crises also get manifested. Finally, the Indian state got dislocated within this new order of things, both as a producer of these components and by being constituted by their effects. I will briefly examine the three components, and unpack the changing rationale and practice of the Indian state.

Neo-liberal Turn in India

The Indian state during the planning era (1951–91) embodied three related beliefs. First, the state—as sovereign—can master the finite totality of the economy and direct socio-economic engineering. Second, the self-regulating character of the market was denied, thereby legitimising the rationalisation of state control of the market economy; the efficiency argument was demoted in favour of state-sponsored allocation of resources. Third, the state embraced another anti-liberal belief that individuals/agents are akin to children, that is, incapable of forming independent decisions that are beneficial for them and for society. These beliefs entailed that the state did not govern for market economy. Instead, it literally governed the market economy.

For Indian policymakers, the above-mentioned beliefs turned out to be important points of departure. Gradually, they found an ideological ally in neo-liberalism which embodied an insurrection against these beliefs and the rationality of the state which telescopes these. Its central critique was that the extant planning/welfare-driven economic order is inefficient, creates market distortions, retards economic growth and denies economic freedom for subjects which is equivalent to political un-freedom under liberalism (Hayek 2001). Neo-liberalism literally coveted a new global order where society and its governance will be modelled on the principle of a competitive market economy. It sought the economisation of the social (Lemke 2001; Chakrabarti, Dhar and Dasgupta 2015: Chapter 4). Neo-liberalism constituted the fundamental precepts of globalisation and the imagined global order. India's economic reforms broadly followed the precepts of neo-liberal globalisation which became the underlying condition for the appearance of a new kind of capitalism in India, global capitalism.

Neo-liberal globalisation involves the transformation of the idea, logic and justification of the state itself. Its fundamental principle demanded that the state govern for the competitive market economy and not govern it per se. Direct intervention and control are anathema to this ideology. Yet, at the cusp of the transition from centralised planning to such an economic structure, we face a paradox.

> Though the eventual and ideal objective of liberalisation is to reduce the state's role in economic life, ironically, it is only the state which can reduce the functions of the state. (Kaviraj 2010: 237)

To this end, the self-transformation of the state entailed that it undertakes concomitant policy in a neo-liberal direction, meaning to (a) create, secure and facilitate the competitive market economy, and then leave that economy—through the free interaction of private agents—to self-regulate itself; (b) provide space for subjects qua homoeconomicus[1] to cultivate themselves, and consequently, exercise their freedom in choice-action in and through a competitive market economy that respects no boundary between economic and non-economic domains (since it is argued that anything can be potentially priced, directly or through imputation); (c) to align these to the global order such that the reference points become global competitive market economy and choices on production, distribution and consumption by the homoeconomicus come to be globally situated or sensitised.

It is important to understand that neo-liberalism is not just about structural adjustment but also refers to a process of subjectification. The neo-liberal homoeconomicus or "rational ability machine" is seen as (a) innately rational, capable of weighing any situation through cost–benefit and through the maximising of welfare in a dynamic field of competing ends, and (b) an entrepreneur capable of taking care of the self, organiser of his own capital, his own producer and source of earnings. A global competitive market economy ruled by the conduct of the mass of neo-liberal homoeconomicus will guarantee a self-regulated and optimal economic structure that will, relative to other competing economic systems, produce higher economic growth and individual welfare.

The state will govern for this self-regulated and optimal competitive market economy. In this context, neo-liberalism does not mean a delinking of state with the individual (or the market through which individuals operate), but reflects a change in the manner of state intervention. Instead of directly appearing within the market or the inner realm of competition in order to direct/control human choice-action, the state strives to *conduct* the conduct of the subject's behaviour (by changing various conditions of existence under which they operate including the specified structure of competition) without impeding on their freedom of choice-action. This is not to say that the sovereign and the disciplinary contexts and conduits of power have disappeared (such as over workers and dissent), but we are highlighting the core contribution of neo-liberalism in the structure of governance.

However gradual and incomplete it may seem, I contend that India's political economy of reform has taken the colour and character of neo-liberalism. Along with an initial spate of privatisation and disinvestment, it concentrated first on freeing, creating and organising the principles and structures of the market and competition (for these are made/unmade and cannot be taken as given). It then allowed markets to operate freely in an increasingly competitive environment (however uneven and incomplete it may seem; that is the long-run tendency), and also authorised the creation of free market in areas which till now had operated in controlled markets or non-market ways (spanning the vast canvas of land, finance and banking, information and communication, water, care-affective labour, old age, body and mental health, art, aesthetics and entertainment, etc). Rules and regulations regarding trade and competition aligned to the global order were set up and authorised. India's integration to a privately-driven global competitive market economy is in the final stage of completion with a few resisting areas in public utilities, agriculture, health, labour, education, defence, retail, banking and infrastructure being presently unlocked for total or partial integration or changed to support the process of integration; even though taxation rules, bureaucracy and corruption still continue to be criticised as problems, there have been concerted attempts lately to address these issues so as to better lubricate the functioning and expansion of global capitalism.

Now, to the question of the subject. We have argued elsewhere on the need to situate homoeconomicus as both a theoretical/epistemological category (the way it is defined and imagined) and as a socio-historical category (how it is actually placed, produced and lived). The problem with studies of neo-liberalism is that the epistemological construct of subject is often assumed as the ontological one, of what the subject essentially is and does (Madra and Özselçuk 2010). Taking the subject as already always neo-liberal is unsatisfactory since it erases the question of subjectivity transformation as a distinct problem of transition; it also evacuates the possibility of theorising subject in a different way. By arguing that the subject is not neo-liberal per se, Kaviraj (2010: 237) decisively captures the issue in the context of Indian economic transition from the pre- to post-reform period:

> Liberalisation might appear to be 'freeing the spirit of enterprise' of economic individuals and groups, but contrary to ideological images of the process, there is nothing spontaneous or natural about it. Treating people as 'economic individuals' with atomistic self-interested inclinations is not a natural human trait but a cultural construct…it means serious reorganisation of economic life, which only the state has the legal ability and the sheer social power to carry through.

The neo-liberal subject cannot be taken as given. Instead, the subject's mental landscape and consciousness has to be reshaped to secure and procreate the altered economic structure and mode of governance being put in place by reforms. This reiterates our point that in the context of India's economic transition, both structural reform (by way of global competitive market economy) and subject formation (by way of neo-liberal homoeconomicus) would have to transpire concurrently, conditions that can generally be created, protected and facilitated by the state. At one level, the protraction and deepening of competitive market economy assist the cultivation of the neo-liberal practice of economic subject (since, within this set-up, the subjects are enticed and persuaded to respond to the call of cost–benefit calculation and human capital generation in various socio-economic matters). But the mere presence of this economic structure cannot suffice for producing the functional subject of/in the global competitive market economy.

Subjective transformation towards rational ability machines must be additionally escorted by a process of cultural transformation from childhood itself. Cultural institutions, apparatuses and meanings pertaining to education, human body, pleasure, etc, have to undergo fundamental change enabling, among other things, the accumulation of neo-liberal brains and abilities to accompany the accumulation of surplus and capital (Rabinow and Rose 2006; Soljar Vrzina 2012; Kumar 2016; Chakrabarti, Dhar and Dasgupta 2015). In a society subjected to the dynamics of market competition, the individuals must be disposed to the spirit of competition long before they arrive at the market. Their assessment of performance, their mode of choosing and acting, their very manner of organising life has to be, to a considerable extent, regulated by the need and desire to be rational ability machine.

Even as we acknowledge the presence and role of state in the production of neo-liberal subject and in conducting the subject's conduct as explained earlier, our analysis also highlights that one must not overlook the fact that the immediate and most potent shield for global competitive market economy is not the state but the mass of neo-liberal subjects who nurture and promote it, as if, of their own free will. The state governs for this global competitive market economy run by the mass of neo-liberal homoeconomicus. That is why, alongside the successful structural reform, the long-run success of neo-liberalism must be accompanied by a corresponding transformation of the subject in the above-mentioned direction. At the beginning of the 1990s, India possessed neither an extensive market economy nor the depth of competition that were anything comparable to the West. Globalisation was non-existent. Finally, the kind of neo-liberal homoeconomicus described above was farthest from realisation in the Indian context. To be successful, India's reform had to enact a change in the Indian economy and society in these directions. To a considerable extent this objective has been achieved.

The change in the character of the Indian state became most profound against the backdrop of this question: "Why must one govern?...What makes government necessary, and what ends must it pursue with regard to society in order to justify its own existence?" (Foucault 2008: 319). The answer is the following in neo-liberalism: *the state exists to govern for society that is modelled in the image of competitive market economy and not for itself.* This changes the basic premise of rationalising the existence of the state, which is now sought by invoking a question of "self-doubt": is state intervention required for society? The state in turn embodies the self-limiting principle; *self-regulation* of governmental practice and a *self-critical* approach towards governmental practice (driven by the question as to whether the state is governing too much).

How far the Indian state has travelled in the last few decades in rethinking the basis of its existence can be gleaned from a quote in the *Economic Survey*:

> In many poor nations the Government takes the stance that, when in doubt about the goodness or badness of two or more adults voluntarily conducting an exchange, stop them. An enabling state, on the contrary, takes the view that, when in doubt, do not interfere. There are, of course, many actions of individuals and groups that will need to be stopped for the welfare of society at large. But the default option of an enabling state is to allow rather than stop, to permit instead of prevent. This *altered conception of the state* can have dramatic effect on the functioning of an economy, in general by promoting greater efficiency and higher productivity. (emphasis added, *Economic Survey* 2009–10: 24)

The deep-seated scepticism about the state's own role in the global competitive market economy is encapsulated in the gradual but steady process of liberalisation, privatisation and disinvestment across sectors in India since 1991, and the self-critical gaze on fiscal policy (captured by the effort to put in place the Fiscal Responsibility and Budget Management Act), and monetary policy (with de-emphasis on its role in growth management and increasing decontrol of interest rates). This is accompanied by growing regulation of state policy by international credit agencies and think tanks tied to global capital leading to questions concerning the autonomy of policymaking. Governmental practices pertaining to the welfare of society concerning production and distribution of public utilities, such as water, health, education and infrastructure (which are also increasingly being privatised and/or made marketable), poverty management and public distribution systems are ever more subjected to efficiency criterion, targeting (as against universal coverage) and individualisation.

March of Global Capital

The economy is decentred and disaggregated into various kinds of class processes of performance, appropriation, distribution and receipt of surplus labour (capitalist, feudal, slave, communist, communitic and independent) which must exist in a relation of mutual constitution with other non-class processes (Resnick and Wolff 1987; Gibson-Graham 2006; Chakrabarti and Cullenberg 2003). In this theory, class process (an economic concept here) is taken as the entry point and is guided by a specific understanding of how it is related to other non-class (economic, cultural, political and natural) processes. This idea of relationship entails that, in any concrete setting, class process of surplus labour cannot exist on its own; it shapes and is in turn shaped by non-class processes such as income, property, caste, gender, race, etc. Each provides the conditions of existence for the other and therefore any kind of reductionism by which one (say, caste) is explained in terms of the other (here, class) is disallowed. This non-reductionist conception of economy implies that the mode of explanation is class-focused and not class-specific or class-reductionist.

By capitalist class process, I mean exploitative organisation of surplus labour/value realised in a scenario where means of production, labour power and final produce are in commodity/value form. Capitalist class process could take state or private form depending upon factors such as whether the mode of appropriation of surplus value is connected to the state (appropriators of surplus connected to the bureaucracy and ministries) or not (appropriators being private). Capitalist class process (state or private) and non-class processes constitute one another to form a capitalist economy; likewise, alongside this capitalist economy, we have independent, feudal, communist economies and so on. Capitalism is thus one component of the otherwise 'mixed' economy.

It is here that the role of the state became decisive. One can interpret the Indian planning era as an instance where state/national capitalism was privileged within this disaggregated (mixed) economy and a concerted attempt made to reconstruct the Indian economy and society through its lens. In the post-planning era, private capitalism took a privileged place and that too within a global competitive market economy; it did not mean that state capitalist enterprises disappeared but their importance was made secondary. The political economy of reform based on the precepts of neo-liberal globalisation emerges as a necessary condition to create global capitalism from within India. What is new is then, a change in the character of capitalism, as also its role and extent.

With the flow of value and class processes fragmented across regions and nations (facilitated by the information technology, transportation and telecommunication revolutions), global capitalist enterprise (industrial, trading and financial, that is, in M-C-M$'$ or M-M$'$ form; henceforth, global capital) was taken in the post-planning period as the primary unit in the reorganisation of the structure of Indian economy. It is deemed as the primary value-creating sector. The policy imperative is to conceptually privilege and provide a central place for global capital in the economic map and then allow the socio-economic space to be re-signified and restructured by the functioning of global capital which in turn institutes a reverse impact on the state and its policy.

Once this privileged position and the role of global capital is accepted, the new Indian economic map that emerges can be construed in terms of "circuits-camp of global capital" and its outside—"world of the third" (Chakrabarti, Dhar and Dasgupta 2015). We define "circuits of global capital" as comprising of all those processes that are directly or indirectly connected with global capitalist enterprises. Local capitalist enterprises and non-capitalist enterprises are intertwined with global capital through local–global markets via instances of outsourcing, subcontracting, offshoring, body shopping and so on. When we refer to local–global markets with reference to a commodity, we mean the chain of "local–local...to...global–global" exchages that make up the value sequence of a commodity. There are enterprises (in production and in circulation, including trading and financial enterprises) which are directly and immediately connected to global capitalist enterprises and together these cluster into what can be provisionally named as the hub of circuits of global capital; while the rest in the chain indirectly connected and some distance away from global capitalist enterprises comprise the margins of the circuits of global capital. The circuits of global capital have been emerging from every pore of the Indian economy, the latest being the hitherto (en)closed bastion of agriculture that is fast crumbling and getting restructured under the relentless barrage of global capital and global markets even as its extant rural lifeworld gets hollowed out by continual internal crisis and migration of its younger population.

As already argued, the neo-liberal turn encapsulates the relocation of subjectivities as also of cultural space, constituting in the process new notions of success, of ways of judging performance and conduct, entrepreneurship and consumerism, customs and norms, etc. What appears is a social cluster of practices, activities and relationships connected to the circuits of global capital; we name it the "camp of global capital". These are instrumental in propelling the reconfiguration of the spatial contour of India's old and new cities and urbanity that is in conformity with neo-liberal values embodying competition, possession and accumulation and that too in a global context; the inauguration of "smart cities" is only the latest addition in the creation of neo-liberal cities. At the same time, the privileging and expansion of the circuits-camp of global capital seeks transformation of the idea of the nation from its extant moorings in critical nationalism and inward-looking nationalism (marked by the trope of self-sufficiency and self-rule) to a nationalism which is tied to global capitalism and its expansion/growth (India as an economic superpower as also a military superpower); as such, the idea of the Indian nation and nationhood itself is undergoing questioning and change (Chakrabarti and Dhar 2012).

The demarcating boundary between the circuits of global capital and "world of the third" crucially depends on the local–global markets. World of the third is a space that is outside the local–global market exchanges. Alongside capitalist enterprises (especially of the simple reproduction type that accumulates little, if any, capital), a huge segment of the enterprises procreating here would fall under non-capitalist forms ranging from independent, feudal, communitic, slave to communist (concentrated in the agriculture sector, the informal sector, the forest economy, etc). Knotted by world of the third markets as well as into non-market exchanges, these enterprises would have their own interlinkages forming a contrasting chain. Together, they form the circuits of the world of the third. Whenever and wherever we locate a space and its forms of life procreating outside the circuits-camp of global capital, we conceptually come face-to-face with the camp of world of the third with its distinct identification of the knowledge-logic–experience–ethos. Importantly, no value judgment (good, bad, useful) can be forwarded with reference to world of the third which itself is a heterogeneous space (containing complex configurations of rich/poor, exploitative/non-exploitative, totalitarian/liberal, etc). Global capital has been expansive, but not necessarily inclusive. It structurally excludes. The exclusion is also perspectival. The world of the third is the name for this spatial and perspectival outside.

The changing map of the Indian economy was driven by, among other things, the primacy accorded to capitalist performance, appropriation and distribution of surplus value which, with greater rates of capital accumulation, resulted in the expansion of the circuits-camp of global capital. The objective of economic growth lubricated by the ideology and implementation of neo-liberal reforms no doubt helped fuel this expansionary logic; high economic growth and material prosperity, especially surrounding the hub of global capital (the rise of the so-called middle class) followed. This sustained income growth is one of the success stories of Indian capitalism even as it has in the process grafted modern abuse onto ancient injustice, new forms of class-caste-ethnic-gender divisions onto their older forms. At the least, it certainly has re-casted the make-up and character of India's rapidly growing working class in a decentred and disaggregated direction thereby throwing in turn challenging questions for class focused politics.

However, this transition process, not surprisingly, was associated with what Marx referred to as "primitive accumulation" of world of the third (which arises in the event of capitalist-induced industrialisation and urbanisation). A rapid process of expropriation of land, forests, rivers, etc, unfolded, which was justified by the idealised trope of the progress of the third world from its so-called decrepitude state; the outside of the world of the third is represented as the devalued "third world" (victim, hapless, evil, utopian, etc) waiting to be rescued through uprooting or uplifting.

The palpable violence against the world of the third is projected as necessary for initiating long-run liberation of the embedded subjects from their own "backward" structures that hold them down. Because the Dalits and particularly Adivasis reside in these areas, they have been subjected to the process of land alienation, dislocations, forced evictions, and displacements. However, what appears as progressive from the perspective of global capital (or the third world) may appear as unjust violence and plunder from the perspective of world of the third, which in turn can and did produce countrywide resistance; the last 25 years have been witness to such resistances and the effort of state–capital nexus to manage and navigate this process.

The response of the state has been manifold. Recognising that mere repression will not do, the state had to initiate a rethinking on the issue of land acquisition and forest rights; laws on these soon followed although the same nation state has since been trying to undercut and undermine those laws. At the same time, there transpired an apparent "securitisation of the economic".

Under the new order, the economy is a security problem in two ways: (a) an economic state of exception, which arises via the crisis emanating from the functioning of a global competitive market capitalist economy (say, following the effect of global economic crisis of 2008); and (b) a political state of exception, which arises due to fundamental dissent or fettering of the process of primitive accumulation.

The former entails state intervention (say, through fiscal, monetary and currency policies) to rescue the capitalist market economy from itself (but only momentarily so as to put it back on track as was the case after the economic crisis). Instead of addressing the source of the economic crisis, which would require questioning the current economic order and its inherent dynamics that procreate in stabilities and vulnerabilities, the governance of economic crisis seem to shift the focus from the disease/cause to its symptom/effect. This is akin to Quesnay's idea of governance, who suggested that "since governing the causes is difficult and expensive, it is more safe and useful to try to govern the effects" (Agamben 2014: 3). Trying to overcome the crisis by governing the effects and thus avoiding the deeper systemic question, as in India's case presently, invariably ends up seeking deeper neo-liberal reforms rather than its truncation or arrest.

On the other hand, the political state of exception paves the way for a securitisation where entire regions and people therein could be classified into a state of exception (Agamben 2005), in the sense that state enjoys the sovereign power to declare illegal the normal rights of these people that is otherwise accorded to ordinary citizens. The post-reform Indian state has acquired an almost imperial authority to, at any time, name and segregate any region/group/person as existing outside the scope of law. It does not matter whether the latter operate outside law (they may or may not). What is material is that the state by this kind of naming, relocates itself outside law. Its right to be outside the rule of law is henceforth rendered legal; that is what allows the political state of exception to emerge and by extension produce the security state. The Indian state is also a security state in this sense.

In this context, it is hardly surprising that the opposition to "Development" gets displaced into a particular political terrain, not for engagement or debate but to be positioned as, and declared, the "enemy of the state". Thus the scope of defining, branding and punishing the "terrorists and secessionists" is being gradually broadened to encompass the "Development dissenters".

At this point, sanctioned politics thrives not on expanding the scope and scale of democratisation within Indian society, but on its growing truncation through the suppression of dissent to the so-called nationalist consensus of "Development". Correspondingly, the Indian state that has emerged as a condition provider for global capitalism uses both ideological and repressive apparatuses, and becomes a complex site of biopolitics, disciplinary politics and sovereign politics.

Balm of Inclusive Development

Inclusive development (as distinct from inclusive growth) addresses three kinds of exclusions: structural, social and income; exclusions from the circuits-camp of global capital, from benefits of growth emanating in the latter and from modern institutions. The state is deemed as the only institution that can possibly take care of this extensive domain that manifests in the world of the third but gets foregrounded via its instituted discourse of the third world. The state does not just uproot but also uplifts by being benevolent.

As we have seen, structural exclusion arises from the very process of making of the world of the third. To address structural exclusion, there is, among other things, a concerted attempt to introduce and deepen the market economy, as also introduce principles of individualism, competition and profit as part of institutional intervention (aimed at subverting and demoting the extant "backward" structures) to transform the production economy of the world of the third and make it dependent on the benevolence of the state. The point is also to increasingly interpellate the world of the third subjects to the signals and signs of market, competition, profit, risk-taking behaviour, etc, thereby initiating a long-drawn process of subject formation in the image of neo-liberal subjectivity.

The disaster of the "Shining India" campaign in the 2004 elections symbolised by the defeat of the Bharatiya Janata Party-led National Democratic Alliance led to a rethinking among policymakers. A realisation dawned that high growth boosted by the circuits of global capital and particularly its hub has been exclusionary not only in the described sense of structural exclusion, but because trickle down is not working sufficiently well leading to a greater income and social divide; it received strength from the argument (theoretical and empirical) that income and social inequalities may undermine the otherwise accepted positive relation between income growth and poverty reduction, and therefore needs to be addressed in 'Development' along with capitalist induced economic growth driven by the neo-liberal policy. This revisionist position made palpable the limitation of the neo-liberalism–global capitalism complex (without denying its central importance), a point which was readily acknowledged by the Indian state under the United Progressive Alliance (UPA) regime.

The subsequent shifting policy paradigm held that high economic growth lubricated by a global competitive economy must be supplemented by inclusive development addressing the mentioned exclusions. Accordingly, the state must combine two seemingly contrasting rationales of neo-liberalism and dirigisme in a coherent but divided manner.

> We need a Government that, when it comes to the market, sets effective, incentive-compatible rules and remains on the sidelines with minimal interference, and at the same time, plays an important role in directly helping the poor by ensuring that they get basic education and health services and receive adequate nutrition and food. This roll back of the government in the former [circuits-camp of global capital] will enable it to devote more energy and resources to and be more effective in the latter [world of the third].
> (*Economic Survey* 2009–10: 23)

Not surprisingly, the problem of redistribution of the benefits of growth to the excluded populace, whether in the form of much discussed social programmes addressing socially excluded groups or redistributive programmes targeting the bottom quintile of the income bracket, laid down the foundation for an additional explanation of the existence of the Indian state. It is held by many scholars that a high growth rate combined with redistribution produced a dramatic fall in income poverty during the UPA regime though hardcore neo-liberal proponents demote the role of redistribution in this outcome. Moreover, regarding its interventionist role within the world of the third, the Indian state inculcates a different menu of techniques and strategies imbibing neo-liberal modes of governance (targeting, cost–benefit approach, modern management techniques, individual responsibility, etc) and in ways that are as far as possible monetised and commercialised (cash transfer as against kind transfer is just an example).

Inclusive development has changed the meaning and contour of Indian politics in another way, especially at the margins of the circuits of global capital and the world of the third. Identity, regional and even class politics are often getting reduced to cries for inclusion, represented by competition to get access to distribution networks; in particular, identity politics (based on region, ethnicity, caste, religion, etc) have acquired growing significance. Politics, including issue-based local politics, is becoming state-centric, a struggle of how and whether groups can get absorbed into the conduits of inclusive development. This deepseated relationship of politics to social programmes also makes demotion of inclusive development, as has been recently suggested in some quarters, a vexed issue.

Crisis: From Economic to Transitional

The new order of things has become the reference point in terms of which further transformation of the economy and society is posited, discussed and evaluated. I will exemplify my point with a brief analysis of the economic crisis.

The response of Indian state to it can be divided into the somewhat groping temporary Keynesian type initial response involving the suspension of reforms (2008–mid-2012) followed subsequently by aggressive neo-liberal policy reassertion. Interestingly, this reassertion of neo-liberalism is posited not merely on account of the economic crisis, but came to be more vigorously premised on what may be referred to as a transition crisis; the former has been telescoped in the latter.

It was argued that the new order has exhibited an inability to move jobs en masse from the low productivity agricultural sector to the more productive industrial sector, particularly of labour absorption in the organised manufacturing sector. This scenario has produced in turn a growing income and social divide. If the present divide between a small organised sector and the large unorganised sector turns out to be permanent then the high economic growth regime will become unsustainable, mal-distribution persistent and serious social strife will ensue. That the Lewisian-type trajectory has got derailed in India's transition is a problem that must be corrected; any valorisation of the unorganised sector is misplaced.

This perceived lacuna makes the neo-liberal proponents question the extant form of circuits-camp of global capital and the lack of job growth in the organised sector which they maintain need to be made more inclusive by propelling an expansion of labour-intensive manufacturing driven growth (such that income, productive employment and opportunities increase and gets relatively evenly spread across socio-economic groups). Inclusion must be at the level of economic structure and cannot be deemed as the primary responsibility of the state. In this context, it is claimed that this redirection of the transitional route can be induced by deepening neo-liberal reforms rather than truncating or arresting them.

Given the unfolding scenario that clearly points to the above, and despite resistances, this looks like a good bet to transpire in the immediate future. Whether or not the reforms succeed in its desired objective and whatever may be the lasting effect on the Indian economy, it seems that, despite recurrent contradictions–crises–resistances, the displacement of the debate on India's economic reform to that of transition crisis has succeeded in securing and augmenting the possibility of the march of Indian capitalism in the immediate future.

Note

1. The homo economicus or "economic man" (seen as an embodiment of post-enlightenment rationality) has been the classic rendition of subject under liberal theory. However, as Foucault argued, "[N]eoliberalism is not Adam Smith; neoliberalism is not market society" (2008: 131). Under neo-liberalism, the meaning of homoeconomicus undergoes an alteration. It is no longer merely a "rational being" but a personification of rational conduct with entrepreneurial human capital which we, following Foucault, summarise pithily in

the following paragraph as rational ability machine (Becker 1976; Foucault 2008; and Chakrabarti, Dhar and Dasgupta 2015: Chapter 4 for details). The subject we are referring to qualifies as homoeconomicus in this altered sense.

References

Agamben, A. (2005): *State of Exception,* London: Chicago University Press.

——— (2014): "The Security State and a Theory of Destituent Power," *Philosophers for Change,* 25 February, https://philosophersforchange.org/ 2014/02/25/ the-security-state-and-a-theory-of-destituent-power

Becker, G.S. (1976): *The Economic Approach to Human Behaviour,* Chicago and London: University of Chicago Press.

Chakrabarti, A. and S. Cullenberg (2003): *Transition and Development in India,* New York : Routledge.

Chakrabarti, A. and A. Dhar (2012): "Gravel in the Shoe: Nationalism and World of the Third," *Rethinking Marxism: A Journal of Economics, Culture & Society,* Vol 24, No 1, pp 106–23.

Chakrabarti, A., A. Dhar and B. Dasgupta (2015): *The Indian Economy in Transition: Globalisation, Capitalism and Development,* Cambridge University Press.

Economic Survey (2009–10): *Economic Survey 2009–10,* Ministry of Finance, Government of India.

Foucault, M. (2008): *The Birth of Biopolitics: Lectures at the College de France 1978–79,* translation Graham Burchell, London: Palgrave Macmillan.

Gibson-Graham, J.K. (2006): *The End of Capitalism (As We Knew It): A Feminist Critique of Political Economy,* Oxford: Blackwell Publishers.

Hayek, F.A. (2001): *The Road to Serfdom,* 1944, Oxon: Routledge.

Kaviraj, S. (2010): *The Trajectories of the Indian State,* Ranikhet: Permanent Black.

Kumar, R. (2016): *Neoliberalism, Critical Pedagogy and Education,* New York: Routledge.

Lemke, T. (2001): "'The Birth of Bio-politics': Michel Foucault's Lecture at the Collège de France on Neo-liberal Governmentality," *Economy & Society,* Vol 30, No 2.

Madra, Y.M. and C. Özselçuk (2010): "Jouissance and Antagonism in the Forms of the Commune: A Critique of Biopolitical Subjectivity," *Rethinking Marxism: A Journal of Economics, Culture & Society,* Vol 22, No 3.

Rabinow, P. and N. Rose (2006): "Biopower Today," *Bio Societies,* Vol 1.

Resnick, S. and R. Wolff (1987): *Knowledge and Class: A Marxian Critique of Political Economy,* Chicago: University of Chicago Press.

Špoljar Vržina, S. (2012): "Brainstorming for Which Brains Are Prohibited: Analysing Our Bio-Neoliberal Realities," *Collegium Antropologicum,* Vol 36, No 4.

TINA, India and Economic Liberalisation

T. Sabri Öncü

Although India has been "reforming" since 1991, almost nobody seems to be satisfied with either the progress or the outcome. The reformers need to put the economy's long-term interests above financial sector short-termism and reorganise the financial system to keep credit productive. They should realise also that banks do not lend existing money but newly create the money they lend, as this has major implications for monetary and fiscal policies, as well as for financial sector reforms.

ζ❧

TINA is an acronym for the term "there is no alternative". It was famously used by Margaret Thatcher when she wrote in the *Daily Telegraph* on 22 May 1980:

> There's no easy popularity in what we are proposing, but it is fundamentally sound. Yet I believe people accept there is no real alternative.

Although Tina is used as a synonym for such terms as "neo-liberalism," "globalisation" and "financialisation," its best synonym appears to be the term "imperialism" defined as a relation between Centre nations and Periphery nations. The Centre nations have power over the Periphery nations so as to bring about a condition of "disharmony of interest" between them (Galtung 1971); by disharmony Galtung means conflict. Why

TINA is synonymous with imperialism will become evident in the later sections of this article.

Transcendental Marketism

In 1994, without referring to either neoliberalism or TINA, Prabhat Patnaik (1994) introduced another synonym, "transcendental marketism". By this, Patnaik meant the ideology in which

> the state's role is reduced to performing three main functions: protecting and sustaining the functioning of markets; using whatever policy instruments are available to entice capital, both foreign and domestic, to come into or stay within the economy; and undertaking certain minimal expenditures *inter alia* to ameliorate the excesses perpetrated by the market, for example, the so-called 'safety-net,' so as to make the regime socially viable. (1994: 683)

He called it "transcendental" because the case for it was made on general principles and identified three main arguments.

The first argument is the usual neoclassical argument of efficient allocation of resources which requires "correctly" determined prices. In this view, since the markets are efficient and therefore market-determined prices are "correct" in the sense that they reflect all "relevant information," any state intervention distorts the prices and results in inefficient allocation of resources. Hence, the market wins.

The second argument is the so-called agency problem between voters (principals) and politicians (agents), and emphasises the intrinsic limitations of the state as an agency for economic intervention: for the state to perform well in its interventions, the bureaucracy must be controlled by elected politicians who are accountable to voters. The voters provide their personal information to the politicians; but monitoring the politicians and holding them accountable is very costly to the voters; further, the chance of personally influencing the election results is negligible, especially in large democracies, so most voters rationally choose to be ignorant and leave the politicians unaccountable. In addition, the voters cannot reasonably exit their relationship with the politicians, at least until the next election, so the voters cannot discipline the politicians. The market, by contrast, is essentially a disciplining device because there the principals can exit their relationship with the agents easily. Hence, the market wins again.

The last argument—which Patnaik called neo-Schumpeterian in fashion—emphasises

> the stifling of enterprise and innovativeness that an economy with pervasive state intervention and ownership. The market, in this view, apart from being a purveyor of appropriate signals, and a disciplining device, is also a mechanism for unleashing enterprise, in the absence of which there is bound to be economic atrophy. (Patnaik 1994: 683)

Hence, the market wins once again.

After presenting these arguments, Patnaik goes into a lengthy theoretical discussion showing that these arguments are false. But that was in 1994. In 2016, there is no need for discussing why these arguments are false at length. This is because the ongoing global economic crisis triggered by the global financial crisis that started in the summer of 2007 has taught us that neither are markets efficient, nor are market prices necessarily correct, nor is the market essentially a disciplining device, nor is it necessarily a mechanism for unleashing enterprise. Hence, transcendental marketism is equivalent to what Patnaik later called "contextual marketism" (1994: 684), which is by his definition, nothing but TINA.

Was Jawaharlal Nehru a Socialist?

Patnaik (1994) dismisses a few other arguments as logically dubious and to those, I add one more, at least in the case of India. This dubious argument is best expressed by Satyajit Das (2012):

> India's poor economic performance was not driven by religious factors but the half-baked socialist policies of its leaders. India's first Prime Minister

Jawaharlal Nehru admired the Soviet Union, becoming one of the few followers of its ultimately unsuccessful economic policies.

The reason why Das referred to "religious factors" was because of his earlier mention of the so-called "Hindu rate of growth"—a derogatory term coined by economist Raj Krishna in 1978 to refer to the low annual growth rate of the Indian economy which averaged about 3.5% from 1950 to 1980, while per capita annual income and population growth rates averaged about 1.3% and 2.2% respectively.

Well, if not socialist policies, then what? Of course, market policies, that is, TINA.

Whether Jawaharlal Nehru admired the Soviet Union or not can be debated. But calling the economic policies of the post-independence/pre-liberalisation Indian leaders socialist is almost equivalent to calling the recent quantitative easing policies of the Federal Reserve (the American central bank) socialist, as many subscribers of the Austrian economic school and other libertarians do these days. Neither Nehru nor other pre-liberalisation Indian leaders had any problems with capitalism. They were influenced more by Keynes than by Marx. They were economic nationalists cooperating with the national bourgeoisie they fostered.

Despite variations across countries for historical, geographical and unequal development reasons, the economic policies post-independence/pre-liberalisation Indian leaders implemented was common place around the globe shortly after the onset of the Great Depression in 1929, gaining momentum with the national independence movements after the World War II and lasting at least until—if not well beyond—the mid-to-late 1960s when capitalism entered its first post-war over-accumulation crisis, that is, when the so-called Golden Age of Capitalism ended. TINA—with its natural outcome of income and wealth inequality which eventually reached unheard proportions as Piketty (2014) demonstrated—is the project the system has been trying to run to overcome this over-accumulation crisis shortly after its onset. The five-year plans by some central planning agency that the adherents of this argument like to mention had been implemented in many other capitalist countries too. One simple example is the hardly-socialist Turkey where socialists usually end up in jail or on the death row rather than in the prime ministry or in the finance ministry.

TINA Comes to India

The "wall" came tumbling down in Eastern Europe in 1989, oil prices shot up in response to the Iraqi invasion of Kuwait in 1990, the Soviet Union collapsed in 1991, and in the same year, India faced a balance of payments crisis. Finance Minister Manmohan Singh in his budget speech on 24 July 1991 said:

> There is no time to lose. Neither the government nor the economy can live beyond its means year after year. The room for manoeuvre, to live on borrowed money or time, does not exist anymore. Any further postponement of macro-economic adjustment, long overdue, would mean that the balance of payments situation, now exceedingly difficult, would become unmanageable and inflation, already high, would exceed limits of tolerance. (Ministry of Finance 1991–92)

What Singh said was more or less along the lines of what Margaret Thatcher said in her speech to the Conservative Party Conference on 14 October 1983:

> One of the great debates of our time is about how much of your money should be spent by the State and how much you should keep to spend on your family. Let us never forget this fundamental truth: the State has no source of money other than money which people earn themselves. If the State wishes to spend more it can do so only by borrowing your savings or by taxing you more. It is no good thinking that someone else will pay—that 'someone else' is you. There is no such thing as public money; there is only taxpayers' money. (Thatcher 1983)

The above is a total misunderstanding of what money is, but I will come back to this topic later. What is important to note at this point is that after

Singh's July 1991 budget speech, towards the end of which he quoted Victor Hugo's famous phrase "no power on earth can stop an idea whose time has come," India became another TINA country.

Although TINA spread around the globe after what David Harvey (2003) called the "Deng–Volcker–Thatcher–Reagan Revolution" that took place between 1978 and 1980, its origins can be traced back to the 1973 coup d'état in Chile after which a group of Chilean economists (who came to be known as the "Chicago Boys" because of the degrees most of them obtained from the University of Chicago where Milton Friedman taught) started implementing their economic reform programme. Often referred to as the "miracle of Chile" after Friedman's 25 January 1982 article in the *Newsweek* where he declared "Chile is an economic miracle," the programme they implemented consisted of three main objectives: economic liberalisation, privatisation of state-owned enterprises, and stabilisation of inflation—or to loosely translate into today's language—financial stability.

Sounds Familiar?

Of course. For example, let us take a look at the structural adjustment programme imposed on Greece by its May 2010 bailout creditors when Greece triggered the ongoing European sovereign debt crisis in early 2010. What were the three components of this programme? They were: "(1) fiscal reforms to 'generate savings,' that is, 'austerity,' (2) structural reforms to 'enhance competitiveness and growth,' such as privatisation of public assets and deregulation of the markets including the labour market, that is, 'labour market flexibility,' and (3) financial reforms to 'enhance financial stability,' such as banking regulations, and bank recapitalisation and resolution mechanisms" (Öncü 2015). Apart from a few new ingredients that came to being after the ongoing global financial crisis, this is the usual recipe imposed on many Third World economies as well as former socialist countries like Russia by their creditors—mainly the International Monetary Fund (IMF) and World Bank—since the beginning of TINA.

India before 1991 BOP Crisis

Before going back to the balance of payments (BOP) crisis of 1991 in India, let us take a quick look at the post-independence Indian economy from independence in 1947 until the onset of the 1991 balance of payment crisis. India's post-independence development strategy until the 1980s was both inward-looking and highly interventionist. Essentially based on import substitution, it consisted of, among other things, complex industrial licensing requirements and substantial public ownership of heavy industry (Cerra and Saxena 2002).

An important tool of this development strategy was the central bank, the Reserve Bank of India (RBI). Established in 1934 under the British rule and privately owned entirely, the RBI was nationalised in 1949. The financial sector, particularly the banking sector, was another tool of this development strategy. The RBI imposed two requirements on the banking sector: priority sector lending (PSL) requirement and the statutory liquidity ratio (SLR). While PSL ensured that banks made a significant portion of their loans to farmers for agriculture, poor people for housing, students for education and the like, the SLR determined the amount of government securities the banks had to hold as percentage of demand and time deposits, and, among other things, ensured that the banks lent to the government.[1]

However, India's macroeconomic policy sought stability through low monetary growth and moderate public sector deficits. Indeed, moderate public sector deficits and low monetary growth went hand-in-hand because the SLR imposed on the banks by the RBI—and hence the availability of government securities—put a boundary on the amount of money banks could create. As a result, inflation remained generally low except in response to unfavourable supply shocks such as oil price increases or poor weather conditions. Low monetary growth and moderate public sector deficits also went hand-in-hand with the previously mentioned Hindu rate of growth. India had run a current account surplus for most years until 1980, with a reasonable cushion of official reserves and official aid dominated capital inflows (Cerra and Saxena 2002).

With the introduction of import replenishment schemes in 1975, India's development strategy started to drift away from import substitution and the government began a process of gradual liberalisation of trade, investment, and financial markets (Cerra and Saxena 2002). While many argue that this was a policy shift from an import substitution-based development strategy to a export-led growth strategy, much of these changes (mostly in the form of import liberalisation of raw materials and intermediate goods) were made with the intention of allowing domestic industries to modernise to meet the pent-up demand in the domestic market, although this gave some thrust to exports too. To sum up, however measured and slow-paced, economic liberalisation in India actually started in 1975, not in 1991, although the changes that followed the 1991 crisis were much more comprehensive.

BOP Crisis of 1991

The first and more cautious phase of India's economic liberalisation lasted until 1985, and in its second half—between 1980 and 1984—India had run a modest current account deficit of about 1.1% of the gross domestic product (GDP) per year on an average. In the second and speedier phase that started in 1985, India's current account deficit and external debt started to grow. Despite a respectable increase in the dollar value of exports during the second phase, the dollar value of imports had increased at a faster rate and the growing current account deficit had become increasingly financed by commercial borrowing and non-resident Indian (NRI) remittances, which meant greater dependence on higher cost, short-term financing.

It should be mentioned that India's changing relationship with the former Soviet Union also played an important role in this situation (Cerra and Saxena 2002). The Soviet Union had been India's largest trade partner until the mid-1980s and the trade between the two countries was conducted in rupees, meaning among other things, India used to make a large part of her oil imports in her own currency which she could create at the stroke of a pen without any external debt. But from the mid-1980s onwards, important political and economic changes had been taking place in the Soviet Union and the Soviet Union eventually collapsed in 1991.

With the turn of 1980, India started to run a current account deficit which lasted until 2001 when India recorded its first current account surplus after 21 years. Starting at about 0.94% of the GDP in 1980, the Indian current account deficit reached a peak of about 2.37% of the GDP in 1988 and was about 2.15% of the GDP at the end of 1990.

While India's foreign debt was $20.5 billion in 1980, it reached $72 billion by 1991, making India the world's third largest debtor after Brazil and Mexico. Medium- and long-term commercial debt jumped from $3 billion in 1984 to $13 billion in 1990 and the stock of NRI deposits rose from $3 billion to $10.5 billion over the same period, while short-term external debt reached about $6 billion and the ratio of debt-service payments to current receipts was close to 30% in 1990 (Cerra and Saxena 2002).

But the biggest worry was the foreign exchange reserves which were hovering at $1.3 billion to $1.5 billion, barely enough to meet the country's import needs for three weeks (Bhattacharya 2011). Hence, by 1991, India had become highly vulnerable to shocks as a result of its growing current account deficit and greater reliance on short-term external financing.

The already mentioned oil price hike in response to the Iraqi invasion of Kuwait in 1990—despite significant import substitution in oil—and the global recession of 1990–91 that hit India's major export partners including the United States (US) were the two "external" shocks. The rising political uncertainty, political disputes centred around caste and religious issues, riots throughout the country, and the assassination of Rajiv Gandhi, the President of the Congress party, on 21 May 1991 were the "internal" factors contributing to the crisis. And barely 10 days after a minority government took its oath, on 2 July 1991, mayhem started. On that day, the rupee was devalued by about 9.5% against the US dollar. The next day, the rupee was devalued by another 11% and in the course of three days, lost 20% of its value against the US dollar.

However, signs of the mayhem had become evident much earlier. For example, in September 1990, the National Front government which fell two months later anticipated the forthcoming trouble and borrowed about $550 million from the IMF under a gold tranche facility (Bhattacharya 2011). Towards the end of 1990, India's credit rating was downgraded, effectively cutting its access to sources of commercial credit and by early 1991, India was on the brink of default. Between 6 July 1991 and 18 July 1991, the government airlifted a total of 47 tonnes of gold to London to be kept with the Bank of England in three rounds as collateral to secure an IMF loan.

Indeed, in the course of 11 months from September 1990 to July 1991 and after three governments, India was ready to surrender. Manmohan Singh's budget speech on 24 July 1991 was to send this message to the IMF, the World Bank and the "international community". About three months later, in October 1991, the government signed a stand-by loan agreement with the IMF in which the Fund pledged about $2.27 billion to be disbursed in eight tranches until May 1993. Then came a structural adjustment loan agreement with the World Bank in which the Bank spelled out the conditionalities of the IMF and World Bank loans and India got bailed out.

25 Years Later

The conditionalities of the IMF and World Bank loans consisted of nothing but TINA and although since then India has been "reforming," almost nobody seems to be satisfied with either the progress or the outcome. A quick look at the domestic and international newspapers, magazines, journals and other media is a clear indication of this.

Let me now go back to imperialism and narrow the broad definition I borrowed from Galtung in the beginning of this essay. Galtung takes his departure from two of the most glaring facts about this world:

[T]he tremendous inequality, within and between nations, in almost every aspects of human living conditions, including the power to decide on those living conditions; and the resistance of this inequality to change. (1971: 81)

According to him, the world consists of Centre and Periphery nations; and each nation, in turn, has its centre and periphery.[2] He then gives his narrow definition of imperialism as a relation between the Centre and Periphery nations such that (a) there is "harmony of interest" between the centre in the Centre nations and the centre in the Periphery nations; (b) there is more disharmony of interest within the Periphery nations than within the Centre nations; (c) there is disharmony of interest between the periphery in the Centre nations and the periphery in the Periphery nations.

Why I claimed TINA and imperialism are synonyms should be clear now. It is up to the peripheries of the Centre and Periphery nations to find a way to unite and resist the power of their centres so as to bring about a condition of disharmony of interest between them in general and TINA in particular.

An important characteristic of imperialism is the dominance of finance capital. Unlike what Lenin claimed, imperialism is not the highest stage of capitalism, but a recurring phase intrinsic to it. This does not mean that history repeats itself, but here is Lenin's definition of imperialism (Lenin 1916): (a) the concentration of production and capital has developed to such a high stage that it has created monopolies which play a decisive role in economic life; (b) the merging of bank capital with industrial capital, and the creation, on the basis of this "finance capital", of a financial oligarchy; (c) the export of capital as distinguished from the export of commodities acquires exceptional importance; (d) the formation of international monopolist capitalist associations which share the world among themselves; and (e) the territorial division of the whole world among the biggest capitalist powers is completed.

If we leave out Lenin's fifth and possibly parts of his fourth points, it appears that Lenin's definition is quite relevant today as well. Indeed, what Galtung called "centre" currently corresponds to what Lenin called "financial oligarchy" and what is called "financialisation" these days is nothing but imperialism.

Let me make one more point. When finance capital enters any country, it does not enter that country for altruistic reasons. Whether it is in the form of "direct" investment or portfolio investment or "hot money," its objective is clear: to grow. And finance capital cannot grow in any country it enters if it does not suck wealth from that country, whether it helped create that wealth or not.

Before closing this section, let me connect imperialism to Minsky's financial instability hypothesis in which Minsky (1980) identified three types of financial postures that contribute to the accumulation of insolvent debt: (a) hedge finance, in which borrowers can meet all debt payments (interest and principal) from their cash flows from investment; (b) speculative finance, in which borrowers can meet their interest payments from investment, but must roll over their debt over to pay back the original loan; and (c) Ponzi finance, when borrowers can neither repay the interest nor the original debt from the original investment, but rely entirely on rising asset prices to allow them continually refinance their debt.

Imperialism—at least, currently—is essentially about Minsky's financial postures of the third kind, that is, Ponzi finance.

Now What?

Since the Deng–Volcker–Thatcher–Reagan Revolution of 1978–80, we have been in a Ponzi finance period during which the financial sector has travelled along an unsustainable path and rent extraction has been financial oligarchy's major source of gain. Rather than becoming more equal, the economies polarised between creditors and debtors, the debt burden shifted from the public sector to the private sector through austerity programmes, and much of this accumulated private sector debt almost everywhere around the globe including India is currently unpayable.

Any economic and financial reform programme must take these facts into account.

Further, there are not many left who still claim that the markets are efficient and while there is no question of the necessity of discipline and accountability in the functioning of any economy, relegating the discipline to the market is not the way to go. Anyone who paid any attention to such scandals as Enron in 2001, Worldcom and Tyco in 2002, AIG in 2005, Lehman in 2008, Satyam in 2009 and a host of many others over the last

15 years would know this (Accounting Degree Review nd). And many have argued that if accountability mechanisms are well designed, an economy with an interventionist state would perform better than markets left to themselves.

However, Indian reformers do not appear to be taking these into account.

Whether one calls it financialisation or imperialism or something else, the reformers need to put the economy's long-term interests above financial sector short-termism, and reorganise banking and financial systems in a way to keep credit productive and within the ability of debtors to pay. Since the question of whether a bank lends existing money or newly creates the money it lends has major implications for monetary and fiscal policies, as well as for financial sector reforms, this question should be debated vigorously. This is because if banks newly create the money they lend, then the money supply is endogenously determined by the economic activity, not the other way around. And there is little doubt that, like almost every other economy these days, India is an endogenous money economy too (Kohli 2016).

A non-exhaustive list of other topics to debate for economic and financial reforms may include: (a) writing down debts in keeping with the ability to pay; (b) taxing rent extraction and capital gains; (c) public provision of all banking; (d) public ownership of natural monopolies; (e) central bank financing of government deficits.

No matter what, one thing is for sure: TINA and its equivalent, transcendental marketism, are fallacies. Their unconditional acceptance is leading to policies that at best are keeping us in economic doldrums with highly undesirable social and environmental consequences. There is no questioning that income and wealth inequality has reached unheard proportions while poverty is getting worse by the day; regional wars and terrorist attacks are now ordinary events that occur almost daily; a variety of fascist, racist, sexist leaders and parties are on the rise in many countries; and environmental degradation and global warming have already become undeniable even for the strictest denialists.

It is time to leave TINA before it gets too late, if it is not too late already.

Notes

1. This is why the loans to deposits ratio of the Indian banking sector has always been below one since 1949 to this day: the credit extended by the banks to the government is not in the form of loans, but in the form of government securities for which the banks create the corresponding deposits for the government.

2. To this, one may add the concept of semi-periphery which in daily parlance may mean "emerging market economies" or "middle classes" as the case may be, but I will stick to Galtung's classification.

References

Accounting Degree Review (nd): "The 10 Worst Corporate Accounting Scandals of All Time," http://www.accounting-degree.org/scandals/.

Bhattacharya, A K (2011): "Two Months that Changed India," *Business Standard*, 2 July, http://www.business-standard.com/article/beyond-business/two-months-that-changed-india -111070200041_ 1.html.

Cerra, V. and S.C. Saxena (2002): "What Caused the 1991 Currency Crisis in India?," *International Monetary Fund Staff Papers*, Vol 49, No 3.

Das, Satyajit (2012): "The Great Pretender—India's Economic Past & Future, Part 1: 'India Shining'," *Naked Capitalism*, http://www.nakedcapitalism.com/2012/05/satyajit-das-the-great-pretender-indias-economic-past-future-part-1-india-shining.html.

Galtung, J. (1971): "A Structural Theory of Imperialism," *Journal of Peace Research*, Vol 8, No 2, pp 81–117.

Harvey, D. (2003): *The New Imperialism*, Oxford: Oxford University Press.

Kohli, V. (2016): "Financial Reforms in an Endogenous Money Economy: The Case of India," *Economic & Political Weekly*, Vol 51, No 12, pp 87–93.

Lenin, V.I. (1916): *Imperialism, The Highest Stage of Capitalism*, Modern History Sourcebook, http://legacy.fordham.edu/halsall/mod/1916lenin-imperialism.html.

Ministry of Finance (1991–92): "Budget Speech 1991–92," 24 July, Ministry of Finance, http://indiabudget.nic.in/bspeech/bs199192.pdf.

Minsky, H.P. (1980), "Finance and Profits: The Changing Nature of American Business Cycles," *The Business Cycle and Public Policy*, Washington DC: US Government Printing Office, pp 209–44.

Öncü, T.S. (2015): "Greece, Its International Creditors and the Euro," *Economic & Political Weekly*, Vol 50, No 7, pp 10–12.

Patnaik, P. (1994): "International Capital and National Economic Policy: A Critique of India's Economic Reforms," *Economic & Political Weekly*, Vol 29, No 12, pp 683–89.

Piketty, T. (2014): "*Capital in the Twenty-first Century,*" Belknap Press.

Thatcher, M. (1983): "Speech to Conservative Party Conference," Thatcher Archive, http://www.margaretthatcher.org document/105454.

Politics of Growth

Script and Postscript

Atul Sood

Challenging the notion that economic reforms have resulted in a non-interventionist neo-liberal state, the relationship between economic and social outcomes is examined. These outcomes result from the interconnections between economic reforms, the responses of the Indian state and the nature of Indian politics. Understanding and evaluating this relationship will contribute to further strengthening the Indian people's engagement with policy choices that the ruling classes make and their contestations and struggles to improve their lives.

❧❀❧

The purpose of this article is to look at the experience of the last 25 years of dominant economic policy thinking and draw lessons for the future. This experience is evaluated on the premise that the governing regimes in India cannot set universal and homogeneous goals for all Indians, who happen to be sharply differentiated across income, region, caste, gender and other social and economic identities. Any outcome evaluation has to be from the vantage point of those who are poor, deprived and marginalized and from the point of view of supporting the democratic struggles that bring about greater equity and social and economic justice. The evaluation of the 25-year period has to be in sync with the Indian people's engagement with these policy choices, the contestations and struggles to make life better today. Furthermore, in order to understand the script and the process of economic reforms in India, we need to look at the Indian state, economic reforms and politics in an interconnected way and not look at the economic policy in isolation.

I will briefly present below how some of the economic parameters have changed over the last quarter century. I begin this article by looking at how those who were the movers and shakers of economic reforms in India now look back at their own achievements, what insight hindsight provides, and then examine in detail how in these 25 years the discourse of policy altered from the past, what have been the changes in public policy goals, how the Indian State has responded to the outcomes of these 25 years and what are the political implications of these changes for those who support a more democratic and inclusive vision for the people of the country.

Reforms, Outcomes and Nature of Growth

The fallout of the union budget presented in July 1991, further pursuance of industrial delicensing, an altered trade policy, exchange rate management announcements and the devaluation of the Indian rupee on 1 July are all part of the historic quarter century we mark this year. The face associated with this momentous change shared his reflections with the nation recently. Former Prime Minister Manmohan Singh, who was then the finance minister, says two things: first, he does not see much originality in these reform ideas, and second, he sees the process of economic reforms in India to be still trapped in the circumstances in which it began, namely, the willingness to act, only when there is a crisis (Vikraman 2016a). So the architect of policy change that led to profound impact on the lives of vast majority of the Indian people, now admits that the policy prescription he used had nothing unique about India in it, and also that the environment of crisis, which these policies were supposed to address, persists even today.

Most commentators—across the political spectrum—writing on the last 25 years suggest that on the growth front the introduction of economic reform was a great success. There are a few commonly identified positive features. Gross domestic product (GDP) has grown 6.3 times today in comparison to its size in 1991; foreign exchange reserves as well as the current account deficit and the centre's outstanding liabilities are in better shape; the composition of exports has changed. We now have lower import tariffs, and access to a larger number of consumables—television sets, automobiles and mobile phones. Remittances from abroad have grown. Poverty and mortality rates have declined and literacy has improved. There has been explosion in the number of private hospitals and private educational institutions and there is a section of the population that can now dream and aspire to access these institutions. The dismantling of the licence raj has led to the emergence of new sectors like information technology (IT) and the democratisation of the market for entrepreneurs is evident in the rise of associations like the Dalit Indian Chamber of Commerce and Industry.

Some of the negative consequences associated with the reforms identified in the mainstream writing include: uneven growth, sustained growth not generating decent employment, growth driven by low value added services generating low skill, low remuneration jobs, small share of jobs requiring high level of skills by passing many even those amongst the dominant castes who lack requisite soft skills, private consumption led growth and declining share of public investment, social and economic inequality, urban centric growth often based on privatisation of natural resources—water, land, etc at the cost of neglect of agriculture and absence of accumulation drivers rooted in investment and innovation. These two sides of growth are seldom seen in any interconnected way and the popular implication drawn is that if we continue with the reforms process, it is only a matter of time that the corrections made will address the negative impacts of the reforms.

Former Finance Minister Yashwant Sinha made two interesting observations (Vikraman 2016b): one, that we still do not understand what leads to sustainable growth (defined by him as 7% and higher, for more than a year, which according to him has happened only twice after the economic reforms of 1991), and second, despite all the reforms, the poor (nearly three-fourths of India's population) continue to be not only poor, but also deprived of basic amenities (potable drinking water, sanitation, toilet facilities, electricity, roads, irrigation, housing) since independence. He finds an explanation for this failure in jobless growth. What explains jobless growth for him is a moot question. The reasons for jobless growth have not been addressed by Sinha and he does not provide any explanation for the reasons why this growth strategy has resulted in jobless growth. Is it rooted in the very nature of the growth strategy or is it just a temporary failure?

Irrespective of what these key players of the economic reforms process say in hindsight, there is an overall consensus that the current growth strategy is good for India. And, it is this focus on achieving growth alone, without discussing the sources, nature and drivers of growth, which has been the one major shift that has occurred in India's public policy debates since the economic reforms began.

There is no recognition in policy circles about some of the important understandings about growth that have evolved globally in recent years. Studying long-term patterns of growth, many economists have now come to the conclusion that inclusive growth cannot be reached simply by the state redistributing the gains from economic growth. There is a need for a redistribution of assets and intervention in market processes to create conditions and opportunities for all to participate in the growth process, particularly those who have been historically disadvantaged. Such challenges in shaping policies are never acknowledged in order to address the unacceptable outcomes of growth. There is talk of inclusive growth without any discussion on redistribution of assets, quantity and quality of jobs, and precarious livelihoods.

The current dominant growth discourse in India does not recognise that growth with high or growing inequalities is less likely to be sustainable, and that inequality can hamper growth. In fact, important contemporary studies on inequality—Thomas Piketty's (2014) *Capital in the Twenty-First Century*, and the equally popular, *Why Nations Fail* by Daron Acemoglu and James A. Robinson (2012)—are widely quoted and debated, and emphasise the need for inclusive institutions for economic transformation.

Given the blind faith in contemporary growth processes by the reformers, there is no question then that India's policy regimes of the last many decades will ever acknowledge what the long time World Bank researcher William Easterly recently said. Sinha is perhaps hinting at the same. Easterly (2013) notes that we know very little about what causes growth, the knowledge of the new growth theory—growth leads to more growth—notwithstanding. Exports, infrastructure, knowledge, labour pooling, agglomeration economies, localisation economies, etc, play a part, of course—but we do not know precisely what part. Swift growth today can easily be reversed tomorrow, with much the same policy regime in place. Easterly says—history and expectations matter—but we do not know how growth begins or where it begins, but once it begins, we know why/how it grows exponentially. When it reverses, we do not know what causes the reversal, but when reversal starts we know what matters.

It is because of the failure to engage with a deep historical understanding about the nature of uncertainty hidden in the contemporary growth process and the denial of possibilities to explore alternative frameworks of growth that Indian policymakers are willing to brutally trample over people's rights in their pursuit of growth.

Changing Goals of Public Policy and Specificities of the Indian State

Public policy in India has gone through major shifts in the recent years. With the implementation of "economic reforms" in the early 1990s, the focus and priorities of development altered in a significant way towards what was termed as "market orientation" compared to the relatively "inward" looking policies of the 1960s and 1970s.[1] These reforms meant greater liberalisation and privatisation that put more faith in the workings of the market in both economic and social spheres. In the early years of the last decade, with the rise of inequalities and deprivation,[2] as a result of economic reforms, along with marginal gains in social inequalities in education, health,[3] nutrition[4] and livelihoods,[5] policymakers started engaging with the idea that growth on its own will not ensure that it benefits all. Exclusion became a well-recognised feature of India's social and economic landscape, as a result. The experience of growth in Gujarat, the most robust and talked about story of growth in India in recent years, further reinforces the exclusionary nature of this growth process (Sood 2012).

Protest movements and civil society action in India constantly reminded the state actors about this dimension of exclusion as part of social reality. In many ways, Indian democracy (and various social movements) provided a consistent counterweight to address these inequalities. This counterweight had to be balanced with state's imperative to pursue economic reforms and consequently ensure greater withdrawal of the state. The idea was to somehow address inequalities of wealth and income and social and economic exclusion in a manner such that incentives for wealth creation do not get compromised. The institutional response that was crafted to address this conflicting and challenging situation is the key message that we need to understand from the 25 years of reforms.

The state is a continuing point of reference for anything that entails economic and social change in India. The role of the state in the context of the neo-liberal economic reform is often minimised. However, the Indian context is clearly different. The state and the market cannot be dichotomously understood in the context of the ongoing economic reforms in India.

The "typical" understandings about neo-liberal economic reforms—the non-interventionist nature of the state and good governance as a prerequisite for the success of economic reforms—are both not true in the Indian context (Sood 2015). The idea that in the phase of economic reforms, the state disengages itself from the economic and social sphere and the other neo-liberal orthodoxy that it can coexist in harmony with the "good governance programme" are both not applicable to India. Some of the features of governance, perceived to be associated with the neo-liberal reforms, especially like minimising rent-seeking and transparent and accountable provision of public goods in line with democratically expressed preferences, have not been achieved in India. The Indian case fits better with the new avatars of the state that are identified with liberalising economies. Evans (1995), for example, argues that the Indian case represents a partial and imperfect approximation of embedded autonomy. This is visible in some of the emerging sectors such as IT in India. However, land which has played a key role in contemporary accumulation dynamics in India does not fit this model. In India, the state is a facilitator and a close ally of private interests in land and it has not demonstrated the autonomy from its entrenched individual players.

The business-friendly Indian state of the 1990s, dependent on its growth synergy on national and international big business, which had internally given up any expectation of redistribution, had to now deal with the experience of enhanced inequalities and political claims made through social collectives and protest movements. Denial of the possibility of exploring alternative growth drivers, the entrenchment of exclusion in India's social and economic landscape and the deepening of the alliance between the big business interests and the Indian State created a serious pressure of legitimacy and acceptability for the political class. This compelled the ruling classes to explore and bring about institutional and political changes, manoeuvring of bureaucratic regulations, and even creating a buffer of non-governmental organisations and non-party politics between the government and the people. This happened along with the continued use by political parties, of religion, region, caste, nationalism and other such identities to conceal the social reality of our much divided and exploitative society.

The "rights-based approach," adopted by the state in the last decade, can also be seen as a part of this larger process to seek legitimacy. Such complex responses and the interventionist strategy of the Indian state to the twin challenges of retaining the drivers of accumulation and meeting people's aspirations, get even more complicated because of the specific features of the political process behind the implementation of economic reforms in India.

The nature of politics in India has ensured that liberalisation, a potentially contentious process, has been less on the agenda than it otherwise would have been. The specifics of liberalisation have tended to be discussed with niche audiences, such as chambers of industry and manufacturers' associations interested in select aspects of the reforms. The larger debate at the popular level in the second half of the last decade was on issues of employment guarantees, the right to food, the women's reservation bill, the impact of large dams, and the challenges of education and health, etc.

In each of the cases, the state always claimed to "stand" with the poor, the deprived and the downtrodden. The Prime Minister's Independence Day speeches, the parliamentary debates, and the content of political mobilisation all suggested that economic reforms were being undertaken for the poor. There have been debates on the privatisation of public utilities, the withdrawal of subsidies, the introduction of user charges and so on. But in popular discourse, these debates often close at public–private partnerships, and the signal sent is that all reforms are to benefit the poor, and nothing is being done in favour of private business interests.

The combined impact of the specificities of the Indian state and the politics of economic reforms established above is that expectations regarding the state in a typical neo-liberal environment, namely—that the state promotes "participatory, accountable and transparent governance in which streamlined bureaucratic institutions work with actors in the market and civil society to ensure liberal growth"—are not met in India (Jenkins 1999). The institutional environment for accumulation is less dependent on building competitiveness through transparency and increased accountability, and more on ensuring continued public legitimacy and robust capital accumulation through the "back door".

Harvey (2004), Perelman (2000) and Patnaik (2005) have all pointed out that in the current phase of global expansion, accumulation by dispossession and accumulation by encroachment have become prominent in some countries, including India. In the context of special economic zones (SEZs) in India, Levien (2011) argues that rather than Harvey's over-accumulated capital searching for new outlets, accumulation by dispossession in India is an extra-economic process of coercive expropriation typically exercised by states to help capitalists overcome barriers to accumulation—in his case, the absence of fully capitalist rural land markets. In SEZs, for example, the dis-accumulation of the peasantry occurs through capitalist rentiers who develop rural land mainly for IT companies and luxury real estate projects and who profit from the appreciation of artificially cheap land acquired by the state.

The result of this "reform by stealth" has been that the dynamics of accumulation and profit in India have been largely characterised by dispossession (of the poor, small landowners, the self-employed, homeworkers, etc) or by encroachment (either on land or forests by the mining companies or on rural and urban land by developers, builders and speculators).

The Current Conjuncture

What are the core economic dimensions of the recent power dispensation and how do we understand the shift in public policy away from inequality, rights and distribution in the light of the discussion on the Indian state and the politics of economic reforms discussed above?

The success of the Bharatiya Janata Party in the 2014 elections for a corporate-led development agenda that has simultaneously created a belief amongst the poor, Dalits, tribal communities, minorities and women that the ruling regime will meet their needs has brought about newer ways of framing the development agenda. The irony of 2014 elections, it appears, is that there is no need to specify one's vantage point. It is the point. So the framing of the agenda for development is now in terms of nation-building; and it is being proposed that the building of the nation will entail major institutional changes. One significant way in which the development agenda is being reframed can be seen by looking at the current discourse on labour laws and centre–state relations.

The "new" agenda is all about regulating labour and deregulating capital (Sood et al 2014). Previously, the Indian state has facilitated accumulation by disengaging from the popular discourse on labour reforms and has instead engaged in seemingly harmless norms of voluntary action and corporate social responsibility. Now, with the recent success of elections and the so-called support for an all-out-for-growth strategy, the attempt is to press for further relaxations and to openly move away from securing and safeguarding the employment conditions of labour in the country.

While the previous regime diluted the labour laws and promoted voluntary regulation, this regime believes it has the mandate to do it upfront. Since labour is a state subject, the "trial" run has been initiated in some of India's states. These reforms will increase the vulnerability of the workforce exponentially.

Similarly, centre–state relations and the federal structure of India have been the other instrument used to hasten the process of economic reforms. They have been used by previous regimes to lay down the necessary conditions to achieve a homogenised framework of development across the different states by the central government. Changes in the criterion for resource transfer to the states from the centre were introduced, where resource transfer becomes a mechanism to control or influence the growth pattern and the policy environment in the states. Transfers based on mobilisation of own resources by the provinces became larger, and economic sustainability was introduced as the chief criterion for "successes" of programmes, schemes and grants.

This increased concern with efficiency lead to privatisation via public–private partnership, even of social programmes. All indirect mechanisms were used in the past to increase the reach of the neo-liberal growth agenda. The fallout of the 2014 elections, like in the case of labour, has made this agenda more explicit. It has already been explicitly suggested, on behalf of the new regime, that if the states amend their laws (for example, on concurrent subjects like land and labour) which is in line with centre's thinking, then it is fine. If they resist change, and for states that do not toe the line, legislation on these subjects as modified by the centre should be applicable (see Panagriya 2014, for this argument). What is implied here is that if the states amend laws that further economic reforms and integrate themselves in the global market then they should be given the freedom to be different from the centre or else they have to follow the prescriptions of the central government.

The implication of the post-2014 policy discussions is to put in place a different institutional mechanism for a centralising, homogenising and corporatist development in India. What could not be done from the front door for the last many years, is now being openly and explicitly articulated and projected as a futuristic plan and those who oppose it are "outdated", not worthy of consideration and even "anti-national".

The interventionist Indian state has moved from manoeuvring and intervening from the back door in defence of big business interests along with some attempt to improve equity and access through institutional change and the discourse of rights to a state that is explicitly working for a foreign direct investment-dependent economic agenda.

The underlying idea behind the current strategy of growth seems to be that to achieve growth, all that is required is to further deregulate various policies that facilitate private investment, liberalise public pension funds for private sector infrastructure investment, loosen environmental standards, ease rules to access cheap land, ease repatriation of profits, and so on. This foreign capital-dependent growth strategy requires the approval of Western capitals of the larger political discourse happening in India led by the party in power. So an openly communal and fascist agenda, like, communal riots and *ghar wapsi*, etc, may not work. At the same time, internally, the openly corporatist agenda that favours the Western capitals is also difficult to sustain, given the complexity and fissures of the Indian society and the "incapacity" of the economic agenda to benefit the ordinary. The current regime continues to facilitate big business interests, trample on people's rights, and reconstruct and create new norms for what is socially just. Its cultural narrative is just the other side of its economic narrative, not its substitute (Sood 2016). Given the limits of Make in India, Start Up-India, Digital India, Smart Cities to mobilize crowds, cadres, emotions a cultural narrative is now even more necessary for political mobilization. The lop-sidedness of the promise of *ache din* and to accommodate the disappointments generated by the mismatch between heightened expectations and more than moderate delivery there is a compelling need for some kind of homogenizing cultural narrative. Dividing or aggregating students, peasants labour and fragmenting democracy in any manner such that it is no longer any threat to the existing order is exactly the role that the contemporary cultural narrative plays. Making common sense of the dominant ideology, the use of the media and the educational apparatus to suppress dissent and legal regulation of democracy are added means to achieve this goal. And that is the core lesson we need to draw from the perspective of the Indian people's struggles against globalisation and for a better life today.

Notes

1. The distinction between inward and outward orientation of economic policy to analyse the policy and practice of the Indian state has been critically challenged by many scholars. The point they make is that Indian state, in order to meet the needs of capital accumulation, has adopted varied forms and features of development in different periods. The Indian state has been in its innermost essence a state that has supported an expanding capitalist system both internally and externally, since a long time ago, and therefore, inward and outward orientation is not something that represents a fundamental shift in India's policy orientation after so-called economic reforms (Singh 2008: ch 6, ch 12). However, I sometimes still use the distinction between inward and outward orientation, as it represents how the popular discourse on policy in India has been constructed.

2. On the face of it, the Indian growth story is quite illustrious, achieving an average growth of 4.1% per annum in the first three decades of independence compared to 6.3% in the last three and a half decades. The source of "new" growth has been rooted in the spread of construction, townships, urban development, IT parks, commercial centres and other service sector activities. Much of this has happened in and around urban and peri-urban centres. The rural economy has experienced very low and often negative growth, and the majority of the poor and marginalised in remote rural hinterlands have been dislocated from their land and settlements to these "new" areas of growth in and around the cities, in search for jobs. To meet these new growth needs, forests and cultivable land have been opened to mining, construction of new airports, roads, dams, IT parks, cantonments, townships and so on (Banerjee and Sood 2012). In all this success of India's growth, there is also a big concern of this growth not being inclusive. Poverty is one indicator on which the government prides its achievements: decline in poverty was 0.74% per annum between 1993 and 2005 and by 2.18% per annum between

2005 and 2012. The number of poor still remain a staggering 270 million. These gains of poverty reduction have not been equal across different social groups and regions in India. The gap between rural and urban poverty is still very large and inequality has increased both in the rural and urban areas in the last two decades or so. The incidence of poverty is higher amongst the caste groups that are in the lower rung of the caste hierarchy by around 10%. The headcount ratio of agriculture labour households is twice that of self-employed. The story of urban poverty is no different. Overall, urban poverty is 14%, it is 22% for Scheduled Castes (SCs) households and 24% of Scheduled Tribes (STs) households are below the poverty line. The sources of livelihoods too reflect the fact that the lower-end caste groups such as the SCs are pushed into low productivity jobs as casual labourers both in the rural and urban areas. The ownership of enterprises too show that the participation of the marginalised caste groups is low. Drèze and Sen (2013) suggest that this growth is "making the country look more and more like islands of California in a sea of sub-Saharan Africa".

3.   The marginalisation of certain social groups has deepened on many fronts during this period. The social gap in outcome indicators in health—the difference between the historically advantaged upper castes and the "other" deprived castes and the gap between men and women—has increased (Drèze and Sen 2013).

4.   The bulk of India's aggregate growth, which has occurred through a disproportionate rise in the incomes of the rich, has left undisturbed the fact that 43% of all Indian children below the age of five are undernourished, and 48% stunted; nearly half of Indian women of childbearing age are anaemic, and more than half of all Indians still defecate in the open.

5.   A major failure of the growth pattern is in not realising the structural changes in the workforce. More than 50% of the workforce is still engaged in the agricultural sector. Long-term growth in employment has been around 2% per annum. Between 1972 and 1983, growth in employment was 2.3% per annum; around the same level between 1983 and 1994; slowed down to 1.47% between 1993 and 2000, was 2.84% between 1999–2000 and 2004–05 and collapsed to 0.10% per annum between 2004 and 2010. This growth in employment has been lower than the growth in labour force, historically, and equal to it in recent years. Growth in employment has undoubtedly not

matched the gains in GDP growth, employment elasticity has declined from 0.53 (mid-1970s to mid-1980s) to 0.40 (mid-1980s to mid-1990s) to 0.33 between 1994–95 and 2009–10. Employment challenge in India is not confined to unemployment, which is mostly high amongst the young, educated and women; but it is mostly about large number of others who are recorded as "employed", but are in the need of new jobs due to their low earnings and low productivity employment. Twenty-one percent of poor in India are "working poor" and 25% of them earn less than half the poverty line income. Those that are "severely underemployed" have no work for more than half the time, and they constitute 2.5% of the labour force. The low level work participation rate, wage disparity, unpaid jobs, low productivity jobs are some of the aspects of the exclusive nature of development in labour market. About 53% of total female workforce is self-employed and another 37% of them are casual labourers and only about 10% are employed in regular jobs. For the vast majority of people, the jobs that have been created are mostly low paying contractual jobs both in formal and informal activities (see for details Sood et al 2014). The Indian economy's growth is driven by the service sector. However, the share of high value-added service jobs is very small. These jobs, are accessible only to a tiny section of society, who have certain skills to participate in the modern economy. It bypasses many even amongst the dominant castes who lack the requisite social and other soft skills.

References

Acemoglu, D. and J.A. Robinson (2012): *Why Nations Fail: The Origins of Power, Prosperity and Poverty*, New York: Crown Business.

Banerjee, Payal and Atul Sood (2012): "The Political Economy of Green Growth in India," *UNRISD-Friedrich Ebert Stiftung*, Occasional Paper 5.

Drèze, Jean and Amartya Sen (2013): *An Uncertain Glory: India and Its Contradictions*, United Kingdom: Allen Lane.

Easterly, William (2013): *The Tyranny of Experts: Economists, Dictators, and the Forgotten Rights of the Poor*, New York: Basic Books.

Evans, P. (1995): *Embedded Autonomy: States and Industrial Transformation*, Princeton, NJ: Princeton University Press.

Harvey, D (2004): *The New Imperialism*, Oxford: Oxford University Press.

Jenkins, R. (1999): *Democratic Politics and Economic Reform in India*, Cambridge: Cambridge University Press.

Levien, Michael (2011): "Special Economic Zones and Accumulation by Dispossession in India," *Journal of Agrarian Change*, Vol 11, No 4, October, pp 454–83.

Panagriya, Arvind (2014): "A Game-changing Reform Strategy," *Times of India*, 5 April, http://timesofindia.indiatimes.com/edit-page/A-game-changing-reform-strategy/articleshow/33248689.cms.

Patnaik, P (2005): "The Economics of the New Phase of Imperialism," *Macroscan*, 26 August, http://www.macroscan.org/anl/aug05/pdf/Economics_New_Phase.pdf.

Perelman, M. (2000): *The Invention of Capitalism: Classical Political Economy and the Secret History of Primitive Accumulation*, Durham: Duke University Press.

Piketty, Thomas (2014): *Capital in the Twenty-First Century*, Cambridge Massachusetts: The Belknap Press of Harvard University.

Singh, Randhir (2008): *Marxism, Socialism and Indian Politics*, New Delhi: Aakar Books.

Sood, Atul (ed) (2012): *Poverty Amidst Prosperity: Essays on the Trajectory of Development in Gujarat*, New Delhi: Aakar Books.

———— (2014): "All About So Called Sins and the Game Plan," *Kafila*, 11 May, http://kafila.org/2014/05/11/are-the-2014-elections.

———— (2015): "Business and Norm-building for Sustainability: What Will Work for Indian Corporations?" *International Journal of Business Governance and Ethics*, Vol 10, No 3–4, pp 324–40.

———— (2016): "Majoritarian Rationale and Common Goals: Rhetoric and Truth," *Economic & Political Weekly*, Vol 51, No 37, pp 36–41.

Sood, Atul, Paaritosh Nath and Sangeeta Ghosh (2014): "Deregulating Capital, Regulating Labour: The Dynamics in Manufacturing Sector in India," *Economic & Political Weekly*, Vol 49, No 26–27, pp 58–68.

Vikraman, Shaji (2016a): "25 Years on, Manmohan Singh Has a Regret: In Crisis, We Act. When It's Over, Back to Status Quo: Manmohan Singh," *Indian Express*, 1 July, http://indianexpress.com/article/india/india-news-india/manmohan-singh-opening-indian-economy-1991-economic-reforms-pv-narasimha-rao-rbi-indian-rupee-devaluation-2886876/.

———— (2016b): "Despite All Reforms, the Poor of India Continue to Be Not Only Poor But Deprived of Basic Amenities: Yashwant Sinha," *Indian Express*, 4 July, http://indianexpress.com/article/india/india-news-india/yashwant-sinha-opening-indian-economy-1991-economic-reforms-poverty-in-india-pv-narasimha-rao-rbi-indian-rupee-devaluation-manmohan-singh-2892159/

Making Reforms Work for the Common People

*Rajiv Kumar**

The reforms of 1991 and 1996 were branded pro-rich as people with better initial endowments benefited disproportionately from the significant positive impacts, thus exacerbating both income and regional inequalities. This must change. Therefore, rather than minimising the role of the state as per the Washington Consensus, the presence of a development state is a necessary condition for implementing structural reforms in India. The State should focus its efforts on improving the delivery of public goods and services like physical infrastructure, housing, education and health as these are essential conditions for ensuring an equality of opportunity for the common people, which is a necessary condition for sustaining a market-based capitalist economy.

౸৽৽৽

That the 1991 reforms marked a major watershed in India's economic history is surely beyond argument. No waiting lists for cars or scooters, no special licenses for securing foreign exchange for studying abroad, no gold smuggling and no more the dread of the customs officer at airports with long queues that took hours to be cleared as each suitcase was opened and rummaged to look for "banned items".

It would have been simply inconceivable prior to 1991 that 10 million Indians would voluntarily give up the subsidy on cooking gas, which prior

* The author gratefully acknowledges the assistance of Ajay Kumar.

to 1991 was a scarce commodity and securing a cooking gas connection required a recommendation from someone influential. The Indian reality has changed and life has become less Kafkaesque. And thankfully, scarcities are no longer the driver of human endeavour in present-day India as it was prior to 1991. One must acknowledge the paradigm shift that was initiated in 1991 and which 25 short years later has resulted in a post-reform generation that is perhaps totally oblivious to the days when one had to wait for three to five years to buy a Bajaj scooter or 10 years to get hold of a Padmini car.

The credit for this must be given to P.V. Narasimha Rao, who as the Prime Minister heading a minority government after the horrendous assassination of Rajiv Gandhi in May 1991, was able to establish the necessary political coalitions in support of the reforms. Rao was successful in putting across to his political opponents and to the people at large, that India was faced not only with an unprecedented economic crisis but also a potentially severe political crisis in case the population did not come together as one in supporting the reforms. His principal secretary A.N. Verma marshalled a highly skeptical bureaucracy to support the effort.

This unity of purpose among the political class and senior bureaucracy provided the necessary condition for the Rao government to successfully reverse the three decades of steadily rising state intervention in all aspects of economic activity that expanded the scope of state capitalism, central planning and bureaucratic over-regulation. Therein lies a lesson for the present government: in a country as diverse as India, leaderships of ruling parties will have to constantly build coalitions both within and outside the Parliament if it is serious about implementing the critically necessary structural reforms. Neither an abdication of reforms nor an attempt to railroad them through the legislatures or even the bureaucracy will yield the necessary growth momentum.

The second necessary condition for the 1991 reforms was the significant amount of academic and intellectual churning that preceded them. Throughout the 1980s, there was a constant battle of ideas between the "liberalisers" and "status-quoists and regulators". The latter would employ the age-old trick of creating a scare about India becoming a "neo-colony" and the demise of domestic industrial capacities if the Indian industry was confronted with global competition.

There were a number of studies undertaken by leading think tanks to refute this vicious argument on the basis of empirical evidence. Some major studies were also published to quantify the benefits that would potentially result from economic liberalisation. For reforms to succeed in India, the intellectual battle has to be won in the public domain. With media explosion and greater openness and participation in public discourse, this is now even more essential than ever. It is a misplaced perception that reforms in India were or can be stealthily undertaken by ministers and bureaucrats acting covertly in the expectation that positive results that are expected to accrue from these reforms will suffice to convert the general public opinion in their favour. Given our vibrant and fiercely competitive democracy, reforms in India will be successful if and only if, sufficient groundwork has been done in advance to mould the public opinion in their support.

It is perhaps redundant after 25 years to argue that reforms cannot be imposed from abroad or by any group of externally oriented experts. India has traversed a long distance and appreciably reinforced its sovereign credentials. But it should also be recognised that even the 1991 reforms had a very large dose of indigenous inputs and were a result of rigorous research and active advocacy domestically. Researchers well versed in the Indian ground realities and its political economy presented these reform measures in a form readily comprehensible to the political leadership, bureaucracy and the political class in general.[1] In the present context, it will be even more critical for the political leadership to ensure that reforms are perceived by the common people to be rooted in the Indian reality and have not been imposed by an external entity.

Major Achievements

A lot has been already written about the positive impact of 1991 reforms (Ninan 2015). Summarily, the best testimony to the success of the 1991 reforms arises from comparing the rate of growth of per capita incomes in the 25 years preceding the reforms and those succeeding it. Between 1965 and 1990, India's average[2] annual gross domestic product (GDP) growth was a mere 4.1%, which translated to a per capita income growth of 1.9% per annum. In the subsequent period (1990 to 2015), this increased to 6.3% and 4.6% respectively. The reforms allowed India to firmly jettison the so-called Hindu rate of growth. It would not be misplaced to assert that without these reforms, the country could have faced acute social and political problems that would have arisen as a result of the economy's inability to generate enough wealth and employment, had the economic growth remained at pre-1991 levels.

A related achievement of the reforms was to integrate the Indian economy more deeply with the global economy. Import tariffs were lowered substantially and some non-tariff barriers on inflows of technology and services were removed facilitating transfer of technology. In the 25 years prior to the reforms, the share of the trade (export and imports of goods and services) in the total GDP was on average a low 11.5%. This increased four times to 48.7% in 2015. This was a direct outcome of policy reform measures being focused largely on the "tradable sectors" of the economy.

Average applied import tariffs have been brought down from about 82% in 1990 to less than 10% in 2014, giving Indian consumers and producers the benefit of lower prices prevailing in global markets. Exports of goods and services (taken together) have increased from a mere $2.0 billion in 1965 and $22.6 billion in 1990 to $522 billion in 2014. The higher level of integration has allowed India to benefit not only from easier access to foreign markets and relatively cheaper intermediate inputs but also from higher inflows of foreign direct investment (FDI) and portfolio investments and technology. This has enhanced the investment capability and raised productivity levels in the economy.

In summary, the 1991 reforms put India on a higher trajectory of economic growth by removing some of the dysfunctional controls and regulations, facilitating imports of intermediate inputs, technology and financial flows thereby moving the economy towards greater integration with the world economy and de-reserving some key sectors from exclusive public sector ownership.

The Pro-Rich Perception

It is generally agreed that policy advance of the early 1990s initiated the programme of structural reforms but left them far from complete. The Rao government lost its reformist élan before it reached the mid-term mark of its five year term, that is, by the beginning of 1994. This was reflected most sharply in two separate incidents.

The first was when the government did not accept the second tranche of the Asian Development Bank's industrial structural adjustment loan that required the completion of a slew of deeper structural reforms, including changes in the labour market and privatisation of public sector enterprises. Having completed some far-reaching reforms like the abolition of the Monopolies and Restrictive Trade Practices (MRTP) Act and Directorate General of Technical Development (DGTD), and sharply reducing the number of sectors reserved for public sector operations (including commercial banks and insurance), the Rao government lost its appetite for further reforms that would have involved taking on both the well-entrenched trade unions and vested interests supporting the continuation of "state capitalism" in the country. This was despite the strong demonstration of the positive impact of de-nationalization in the telecom sector, in which public sector monopoly was eliminated and private investment was actively invited.

The second manifestation of the loss of reformist verve was the extreme reluctance of the government to privatize even the loss-making public sector enterprises. Privatisation became a derogatory term and was replaced by disinvestment or de-nationalization. It was clear early on that the Rao government was not prepared to take on the public sector trade unions or roll back the dysfunctional expansion of the government in commercial activities. This reluctance to reform the public sector enterprises either through strategic privatisation or by instituting more accountable governance and efficient operations has persisted with successive governments, except for a brief interlude under Atal Bihari Vajpayee.

The reform effort was sustained and actually given a fresh momentum during the Vajpayee government (1999–2004) especially under Yashwant Sinha as finance minister and Arun Shourie as minister in charge of disinvestment (Sinha 2007). Murasoli Maran, the minister of industry and commerce in that government was, however, not a reformist and spent his energies largely in defending India's position in the Doha Development Round.

However, the rather bitter truth was that the 1991 reforms or those undertaken subsequently by the Vajpayee National Democratic Alliance (NDA) government, despite their success in pushing the GDP growth rate higher, neither guaranteed nor were seen to guarantee electoral success. If anything, the unfortunate fate of the Vajpayee government in Delhi and of Chandrababu Naidu government in undivided Andhra Pradesh led the political class to draw the lesson that economic reforms targeted at liberalising the economy were to be left well alone if the political fray had to be won. This was a result of the palpable inability of successive governments and assorted political formations in building a case in the public domain that reforms yielded widespread welfare gains including lifting substantial numbers above the poverty line.

The liberal, open economic policy regime continued to be seen as being pro-rich and not serving the interests of the poor. This is in complete denial of the reality that during the 25 years after reforms, India has been successful in reducing the share of population living in abject poverty from 56% of the total population in 1973 and 46% in 1993 to (a still unacceptable) 22% in 2011. This implies bringing more than 150 million people out of rank poverty as compared to an increase in the number of poor from around 326 million to 416 million, between 1973 and 1993, that is, in the period prior to the 1991 reforms. This negative public perception about the reforms that is reflected rather widely also in the political classes, despite the positive economic outcomes, needs explanation.

Therefore, in its bid to wrest power back from the NDA, the Sonia Gandhi-led United Progressive Alliance (UPA) government that succeeded the Vajpayee government in office for 10 years (2004–14) gave up the reform effort and instead tried to maximize its longevity in office by pursuing populist policies that were focused on improving distribution and entitlements. The Sonia Gandhi-led National Advisory Committee, that ironically called the shots on economic policy, despite the government being led by a professional economist, worked on the assumption that economic growth of 7% to 8% had been assured by the reforms already undertaken in the past and so did not need further reform push to be sustained. Instead, the focus was principally, if not exclusively, on establishing higher entitlements and expanding the social security net in the firm belief that this would yield successive electoral victories. The disappointing result was a marked loss of reform momentum and concomitantly of growth momentum as well. The economy is still struggling to emerge out of that slowdown.

Having been successful both in 2004 and 2009, the Congress Party, led by Rahul Gandhi, repeated the populist strategy once again in 2014. This time however, the strategy met with disastrous results for the Congress, whose appeal based on further enhancing entitlements fell far short of a young electorate's rising aspirations (Kumar 2014). The Congress leadership perhaps overlooked the fact that by 2014, a very large cohort of the post-1991 generation had entered the workforce and acquired voting rights. This generation was not aware of the scarcities and deprivations of the pre-1991 period and hence was not impressed with the Congress Party's promise of removing poverty and securing further entitlements. It is also worth noting that the number of Indians living below the official poverty line had also declined precipitously to less than 20% by 2014.

Changing the Pro-Rich Perception

There are to my mind two principal reasons of 1991 reforms being not only perceived as pro-rich but also having produced an inequitable outcome.

First, the growing income inequality in the country since 1991 as compared to the first four decades after independence. The second factor has been the widespread incidence of large-scale corruption that threatened to become systemic as a result of an ever-strengthening nexus of the political classes with crony capitalists. Both anecdotal and empirical examples (rising values of Gini coefficients in the post-reform period) point unmistakably to the rising inequality in the society during the last 25 years. This has happened across both interpersonal and interregional space with some of the poorer states being left behind unmistakably. This trend is counter-intuitive. An open and liberal economic regime should theoretically promote convergence and close the income gaps, especially across regions. The actual outcome was quite the reverse as reforms were seen to increase inequality rather than bring about greater convergence.

The reason is not far to seek. The reforms of 1991 and those which succeeded them during the Vajpayee regime, opened up new opportunities for those already better endowed with financial and human capital. They did so by providing expanded opportunities both in terms of greater access to foreign markets and by facilitating imports of technology, finance capital and intermediate inputs to those already poised for expanding capacities. By unleashing massive export opportunities for software firms, and at the same time, encouraging supply response from the private sector which was allowed entry into the telecom sector, these reforms exponentially increased returns on education and vocational training. Thus, they strongly favoured those who were already in possession of the required human capital. Thus, the reforms accelerated incomes for those individuals, firms and regions already well endowed by connecting them more intimately with global flows and markets.

However, the 1991 reforms did practically nothing for those whose initial conditions or given endowments were poor or non-existing as is the case for those who live in abject poverty. This lack of focus on improving the delivery of essential public services like primary education, basic health and public transport and infrastructure that offers better mobility to those living in backward regions, has been the major failure of India's structural reform efforts. The state simply abdicated its responsibility in these crucial areas by not even attempting to restructure and bring about a modicum of improvement in the two crucial areas of education and health.

In infrastructure too, except for the Pradhan Mantri Gram Sadak Yojana (PMGSY) which sought to connect villages (even remote ones) to state highways and nearby towns, the dominant effort was focused principally on facilitating the mobility of the well-off by developing a network of national highways under the Golden Quadrilateral programme. There has been a notable lack of effort on modernising the railways, and inner-city public transportation, which would have been more accessible to the poor and lower middle classes. In short, the 1991 and subsequent reforms have favoured the middle and rich classes and therefore, by definition, excluded the poorer segments of the population from their coverage.

This is reinforced by the near complete lack of attention to modernizing agriculture and raising yields and productivity of Indian crops. Public investment in agriculture has continued to decline in the last 25 years, reaching an abysmal level of 0.4% of the GDP in 2015. At the same time, the quantum of subsidies on account of fertilisers and electricity have risen many times from around Rs 9,000 crore in 1991 to over Rs 83,000 crore in 2015. Unlike public infrastructure that would be more accessible and help the poor and marginal farmers, these subsidies which seem to have pushed out public investment are largely usurped by the middle and rich farmers. Lack of public irrigation, inability of the public sector agencies to supply reasonably priced seeds, and the near complete breakdown of agro-extension services have implied that agriculture, supporting nearly 50% of the population, remains trapped in backwardness and contributes to rising income inequalities in the country. This has also reinforced the public perception that reforms favour the rich.

The 1991 reforms were essentially directed at the 'tradable sectors' which, as discussed above, provide greater economic opportunities to those already well endowed and well positioned to take advantage of economic liberalization. Reforms did nothing for the 'non-tradable' sectors like physical infrastructure, education, health and public irrigation systems or R&D inputs for agriculture. This lack of policy attention extended to crucial aspects like urbanization and labour market reforms as well. 1991 reforms thus left untouched the 'dualistic nature' of the Indian economy that is commonly perceived as the persistent distinction between India and Bharat. This dualism has several implications. In the labour market it is reflected in only 8% of the workforce being employed in the 'formal sector' with the remaining 92% continuing to work in the 'informal sector', which is characterized by a near complete absence of regulations on minimum wages, working conditions, fixity of tenure or social security provisions. This abnormally high degree of 'informalisation' in the Indian economy has resulted in its inability to raise productivity levels in the great majority of productive sectors, thereby being unable to either compete globally or even become a part of regional and global production networks. On the other hand, for those operating in the formal segment of the economy, including public sector enterprises and large private corporate houses multiple levies on account of social security provisions and the procedural difficulties in laying off any part of the workforce have significantly raised labour costs. This has rendered many of these firms globally uncompetitive and substantially explains India's inability to raise its share in global export markets, which continues to stagnate at less than 2%.

There was a major effort during the 1990s and subsequently to reform and simplify the indirect tax structure. This saw the lowering and rationalisation of both import tariffs and excise duty structures. The modified valued added tax was successfully introduced and the grounds laid for the much awaited Goods and Services Tax (GST). With the GST, the entire country would be covered by a single uniform tax imposed equally on goods and services.

Unfortunately, however, the same cannot be said for the system of direct (personal income and corporate) taxes. Rather than being simplified and rationalised (for example, by removing the surfeit of exemptions), these have been made more complicated and draconian with the introduction of, for example, "retrospective taxation". The result is that the personal income tax net is confined to 37 million taxpayers. Even if we assume that each income taxpayer represents one household (a liberal assumption because there are a large number of households in which there are more than one income tax payers), it represents merely 15% of the total number of 250 million households in the country. Surely the tax net can be widened.

Similarly, the effective corporate income tax (total tax divided by taxable corporate income) is estimated at 22% while the nominal rate is nearly 34%. Removing the exemptions, that will help the micro, small and medium enterprises (MSMEs) by simplifying the tax process, would surely remove this bias in favour of richer corporates.

Finally, according to the Central Board of Direct Taxes (CBDT), the number of taxpayers with incomes above Rs 1 crore is only 17,515. This number can be and should be increased manifold in the present-day economy which boasts of a very large number of billionaires and multimillionaires. The inequity in the direct tax system further reinforces the perception of unfairness and deepens inequality. The inability to collect taxes from the rich, who also inherit wealth without paying any estate duty on inheritance, implies a greater dependence on the relatively more regressive indirect taxes. By not tackling the direct tax system over these 25 years, the reformists have opened themselves to charges of being strongly biased in favour of the rich, rentiers and the prosperous. This must change.

The second weakness referred to above has been the overt emergence of a "politician–crony capitalist" nexus that has seen a manifold expansion of corruption throughout the system even at times endangering the country's security. This has been one of the negative fallouts of the push for public–private participation in infrastructure and other sectors. The basic, though faulty premise underlying this phenomenon was to accept one of the tenets of the Washington Consensus that sought to minimise the presence of the government (or the state) in both undertaking, and effectively regulating economic activity.

Under the convenient garb of pushing back the state from even its legitimate and critical activity in support of development, political leaders and bureaucrats have sought to replace the state with a coalition in which the distinction between the public and private interests is largely blurred if not eliminated. Thus, in the education sector, politicians can beat or circumvent the plethora of regulations because of their proximity to the regulator.

In the health sector, private hospitals with their rampant commercialisation can get away with minimal oversight on meeting their mandated social goals. The growing nexus of those "within the establishment" with private sector providers has promoted a widespread culture of "finding private solutions to public problems". This breeds regulatory corruption at all levels and at the same time weakens the state's capacity to deliver on its development agenda.

The poor, who are by definition, excluded from this private provision of services are often the victims of this unholy nexus. For example, the breakdown in public education at all levels implies that increasing recourse is taken to private tuitions and crammers. The poor cannot afford these. Similarly, the replacement of government security machinery by private security providers (reportedly one of the fastest growing industries in India) has implied that the poor are left vulnerable to the vagaries of thugs and unscrupulous local political and official goons often with unacceptable dehumanising consequences.

The above two weaknesses taken together are symptomatic of a more deep-rooted malaise that has remained untackled over these 25 years and represents to my mind the biggest weakness of the reform effort. This refers to the lack of even the effort to improve governance and implement the critically required reforms in the administrative and judicial systems. This has stymied overall economic progress and has resulted in a growing de-legitimisation of the state. India would not be only emerging country where the state has effectively withdrawn and become discredited over time (Sud 2012). This phenomenon can be noticed in an increasing number of emerging economies across all continents. The Indian state too has become increasingly characterised by rampant corruption within the executive and political establishments, policy paralysis at all levels, and an unimaginably long pendency of legal cases which does not seem to bother the judiciary in which corruption is rife, especially among the lower echelons. Governance has badly broken down across the country.

The governance crisis was simply accepted as a given condition by the followers of Washington Consensus. Rather than try and tackle the governance deficit and unarguably influenced by the Reagan-Thatcher ideological premise of withdrawing the State from the economy, the Indian policy makers in the post 1991 period pointed to the "governance failure" to argue the case for enhanced role of private enterprises even in sectors such as infrastructure, education and health. This effectively implied taking recourse to private solutions for public problems. Such an approach essentially implied an abdication of its traditional role by the government as a provider of public services including the maintenance of law and order. An enhanced role of the private sector in the provision of public services has effectively implied excluding the relatively poorer population segments from availing these services, which is a necessary condition of overcoming their inherited weaknesses and poor endowment of human capital. This exacerbated relative inequalities, specially equality of opportunity, which is the necessary condition for sustaining a market based capitalist economy.

Reforming the governance system and making it more accountable and transparent was not on the reform agenda until Narendra Modi brought it right in the center of his electoral campaign and subsequently followed it up in practice since taking office (Kumar 2016). Reforming governance is the necessary condition for improving delivery of public services that will make economic growth less exclusionary. Better (accountable, consistent and transparent) governance is also at the heart of improving the conditions for doing business and making India a more investor-friendly environment.

Better project execution capabilities in the public sector would also result in a more rapid expansion of physical infrastructure capacities that also help the poor by enhancing their mobility, connectivity and productivity. More accountable governance also reduces the distance between the governors and the governed, thereby deepening our democracy and liberating it from the feudal overtones that currently characterise it. While the present government's rhetorical emphasis on better governance is most welcome, it will have to be translated into actual practice for it to have a positive impact on general welfare. This is not yet in evidence.

Concluding Remarks

The last 25 years, though representing a period of significant economic achievements, have also brought forth several important lessons for the future.

First, India is not suited to the application of the Washington Consensus. Given India's wide ranging diversity of economic endowment across regions and across different population segments, the State, far from being withdrawn, will have to lead the effort in ensuring that growth is inclusive by ensuring that the delivery of public services is efficient and subsidies are effectively targeted and not usurped by the non-deserving. However, this certainly does not imply that the government continues to own and manage commercial undertakings that are best run by the private sector in a competitive market framework. A "Development State", as was established in East Asian econo- mies like Japan, Korea and Taiwan, is the need of the hour in India.

Second, necessary administrative reforms and those needed desperately in the judicial sector must be expeditiously undertaken. These are essential conditions for establishing a development state.

Third, apart from governance, policy attention now needs to be focused on other non-tradable sectors like education, health, direct taxation and infrastructure as these are key to making Indian industry globally competi- tive and economic growth more inclusive and employment intensive.

Finally, a wider and more engaged public discourse on the effective- ness of structural economic reforms in raising the welfare of the general population is now urgently required. The outcome of such an engaged and sustained public discussion on the need for reforms will hopefully result in their wider acceptance. This will ensure that all stakeholders pull together in the same direction for ensuring India's successful emergence as one of the three leading economies in the world by 2046, the centenary year of our independence.

Notes

1. A particular example was the study prepared by Kelkar, Kumar and Nangia for the Asian Development Bank in 1989. This study not only rigorously analysed the weaknesses in India's macroeconomy, but also laid out a plan of action for structural reforms. It is noteworthy that many of these measures were replicated in the structural reform matrix presented by the International Monetary Fund as the set of its conditionality while extending the structural adjustment facility to India to help overcome its external finance crisis that had engulfed it in 1990 and 1991 (Kumar and Kelkar 1990).

2. Compound Annual Average Growth Rate (CAGR) at constant prices of 2004–05.

References

Kumar, Rajiv and V.L. Kelkar (1990): "Industrial Growth in the Eighties: Emerging Policy Issues," *Economic & Political Weekly*, Vol 25, No 4, pp 209–22.

Kumar, Rajiv (2014): *Exploding Aspirations: Unlocking India's Future,* New Delhi: Academic Foundation.

——— (2016): *Modi and His Challenges,* New Delhi: Bloomsbury.

Ninan, T.N. (2015): *The Turn of the Tortoise: The Challenge and Promise of India's Future,* New Delhi: Penguin Books.

Sinha, Yashwant (2007): *Confessions of a Swadeshi Reformer: My Years as a Finance Minister,* New Delhi: Penguin India.

Sud, Nikita (2012): *Liberalisation, Hindu Nationalism and the State: A Biography of Gujarat,* New Delhi: Oxford University Press.

III

REFORMS, STATE INTERVENTION
AND THE MARKET

Markets, Growth and Social Opportunity

India since 1991

Pulapre Balakrishnan*

Since 1991, there has been an acceleration of economic growth accompanied by a widening of the range of consumer goods produced, together with improvement in the quality of services available. Furthermore, the economy has passed through the longest period since 1947 without facing balance-of-payments stress. However, not all sectors of the economy have shown the same dynamism, with the performance of agriculture actually becoming a cause for concern. The unequal distribution of social opportunity has meant that this shortcoming has left a significant section of the population in a low-income trap. What underlies this outcome is examined and what is needed to correct the imbalance is proposed.

※

India has by now seen a quarter century of what may be termed market reforms. In 1991, the government had embarked upon an economic reform programme that was largely propelled by an external payments

*This article originated in a paper written for the Indian Council for Research on International Economic Relations. I am grateful to Rajeev Kumar, its then director, for the invitation to write it and for arranging for four anonymous reviews of the same. Subsequently, it was presented as the first of three lectures on India's economy delivered at the Indian Institute of Advanced Study, Shimla in June 2016 at the invitation of its director, Chetan Singh. Any errors would be my responsibility.

crisis. The focus of the reform, then, was mainly the economy's trade and industrial policy regime. Though widely believed to have been dictated by multilateral agencies (read the International Monetary Fund and World Bank) to which India had to turn for balance-of-payments support, it needs to be remembered that the government had been pursuing a mildly liberalising approach to the economic policy since the 1980s.[1] An impetus to liberalisation other than the immediate balance-of-payments crisis was the definitive collapse of the Soviet economic model. This had made it that much more difficult to justify any form of economic restriction.

The structural reforms commencing in 1991 in India may be approached in terms of their focus on the internal and external sectors of the economy. As far as the domestic economy was concerned, the most important change made in 1991 was that industrial licensing was rescinded and private entry permitted in almost all areas of the economy other than the railways, ports, defence, and atomic energy. In subsequent reforms, private investment has been permitted in all areas other than the last. Though clearly intended to increase competition and productivity—defined widely enough to include also the quality and variety of goods, and therefore believed to potentially benefit mainly the consumer—in the space of entrepreneurial activity, the move may be viewed as contributing to inclusion. After all, investment licensing, irrespective of its motivation, implies a winner-takes-all outcome. Though delicensing is among the rare instances when market liberalisation is per se inclusive, this feature must nevertheless be acknowledged. In academic parlance, it is a move towards a more competitive market structure.

As far as the external sector was concerned, the main changes of 1991 amounted to lowering substantially, if not entirely eliminating, the protection to the domestic industry. A significant across-the-board reduction of the import tariff was implemented. This was staggered over time, with the reduction itself continuing well into the decade, when finally the average rate stabilised at a level far below what it had been, though in some cases yet higher than that in the other non-Organization for Economic Cooperation and Development (OECD) economies. More than two decades after the onset of the reforms, India is a far more open economy than it was in 1991 even though the rupee is not yet fully convertible on the capital account.

However, the extent of capital-account liberalisation must not be understated either. Foreign direct investment is encouraged. Portfolio capital flow alone is controlled, that too with an asymmetry, with restrictions placed on domestic investors while international financial institutions and non-resident Indians are permitted to move their capital freely across the border. In particular, quantitative restrictions on trade have disappeared, though this has come about via an international move towards a more open global trade regime under the dispensation of the World Trade Organization, rather than having been unilaterally administered by India as part of its policy of economic liberalisation. Viewed from the angle of the character of the policy regime, therefore, India's economy is by now far more integrated with the rest of the world. However, economists remain divided on the question of whether openness is to be judged in terms of the restrictiveness of the trade regime or in terms of outcome indicators such as exports and imports as a share of gross domestic product (GDP). Keeping this in mind, we may point out that trade, that is, exports plus imports, as a share of output has increased very significantly in India since 1991.

Overall, combining the implication of industrial delicensing and the opening up of the economy to global trade flows, market liberalisation has proceeded quite far in India since 1991. As India is increasingly transforming into a major economic entity, at least in terms of its size, we would be interested to know the consequences of this development. The rest of this article is concerned with two questions. First, it is sought to be known whether the reforms have yielded results in line with the stated objectives of the government. Second, it is investigated whether market liberalisation has spread opportunities evenly across the economy.

Faster Growth, Greater Efficiency

Two goals had motivated the economic reforms as launched in 1991: faster growth and greater efficiency.[2] The precise relationship imagined between the two was not adequately revealed. However, there was the claim that greater competition following market liberalisation would lead to faster productivity growth. Actually, even outside the government and within the wider ambit of the profession itself, for a concept so central to the discourse on economic policy, agreement on a measure of productivity is scarcely found.[3] For instance, what are we to make of productivity growth in the services sector where output is measured by factor payments? This is particularly relevant for India today, an economy coming to be increasingly dominated by its services sector. For this reason, in this article, we focus on economic growth, the measurement of which is relatively uncontroversial.

Over the two decades since 1991 the growth rate of the economy has definitely accelerated. For five years from 2003–04, India registered unprecedented high growth rates, though not quite attaining the double-digit bracket aspired to by the policymakers. This phase ended abruptly with the onset of the global financial crisis.[4] However, despite the slowing of growth in India from 2008 onwards, the country is today the fastest growing economy in the world, and this position appears unlikely to change very soon. But, it is the nature of growth in India that is interesting, especially from the point of view of its capacity for spreading opportunity and thus advancing social inclusion. While it is the manufacturing sector that the reforms had focused on, directly in terms of the restructuring of the trade and industrial policy, and indirectly via the financial sector reforms, it is services that have grown the fastest. After 2008, manufacturing has grown tardily. As for the agricultural sector, growth here has not only fluctuated, but in the case of foodgrains the growth of production has not kept pace with the rate of growth of the population.

For the first time in about five decades, the per capita availability of foodgrains in the country has been declining.[5] While this is a cause for grave concern, there is reason to doubt that the slowing of agricultural growth is related solely to market liberalisation per se. According to an influential line of reasoning, in a two-sector economy, the protection of industry is tantamount to a bias against agriculture. Now, liberalising trade and industrial policy reforms are expected to shift the terms of trade, and thereby income, towards agriculture. This is believed to create the incentives for producers to expand output in this sector.[6]

We now move on to a qualitative assessment of the growth that has taken place in India since market liberalisation. First, though industrial growth has not till well after 1991 shown the marked acceleration that was expected of it, segments within manufacturing have experienced remarkable growth and transformation. Automobiles are a case in point. Here, not only is fast growth evident, but a growing sophistication suggests a potential for India to become a global manufacturing hub. A further development, though not confined to manufacturing, is that of India becoming a preferred international location for research and development, some of it for global manufacturing giants, but even more prominently for information technology firms from IBM to Microsoft. In manufacturing, India is also being seen as a site for both high-end design and re-engineering of manufacturing processes.

Some of this is related to the development of cheap international communication networks, including the internet, which has made it possible to leverage the globally competitive skill base built up over the long haul in India, rather than market liberalisation per se. But, it is also true that some of the import liberalisation has helped and that there has been a shift in the understanding of the role of the government.[7] This role has since 1991 got reinterpreted to mean the enabling of business. That this may have taken the form of a relatively greater attention to foreign over domestic investment, and among domestic investors to large corporate houses over smaller enterprises, cannot be ignored, however. The increased presence of the prominent global firms in India is of course related to the liberalisation of foreign direct investment.

To conclude this section, it may be said that the map of material production gives the impression of dynamic enclaves within manufacturing and a stagnant hinterland represented by slow-growing agriculture. This is significant from the point of view of inclusive growth as the largest number of India's workers is located in agriculture, even as the sector is shrinking relative to the rest of the economy.

But, what of the "quality of life," and how may have market liberalisation contributed to its advance in India? This profoundly important issue was not explicitly on the agenda of the government when the reforms were launched in 1991. It would, however, be improper to assume that the government was indifferent to the question, only that it appears to have assumed that growth was what was needed to be focused on. However, the question itself is of essence, as we tend to be interested in economic growth only from the point of view of human well-being.

Nevertheless, in fairness to the policymakers, silence may be related to the understanding that "the quality of life" must come into our reckoning only after the issue of employment is sorted out; a direct relationship between faster growth and a widespread growth of employment apparently having been assumed. Despite the ambiguity of its definition and the woeful paucity of statistics, we make some effort, here, to assess the contribution of market liberalisation to the quality of life in India.

'Quality of Life' and 'Public Goods'

Casual observation suggests that, in some spaces, the quality of life in India has improved. Thus, there has been a very substantial improvement in the range, quality and availability of manufactured goods produced in the country. This is undoubtedly related to the liberalisation of entry into the sector. Interestingly it appears to have been achieved without much foreign entry, either in the form of foreign direct investment or imports. We also see an improvement in the quality of services, notably of air travel and telephony. The mobile phone revolution has swept the country and transformed the opportunities for both business and interpersonal communication. Here, the wherewithal for the hardware had initially come from overseas and the liberalisation of foreign direct investment has had a major role to play.

A similar transformation is also to be seen in air travel with direct benefits in the form of reduced cost and greater choice. This owes to the liberalisation of entry into this sector. Interestingly, here, while all the private capital is domestic, some part of the professional services—both of pilots and managers—has on occasion been international. The entry of private players in airlines, telecommunications and banking has had a tangible impact on the quality of services offered to the Indian public. To a lesser extent, this has extended to an improvement in the quality of services rendered by the rival public utilities, which had hitherto been monopolies.

It appears then, that to an extent the assumed strategic role of privatisation, defined broadly to include entry, in India has been borne out. It may safely be assumed though that, except for telecommunications, this improvement in the quality of services is largely confined to the services consumed by the social strata extending from the middle classes and above. This can be inferred by imagining the cohort that uses banking services or relies on the airlines for transportation. Thus, the reforms have certainly ensured that the aspiration of a part of the Indian middle class to global standards in consumption of manufactured goods and access to quality services has, at least to a degree, been satisfied. When flagging this, though, it is important to recognise that even as the numbers may be sizeable, the proportion involved is not so large.

While on the topic of the quality of life, that constitutive of a good life are goods and services beyond banking and the airlines would be agreed on readily. Examples of these range from the courts of law to urban governance and physical infrastructure, from roads to sewerage. Economists refer to these broadly as "public goods". They are public in the sense that, given their characteristics of non-rivalrousness and non-excludability in consumption, they have to be publicly provided. There is little evidence of either the quality or quantity of public goods having increased substantially in India since 1991. On the other hand, we have reason to believe that faster growth may have stretched the limits of the meagre infrastructure in existence. Even the most basic awareness of economic theory would remind us that the fixity of public goods in India, despite a more liberal economic regime and indeed faster economic growth, is not a matter of surprise. After all, the goods are referred to as "public," harbouring the presumption that the market on its own is unlikely to deliver them optimally. We may safely assume, therefore, that their emergence in India in sufficient quantities would require specific interventions beyond the market liberalisation implemented in this country since 1991.

Given the concerns of this note, however, public goods assume an importance that goes beyond their contribution to the quality of life of those already in employment. If the problem of ensuring inclusive growth is to draw much larger numbers into employment, then public goods would be central to inclusive growth. There are instances when agricultural produce rots due to the absence of a road network, or absent irrigation lowers the productive capacity of land. The role of public goods in the sphere of production, as opposed to consumption, has tended to be underestimated in the discourse on growth and development in India.

The first round of reforms in India had, to some extent rightly, focused on incentives for investment or expansion of output, but the time may have come for economic policy to focus aggressively on the factors that enable the production process itself. Where such enabling factors are absent, a favourable incentive structure represented by prices faced by the producer would make little difference. Examples in India range from the water-starved peasantry of Marathwada to the power-short small entrepreneur in Karnataka.[8] By comparison, with statistics on income, and therefore on poverty, we have no summary statistics on the availability and distribution of public goods and services in India. We must perforce rely on piecemeal reports in the media, and these are not reassuring. The flooding of Chennai in November 2015 is a case in point. Some years prior to this event, the entire electricity grid of northern India melted down temporarily.

Surprises, Pleasant and Unpleasant

While faster growth of the economy has been in accordance with the predictions of the managers of the reform process in India, there have also been some surprises. First, the greater integration of India's economy with the rest of the world has been far smoother than anticipated. Though the balance of payments in 2009–10 have recorded the largest deficit in six decades, private capital flows have been abundant and the country has been able to finance its payments far more smoothly than was claimed to be ever possible by critics of external liberalisation. Capital inflow poses its own problems for macroeconomic management, but it also reflects a confidence of the rest of the world in the recipient's economy. The fact that India has withstood exposure to both the goods and the capital markets of the world economy speaks of both the inherent resilience of its economy and the quality of its macroeconomic management. In particular, the 25 years since 1991 has been the longest period India has witnessed without experiencing a foreign exchange crisis. Earlier, there had been an acute shortage once in every decade.

The improvement in India's balance of payments has pleasantly surprised some observers (Chisti 2010). But, there have been unpleasant surprises too. Most unexpected has been the performance of the agricultural sector, where, when growth has not been lacklustre, it has been volatile as it has been since 2008. Altogether, since 1991 agricultural growth has on average barely kept up with the rate of growth of the population. For an economy with low levels of food consumption per capita by global standards, this is disappointing at a time of high growth of the economy. In fact, a high overall growth rate has masked the failure on the agricultural front.

Evaluations of India's economic performance since market liberalisation have tended to overlook that, over the historian's *longue durée,* the richest countries of the world are those that have succeeded in making food plentiful and cheap for their populations.[9] An indicator of this is the low share of food in average household expenditure in rich economies. In a cross-country comparison, we would find a strong inverse correlation between the level of GDP per capita and the share of food in household expenditure.[10] At least, from the time of David Ricardo economists have had an understanding of what underlies this relationship. It represents the mechanism whereby cheaper food releases demand for other goods and services, implying that, at least for poor economies, continuous improvement in agricultural productivity can be an engine of growth at least for a while. In fact, in the absence of international competitiveness in manufacturing agricultural productivity is the one that holds the most promise.

Contrary to the historical experience of the rich economies of the world, in India not only has the real price of food not declined since 1991, it has actually increased since 2009. Food price inflation has been very high during phases in the last decade and though it has abated more recently, it leads among other factors in contributing to a rising general price level. Persistent food-price inflation is unexpected for a country being hailed by some as a rising economic power.

Of course, higher food prices could well have been more than compensated by rising incomes. Whether this has actually been the case is best answered by looking at the trend in poverty. For this, I draw upon the investigation by A Deaton and J Drèze (2002). It helps the cause of our enquiry in that the authors take a slightly wider view of what constitutes poverty by focusing on development indicators such as health and education in addition to the standard emphasis on consumption expenditure. Their estimates show that "poverty decline in the 1990s proceeded more or less in line with earlier trends". On development they conclude that "most indicators have continued to improve in the nineties, but social progress has followed very diverse patterns, ranging from accelerated progress in some fields to slowdown and even regression in others. We find no support for sweeping claims that the nineties have been a period of 'unprecedented improvement' or 'widespread impoverishment'" (Deaton and Drèze 2002: 3729).

Alas, there is no comparable study of the progress of living standards in the subsequent decade. Though focusing on the early post-reform phase, the Deaton and Drèze study is particularly relevant to the argument in this article that accelerated growth per se is unlikely to deliver greater equality. Quite simply, the condition of the poor may not be worsening but the better-off may yet be doing better, thus contributing to widening inequality. We have reason to believe that this characterises India since 1991.

Finally, the government's budgetary policy holds clues as to the section of the population that is gaining from overall economic policy in the era of market reforms. While in the absence of specific empirical investigation such commentary can only be tentative, it may be observed that much of the central government's budgetary allocations since 1991 may have disproportionately favoured the middle classes. Note the reduction in the tax rate, the expansion of higher education—especially the new Indian Institutes of Technology and Indian Institutes of Management—and even the farm-loan waivers. As if to compensate, as it were, governments have targeted the poor via the Mahatma Gandhi National Rural Employment Guarantee Act.

Economic Reforms and Social Opportunity

Social opportunity refers to the idea that the opportunities available to an individual are circumscribed by her location in the socio-economic grid. From this vantage point, it would be of interest to know whether the outcome of the reforms is consistent with the spread of opportunity more or less equally across the Indian population.[11] One approach to this question would be to see how the increase in income has been distributed across the various sectors of the economy.

We find that, since 1991, measured in terms of the rate of growth of output, the agricultural sector has performed far less well than the other two sectors, namely, industry and services. However, the greater part of the workforce, that is, over 50%, is concentrated in the agricultural sector. So, agricultural income per worker has grown more slowly than per capita income in the other sectors. Under present trends, a significant section of agricultural workers would have to move to non-agricultural sectors if they are to have an equal opportunity to earn the incomes rising faster in the latter.

This, however, is not a matter of will. Two conditions are entailed here. First, with the exception of manual labour deployed in construction, participating in the non-agricultural sector requires a higher level of education and a certain degree of skilling for the worker contemplating such a move. This is especially true of manufacturing activity, where in a globalised world firms compete on the basis of labour productivity as the other variable inputs are tradable, implying that firms have equal access to them. Immigration controls ensure that labour is national. Now, firms compete on labour cost, which is determined by productivity. The skilling needed for the labour movement envisaged is not acquired costlessly. Either the firms would have to pay for the training of workers or the workers equip themselves with the skill. Historically, by European standards for instance, firms in India have been quite reluctant to train workers. I do not speak of the quality of the training, but the mere willingness to offer it at all. On the other hand, much of the rural landless labour, which is the relevant cohort here, is pretty much destitute and incapable of training itself. It is obvious that under the circumstances the state would have to step in.

The second factor to reckon with is that the increased nonagricultural production of the migrating labour has to find a market. I digress to place this proposition in perspective. The central insight of the Keynesian Revolution in economic theory, now eclipsed by the reinstallation of Classical economics in the anglophone world, and thus by reflexity in India, was that the demand of labour is a derived one, that is, there is demand for labour only if there is a demand for goods. This implication of the market economy is overlooked by both enthusiasts for the free market economy and their opponents. So, the transfer of workers to the non-agricultural sector cannot merely be wished for. It would have to be dovetailed with developments elsewhere in the economy, to enable which coordination by the state may well be necessary.

In the first instance, the market for expanded non-agricultural production would have to be provided by the growth of agriculture. For, while in principle the demand could come from the rest of the world, a slowing world economy today suggests that external demand cannot be relied upon to enable the desired transition. Does this make me an "export pessimist," among economists—a taint perhaps more shaming than "non-nationalist" is in Indian politics today? I believe that it does not! My observation has been made in the light of the fact that in mid-2016 exports from India were still recovering from 17 consecutive months of decline, reflecting the global slowing down. Nevertheless, it is important to not be bound by the present as a guide to action, and everything ought to be done to develop the international competitiveness of Indian enterprises. But, this brings us back to what I have already highlighted as a constraint to achieving it, namely, the skill level of our workforce.

To sum up, I have said that while there are two sources of demand for an economy's goods, namely, the domestic and the external, in the immediate present we would have to rely on the former, and sustained steady agricultural growth is a necessary part of such a strategy. But, if agriculture is to serve as an engine of growth at least for a while, it would have to expand without an increase in the price, for a rise in agricultural prices will stymie the growth of demand for manufactures envisaged in such a strategy. Agricultural expansion without a rise in prices would yet be profitable if there is a concomitant growth of yield. Before I come to the question of what can be done to raise agricultural productivity, I would mention an important reason, beyond the pursuit of equal opportunity, as to why we must reduce overcrowding in agriculture. Indian agriculture is witnessing a progressive decline in the average farm size due to fragmentation. If this were to continue, household income from farming will shrink even if the yield is constant. We would be advised to treat this as an important instance of how our prospects are constrained by natural resources, a possibility yet again scarcely imagined at both ends of the political spectrum.

Increasing agricultural productivity would require at least three interventions by the government. First, an effective physical infrastructure will have to be provided. This can come only from the government. Here, I wish to briefly clarify what I mean by "effective". It refers to the actual availability of the input. It has been pointed out that official statistics in India may not reflect the true position with respect to availability. Scepticism has ranged from the data on irrigation statistics to the food stocks of the Government of India.

Second, a far greater agronomic input is required from India's extensive archipelago of agricultural research institutions. Recall that these had been in the forefront of the green revolution in the 1960s and nothing but a governance deficit explains their current dormancy. The reference to the green revolution should also remind us that the last major agricultural thrust in India was made 50 years ago. Finally, education matters not only to manufacturing. Increasing agricultural productivity requires a more educated farmer as farming will have to be increasingly undertaken under conditions of natural resource adversity due to climate change, and economic uncertainty due to the integration of markets.

Conclusions

So, how are we to assess the economic reforms on their 25th anniversary? First, it must be acknowledged that India's balance of payments constraint has been eased. A payments crisis had triggered the reforms of 1991, and to have strengthened India's external position is a substantial achievement. Next, both growth and poverty have continued to decline. In this way the reforms have maintained a trend while providing macroeconomic stability. But, 25 years since, India continues to have an unacceptable level of poverty even as it is measured according to a low international standard. The progress made on this front is disappointing given the claim that the reforms mark a sea change in India. Finally, the spread of opportunity has been uneven going by the fact that the sector containing the largest number of workers has been the one growing the slowest. I have emphasised the importance of far greater dynamism in the agricultural sector if we are to move towards an equalisation of opportunities across the economy. Needless to mention, this would also take the economy closer to the dreamt-of double-digit growth. The importance of agriculture for both poverty reduction and growth is evident to us from both the history of East Asia (Hayami and Godo 2005) and the experience of India's economy during the phase of high growth during 2003–08.

What can we expect with respect to the spread of opportunity from the economic reforms as practised in more or less similar fashion by the two coalitions that have governed India over the past two decades? Not much, if the present situation is any guide. The analysis in this article shows us why this must be so. First, there is perhaps excessive focus on the interface of India with the rest of the world, when outward orientation is not going to provide the solution to the most pressing of India's problems today. Historically, countries have solved their problems of agricultural supply shortfall and large-scale physical infrastructure provision on their own. China is perhaps the best example. Second, there is excessive focus on higher education compared to schooling. Finally, the approach to the macroeconomic policy is dogmatic, emphasising fiscal consolidation over capital formation, making it difficult for the state to make a difference via the provision of infrastructure on a significant scale.

Actually, Make in India, a flagship programme of the present government, reflects a failure of the reforms to make a serious dent in the very area in which it focused the most, that is, manufacturing. The failure has also to do with the failure to recognise the importance of demand. Much of the focus, it appears, is on the "ease of doing business". While this is hardly irrelevant as a consideration, the dramatic decline in manufacturing growth after close to double-digit growth over 2003–08 suggests that the supply side is unlikely to be the issue.

The wait for a just economy in India could turn out to be long, but we can start by critically engaging with the economic policy encapsulated in the reforms being pursued by both the political formations at the level of the central government. I hope that this article has been able to show exactly what needs to be done.

Notes

1. For a discussion of the economics and politics of the regime change in 1991 see P. Balakrishnan (2010).
2. The government's view on the rationale of the reforms may be gathered from the *Economic Survey* of July 1991 and February 1992.
3. For a discussion of the issues involved in the use of the much-used index "total factor productivity," see Balakrishnan (2010).
4. For information on the growth of the Indian economy in this period, see "Economic Survey 2009–10," Government of India, New Delhi.
5. Evidence, based on reports of the Government of India, on the decline of the growth rate in the agricultural sector may be found in S.M. Dev (2008). For evidence on foodgrain availability since 1991 see Deaton and Drèze (2002).

6. The view has been articulated in a public lecture by Manmohan Singh, when he was finance minster, see Singh (1995). For an empirical assessment of the relative role of structural factors and the changed policy regime in determining agricultural growth since 1991, which concludes that the former are likely to have been more important, see Balakrishnan et al (2008).

7. See, Narayana Murthy (2004), though his argument is perhaps more pertinent for software.

8. Though water and electricity are not strictly speaking public goods, relieving the environmental constraint and enhancing infrastructure almost inevitably requires an element of what economists refer to as "collective action," as purely market solutions have limited potential.

9. See D.G. Johnson (2000) for a global history extending over half a millennium.

10. Evident from the United Nation's cross-country data presented at http://www.data.un.org.

11. Evidence of the concern on the part of India's political class that social justice can no longer be ignored as a criterion by which public policy is to be judged may be seen in the importance given to inclusive growth in the agenda of the United Progressive Alliance–2 and in the proclamation "sabka saath, sabka vikas" of the National Democratic Alliance–2.

References

Balakrishnan, P. (2010): *Economic Growth in India: History and Prospect*, Delhi: Oxford University Press.

Balakrishnan, P., R. Golait and P. Kumar (2008): "Agricultural Growth in India since 1991," Development Research Group Study No 27, Department of Economic Analysis and Policy, Reserve Bank of India, Mumbai.

Chisti, S. (2010): "A Reversal of Fortune: India Lends to the IMF," *Indian Express*, 7 June, viewed on 26 October 2016, http://archive.indianexpress.comnews/a-reversal-of-fortune-india-lends-to-imf/630443/

Deaton, A. and J. Drèze (2002): "Poverty and Inequality in India: A Re-Examination," *Economic & Political Weekly*, Vol 37, No 36, pp 3729–48.

Dev, S.M. (2008): "Challenges for Revival of Indian Agriculture," First Dayanatha Jha Memorial Lecture, mimeo, National Centre for Agricultural Economics and Policy Research, New Delhi.

Hayami, Y. and Y. Godo (2005): *Development Economics: From the Poverty to the Wealth of Nations*, third edition, New York: Oxford University Press.

Johnson, D.G. (2000): "Population, Food and Knowledge," *American Economic Review*, Vol 90, No 1, pp 1–14.

Murthy Narayana, N.R. (2004): "The Impact of Economic Reforms on Industry in India: A Case Study of the Software Industry," *India's Emerging Economy: Performance and Prospects in the 1990s and Beyond*, K. Basu (ed), Cambridge, MA: MIT Press, pp 217–22.

Singh, M. (1995): "Inaugural Address," delivered at the 54th Annual Conference of the Indian Society of Agricultural Economics held at Shivaji University, Kolhapur, Maharashtra, 26 November 1994 [published in *Indian Journal of Agricultural Economics*, Vol 50, No 1].

'Fiscal Federalism' in India since 1991

Infirmities of Sound Finance Paradigm

*Chirashree Das Gupta, Surajit Mazumdar**

The "reforms" in 1991 laid out a new trajectory in which federalism was dichotomised into two parts—political and fiscal. The fiscal was privileged and used to undermine the political. Fiscal federalism in India since 1991 rests on the contradictions generated by the theoretical infirmities of the sound finance paradigm along with a concerted undermining of federal provisions. This political drive is in keeping with the agenda since 1991, eroding the relative autonomy of the state to turn it into a facilitator of a macroeconomic expansion process in which the wage–surplus distribution becomes more and more favourable to capital.

⁂

Widening regional disparity has been a feature of India's social and economic trajectory at least since the 1960s. The process of economic reforms since 1991 has certainly accentuated it—both between and within states—in sectoral as well as social dimensions. This intensification of regional disparity is also characterised by wider sectoral disparities, especially between agriculture and non-agriculture, among different regions, and widening social disparity along with wider rural–urban disparities.

*The authors gratefully acknowledge Mohit Kumar Gupta's assistance for this article.

The relative ranks of different states in terms of their per capita income levels have remained practically unchanged in the last three decades, with very moderate changes in the ranks of middle- or high-income states within their respective groups. This secular homogeneity among the poorer and richer regions of India has been resolute in continuity across national policy regimes since independence right up to the present period. Moreover, these geographical variations in prosperity have almost no correlation with the natural endowment of the different states (Krishna 2004; Ghosh and Das Gupta 2009; Sood 2016).

Since 2005, for a period of about five years, four low-income states of India started growing faster than the national average. This indeed was a significant change from the past—a phenomenon that has hardly been studied in detail. Bihar was the only state that was noticed and was designated as a "miracle" in the corporate media after the first National Democratic Alliance (NDA) government came to power in November 2005, even though the growth acceleration preceded the formation of the government by at least two years (Das Gupta 2010).

Moreover, the reliance of the Bihar government on central resources for development expenditure increased in this period along with an evident negative divergence in per capita development expenditure from the national average by 2010–11. Tax to gross state domestic product (GSDP) ratios have remained stagnant at very low levels showing sturdy resistance to any buoyant response to economic growth (Das Gupta 2012). Needless to point out that the content of growth in low-income states have had very little impact on social disparities within these states even in terms of the minimum indices of human development, similar to the growth and development contradictions in almost every part of India.

The Sound Finance Paradigm

Given this context, it is indeed ironical that 25 years after the economic reforms in India, the questions and debates around federalism that informed not only the making of the Indian Constitution and its subsequent amendments, but also shaped the politics of centre–state relations, have become muted. Federalism after independence entailed political contestation on the question of the units of the federation, constitutional asymmetries, land reforms, freight equalisation, the regional asymmetry of industrial credit and development expenditure, industrial policy, and especially, conflict over location of industry and policy on items in the concurrent list (Toye 1981; Saxena 2012; Das Gupta 2016a).

The 1991 "reforms" put paid to these political conflicts and laid out a new trajectory in which federalism was dichotomised into two parts: political and fiscal. The asymmetries of political federalism in India were relegated to oblivion with the tussles around fiscal federalism considered to be the sole contention construed as efficient organisation of a multilevel fiscal system (Govinda Rao and Jena 2005; Govind Rao 2015).

The shift in this materiality of academic discourse after 1991 lay in the replacing of the politics of conflict negotiation with that of techno-managerialism. The neo-liberal compact that emerged after 1991 reduced the role of the state to a facilitator of private investment. It shifted from the multidimensional understanding of the fiscal constraint in India since independence, and relied on pushing fiscal compression as the only way to circumvent the perceived problem of "fiscal profligacy". Thus, the narrowing of the class basis of the state entailed a fiscal paradigm that sought its basis in "sound finance". Are states necessarily profligate? The answer to this is based on a behavioural analysis of the state within the sound finance paradigm in which states behave exactly like individual agents operating in a free market on the premises of "bounded rationality". Sound finance did not need a theory of the state. The state was supposed to be what the state does (Byres 1997).

By the next decade with the recognition of the hard version of neo-liberalism institutionalising and intensifying disparities, fiscal federalism was redefined as an "optimal institutional framework for the provision of public services" (Rao 2015: 30–35). This perspective on fiscal federalism, still rooted in the sound finance paradigm, conflated decentralisation with devolution. Intergovernmental competition at the subnational level was supposed to bring about "efficiency" of organisation of the state in its capacity to deliver public services. Figuring out the optimal size of the units of the federation became the precepts of the "design".

The fiscal orthodoxy of the neo-liberal sound finance paradigm has been based on unsound economics which saw a monetised fiscal deficit as more money chasing less goods. It claimed that the fiscal deficit if monetised would lead to higher inflation and would crowd out private investments. This condition is valid only if an economy is at full employment. At a time when the economy is growing, the new money stock would be chasing a larger stock of goods as output of goods may increase through deficit financing in a demand-constrained economy. Also the rate at which money chases goods varies as a result of changes in other economic variables. Money that transforms into capital can have different turnover periods. Thus, even if a part of the fiscal deficit translates into a larger money stock, it need not lead to inflation. If the fiscal deficit was non-monetised, it was argued it would lead to a rise in interest rate that would crowd out private investment. This assertion assumed that a money supply-constrained level of output is necessarily a full-employment level of output without any economic rationale for why it should be so (Bhattacharya 2002; Patnaik 2006).

Despite the infirm economics of the sound finance paradigm, advocacy for fiscal austerity and cuts in expenditure since 1991 had paved the way for "fiscal responsibility and budget management" by 2004 through the aegis of the Twelfth and Thirteenth Finance Commissions. A techno-managerial approach (supposedly "free of ideology") became the premise of constructing methods by which fiscal responsibility legislation was made mandatory for states through both the carrot of debt write-off, and the stick of performance-related riders. These were once again modelled on the managerial appraisal of individual workers in corporate entities. It must be noted that even proponents of the sound finance paradigm (for example, Rao 2007) noted that there is no economic rationale for the setting of the specific quantitative targets at the centre- and the state-level fiscal responsibility legislations, except for a mechanical replication from the Maastricht Treaty of 1992 of the European Union.

The fiscal responsibility legislations were part of a larger set of fiscal reforms. The stated aims of these reforms had been to step up planned expenditure with a high component of capital expenditure as well as expenditure on operation and maintenance. The stated objective was to finance this expenditure as far as possible from internal resources without resorting to huge borrowing along with institutionalising of fiscal responsibility norms at both the central and state levels through the aegis of the union government based on the architecture of sound finance. Thus, fiscal federalism entailed an incentivisation of severe expenditure compression by the centre for all Indian states through the aegis of the last three finance commissions and the conditions attached to plan grants regardless of the specific macroeconomic context. This, in a substantive way, put paid to even the narrowest definition of "federalism" in the construction of "fiscal federalism".

Expenditure Compression

The paradigm of sound finance accompanying the opening of the Indian economy translated into a simultaneous pressure to keep taxes as well as the fiscal deficit within limits. This resulted in a strong expenditure compressing tendency which contributed to, as well as reinforced, a growth trajectory marked by sharply increasing inequality.

On the growth side, the period after 1991 witnessed an unprecedented expansion of the private corporate sector dominated by a relatively small number of business groups (Mazumdar 2014b). The faster growth of this sector than the rest of the economy was accompanied by a quite dramatic redistribution of income within the sector in favour of the surplus component. The share of compensation of employees in the net domestic product of the sector came down from about 55% in the early 1990s to a third or less by 2007–08, despite significant increases in salaries experienced by some categories of white collar employees.

Wage compression, exemplified by the complete stagnation in real wages in the organised factory sector and a sharp decline in the share of wages in its value added (Muralidharan et al 2014; Sood et al 2014), provided the basis for this redistribution. Behind this real wage stagnation had to be a larger labour market situation, to which the onset of a deep-rooted agrarian crisis since the mid-1990s (Patnaik 2007; Reddy and Mishra 2008; Government of India 2007; Ramakumar 2014) was a major contributory factor. It created a push out of agriculture and the swelling of an already vast labour reserve which then also held down the reservation wage in non-agricultural activities. A polarising growth was inevitable under such circumstances, from which the corporate sector benefited tremendously and the share of corporate profits in the total income of the economy experienced a dramatic increase.

Despite growth and increasing inequality after 1991, the improvement in the combined tax mobilisation of the central and state governments was poorer in the period after 1991 than earlier. The combined tax–GDP ratio had moved from about 6% in 1950–51 to about 10–11% by the beginning of the 1970s, and to 15–15.5% by the end of the 1980s. This slow but steady trend of increase was arrested in the 1990s, a decade in which the ratio if anything tended to remain below the late 1980s level. The only period of some improvement in the tax–GDP ratio was the five-year high growth period preceding the outbreak of the global crisis. Thereafter, there was again a dip, and even the subsequent improvement has not restored the tax–GDP ratio to the 2007–08 level.

Interestingly, the tax mobilisation picture has been worse for central taxes than for state taxes taken as an aggregate. Own taxes of states rather than central taxes have performed better in shoring up the country's tax–GDP ratio, particularly after 2007–08. Of course, there has also been some change in the composition of taxes, more sharply in central taxes, with the share of direct taxes increasing in total tax–revenue compared to the position before 1991.

The point, however, is that while a decline in the ratio of indirect taxes to GDP was the inevitable consequence of liberalisation, the increase in direct taxes did not adequately compensate for that decline. This took place although increasing inequality raised the share of taxable incomes in total income. Indeed, the rise in the tax–GDP ratio up to 2007–08 was based significantly on a boom in corporate profits rather than any increase in tax rates. After 2007–08, however, even this "improvement" in the composition of tax revenue ceased.

Under these circumstances, there was little scope for any significant stepping-up of public expenditure. Instead, expenditure always remained held down, with the combined expenditure–GDP ratio remaining generally below the level reached by 1991. When the revenue situation improved, as in the period 2002–03 to 2007–08, it was used mainly to bring down the fiscal deficit by holding expenditure growth in check. When revenue mobilisation suffered, expenditure bore a disproportionate responsibility for bringing down the deficit, as has been clearly observed in the period of reversal from the post-crisis fiscal stimulus. Expenditure compression—as an important causal factor behind the agrarian crisis, as well as by constraining the social sector and capital expenditures—has been at the heart of economic polarisation that has emerged in India over the last 25 years.

Trends in Taxation

Thus, expenditure compression is the raison d'etre of fiscal federalism in India since 1991 as this is an important means of sustaining India's process of integration over the last three decades solely on the basis of labour cheapening. Concomitant to this, fiscal federalism after 1991 has also entailed a certain silence on the trend in effective direct taxation rates.

In a situation where the direct market-based distribution of the economic surplus is highly skewed against labour and is largely reliant on the extraction of unpaid labour of various kinds, resource mobilisation of the state through a progressive direct taxation regime has been the classical option in capitalism. This is to provide for not only a minimum socially acceptable level of nutrition, health, education, housing, sanitation and social security, but also to reduce the amount of unpaid labour that forms the basis of production which powers the macroeconomy. However, tax reforms in India were formulated in keeping with the state's role as a facilitator of private investment.

The problem of tax mobilisation in India in the post-liberalisation phase was attributed to high rates of taxation and sources of "inefficiency" traced to the administrative structure of taxation and proliferation of multiple taxes by the Tax Reforms Committee headed by Raja Chelliah which submitted its interim report in 1991 (Gurumurthy 1993; Academic Foundation 2003). Thus, the emphasis has been on "rationalisation" of tax rates in the architecture of tax reforms. Along with this, the post-liberalisation period has seen tax exemptions and tax subsidies being awarded to corporates (Mazumdar 2014a) as a major incentivising policy tool.

This process has generated a large amount of opinion without consistent empirical evidence of the fallout on effective rates of taxation. One reason for the lack of empirical evidence is the significant change in the process of data dissemination on direct taxes in India. The Central Board of Direct Taxes (CBDT) under the Ministry of Finance has stopped releasing state-level data classified by taxation units after 1989–90. It has also stopped dissemination of national-level data on actual income assessed and tax collected for various taxation units after 1999–2000. After a gap of more than a decade, the CBDT has recently released some data for 2012–14.

Thus, in the very period in which the debate on taxation and tax mobilisation in India has gained ground, and in a period when the ratio of direct tax to indirect tax collection has moved marginally in favour of direct tax, the full import of these trends are not available for analysis. Within these constraints, we have compiled income tax data from various volumes of the Statistical Abstract of India and computed effective rates of income tax for the different assessees in India.

It must be noted that the reporting of taxation data reflects the dichotomy of taxation and corporate governance structures in India. This is because income tax reporting assumes five types of units/assessees which are reported as separate and distinct without any relationship to each other. Our analysis of the institutional structure of corporate governance shows that the institution of the family-owned business group operates through a complex maze of interlocked ownership and control spread across all the five categories (Mazumdar 2006; Das Gupta 2016a).

The various reports on tax reforms in the last 20 years also reflect this dichotomy in which the institutional assumptions of corporate tax rationalisation completely occludes the purview of the system of self-rationalisation offered by the interlocking tax entities. Thus, analyses based on sources like the PROWESS database capture the larger picture of 60–71% of "firms" reporting positive profit before taxes showing effective taxation rates below 25% in the last five-year period, and larger firms facing lower effective tax rates (Rao 2015). While this corroborates our findings discussed below, databases such as PROWESS do not take into account the institutional type and nature of firm, the interlocking relationships between firms, the interlocks between firms and Hindu Undivided Family (HUF) accounts, and the differential impact of changes in tax policy on different tax entities.

There are three broad trends evident from the figures of effective tax rates (ETRs) for the various tax paying categories in Table 1. From 1954 to 1965, in the Nehru–Mahalonobis regime, effective rates of taxation were largely constant at different levels for all categories except the registered firms (sole proprietorships and partnerships) which showed a steady increase in the last part of the period.

Table 1   Annual Effective Income Tax Rate by Type of Assessees (in per cent)

Years	Individuals	HUF	Registered Firms (Sole Proprietors/ Partnerships)	Others (Trusts/ Cooperatives/ Registered Societies, etc)	Companies (Private and Public Limited)
1954–55	15.55	17.33		22.82	43.94
1955–56	15.86	17.74		26.53	43.83
1956–57	15.87	17.41	3.03	24.21	45.98
1957–58	14.93	15.97	3.03	19.61	50.30

(*Cont'd*)

Table 1   *(Cont'd)*

Years	Individuals	HUF	Registered Firms (Sole Proprietors/ Partnerships)	Others (Trusts/ Cooperatives/ Registered Societies, etc)	Companies (Private and Public Limited)
1958–59	13.61	13.85	3.03	19.51	51.69
1959–60	13.00	14.12	3.15	21.85	51.45
1960–61	12.61	13.56	3.24	19.52	48.48
1961–62	12.73	15.74	3.27	22.24	48.41
1962–63	12.82	14.78	3.95	20.58	48.48
1963–64	12.08	14.27	4.56	21.87	50.15
1964–65	11.73	15.12	5.02	23.36	47.56
1965–66	11.26	13.62	5.21	27.62	47.95
1966–67	13.23	16.91	6.03	29.57	50.51
1967–68	14.11	18.57	6.43	29.40	50.69
1968–69	13.73	17.35	6.75	29.69	53.56
1969–70	13.92	18.68	7.63	31.15	53.92
1971–72	15.45	22.31	10.13	39.74	56.50
1972–73	15.30	20.50	9.59	38.39	57.06
1974–75	14.87	23.53	9.68	44.25	58.65
1 975–76	14.27	23.84	10.05	44.19	58.53
1 976–77	15.31	23.90	10.15	40.63	59.96
1977–78	14.61	24.42	10.35	45.68	58.96
1978–79	16.09	24.15	10.55	38.95	57.54
1979–80	16.19	23.25	10.97	40.80	53.21
1980–81	18.19	24.99	11.66	40.54	58.03
1981–82	17.60	24.99	11.23	39.75	52.67
1982–83	17.67	26.05	10.19	35.38	53.71
1983–84	19.58	23.98	10.23	32.19	51.11
1984–85	16.67	31.85	9.88	21.08	54.78
1985–86	17.56	25.68	10.71	31.49	57.00

(Cont'd)

Table 1   (Cont'd)

Years	Individuals	HUF	Registered Firms (Sole Proprietors/ Partnerships)	Others (Trusts/ Cooperatives/ Registered Societies, etc)	Companies (Private and Public Limited)
1986–87	16.39	23.00	9.90	30.41	42.27
1987–88	17.81	23.58	10.36	30.97	40.32
1988–89	19.55	23.78	10.55	31.30	52.59
1989–90	18.48	19.98	11.42	30.35	45.30
1990–91	18.19	19.84	11.46	30.06	45.40
1991–92	16.97	24.78	14.70	24.42	53.27
1992–93	16.81	24.76	14.23	24.41	53.28
1993–94	18.58	25.57	14.79	24.16	49.59
1994–95	18.39	27.55	16.17	28.21	46.01
1995–96	9.05	18.09	32.55	32.81	34.76
1996–97	15.19	16.35	28.84	32.86	35.61
1997–98	14.35	13.05	35.59	10.78	37.72
1998–99	18.00	16.78	28.48	2.70	22.87
1999–00	8.26	11.71	21.22	12.76	7.68
2 012–13	10.39	8.65	30.54	27.64	30.29

Source: Calculated from data extracted from the Statistical Abstracts of India (various years); Central Board of Direct Taxes for 2012–13.[1]

From 1972–73, the ETRs for all units of taxation increased till 1975, coinciding with the period of monopoly regulation with the implementation of the Monopolies and Restrictive Trade Practices (MRTP) Act. From 1974–75, there is a significant divergence in trends. Between 1972 and 1985, the ETR of HUF shows a steady increase. This could be explained by two significant policy changes: the equalisation of rates of taxation for HUF as compared to individuals, and the doing away of special privileges of HUF in Kerala and Andhra Pradesh.[2] After 1991, the ETRs for individuals and HUFs have been declining.

However, it is also clear that from the mid-1970s, limited liability companies and others (trusts, cooperatives, registered societies, etc) have seen a steep decline in ETRs right up to 1999–2000 with limited liability companies recording an ETR of less than 10% in 2000. Also, registered firms (with unlimited liability, that is, partnerships) had the lowest ETR at independence while limited liability companies had the highest ETR.

This pattern gets reversed significantly in the ensuing decades. The registered firms have seen a gradual but continuous rise in effective rates of taxation across policy regimes, while the limited liability companies have seen a steep decline since 1991. This pattern has intensified after 1991. Thus by 2000, registered firms showed higher ETRs compared to limited liability companies. Moreover, the ETR for HUF had converged with that of individuals.

Two methodological propositions follow. First, the ETR trends do not show much policy responsiveness after 1991 as the trends largely pre-date the "tax reform" agenda of the last two decades by a good decade and a half. Thus, the dominant macro policy paradigm and attempts to find causal explanations within the paradigm are methodologically futile to establish either correlation or causality.

Second, the institutional structure of asset, wealth and property holding in India being a maze of interlocked family and business entities spanning all five categories needs to be recognised as the comprehensive unit of taxation. However, the only legislation in India that recognised this comprehensive unit (the MRTP Act) was one of the first regulations to be repealed in 1991 after the strategic dilution of monopoly regulation since the late 1970s (Mazumdar 2006; Das Gupta 2016a). Moreover, there is no systemic compilation of data by the Indian state on interlocking tax entities and extent of direct and indirect ownership of economic assets and property by family-owned business groups.

Figure 1 (p 160) demonstrates that India's income tax structure remains intensely regressive after two and a half decades of tax rationalisation and tax reforms with effective rates of taxation of income declining dramatically with the rise in the income range for all corporate entities.

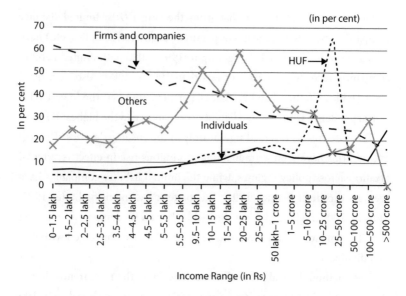

Figure 1 Effective Income Taxation Rates according to Income Range (2012–15) (in Rs)

Source: Data extracted from the Central Board of Direct Taxes, 2016.

If market-led competition indeed has to be the basis of the macro-economy as envisaged by the dominant paradigm, creation of information systems geared towards measuring the extent of monopoly and oligopoly in India and the ETRs of such entities is a task in hand.

This trend of regressive, declining effective direct taxation of income is also evident in the taxation of property and wealth. These trends since 1975–76 which intensified after 1991 are one of the causal explanations of the so-called resource crunch in the economy despite the high growth decade of the 2000s. The state's role in the labour cheapening process by increasing the burden of unpaid labour for social reproduction is combined with declining support for paid employment-enhancing production. This is evident in the conscious fiscal paradigm founded on different ways of lowering effective taxation rates for big corporate entities to drive economic growth after 1991.

From VAT to GST

The last component of the construction of fiscal federalism in India after 1991 lies in the design of eroding the fiscal powers of the state-level governments through the efficiency claim of a single tax at a rationalised rate. The subsuming of all indirect taxes at the central and state taxes to create one single tax—the Goods and Services Tax (GST) under the aegis of the states by the 122nd Constitutional Amendment (GST) Bill, 2014—has led to a renewed examination of the centralising premises of fiscal federalism in India in the current conjuncture.

The introduction of GST is claimed to be a significant step towards creating a "common national market" and creating a harmonious tax system. The United States, which is the largest economy in the world, has not implemented the value added tax (VAT)/GST regime, and has a sales tax which varies across the states and is decided by the states. Why has it not felt the importance and need for a common national market?

This goal of fiscal federalism in India to create a common market follows once again from the Maastricht Treaty that led the basis of the formation of the European common market. This was an attempt to create a political and economic union of sovereign nation states in Europe—an experiment that is now in crisis due to inherent contradictions. The blind import of the understanding of a common market in the professed goal of creating one in India is testimony to our earlier observation of the lack of a theory of the state and especially the nation state in the rubric of the "sound finance architecture".

In Europe, the question of a common market was important as it was an amalgam of markets separated by boundaries of the nation state, but with a relatively homogeneous consumption structure. The claim of "home-grown reforms" (Ahluwalia 2016) stands questioned in the inexplicable conflation of a formulaic prescription of taxation principles in the architecture of fiscal federalism within a sovereign nation state like India (with federal subnational units with very heterogeneous consumption structures) with that of Europe. Even within that, the transition economies of Europe, where the consumption base was much more heterogeneous compared to other countries of Europe, the VAT/GST regime came as a conditionality to join the European Union (Das Gupta 2016b).

It is only in the "developing" economies of Asia and Africa that the economic rationale for the VAT/GST regime has been based on the "efficiency" argument. Thus, contrary to dominant assertions, universal efficiency considerations did not inform the design and implementation of the VAT/GST regime in various parts of the world. Efficiency under stringent assumptions of full-employment—conditions which are simply not possible to be assumed within the social structures of India's economy (Patnaik 2016)—has been reduced to "ease of business" in the design of GST in India. Thus, the shift in the class basis of the state is the only explanation for this paradigm and not this or that economic theory.

The cavalier pushing through the GST shows that there is a collective blinker on the experience of VAT implementation in India which was the first of the two steps in the shift towards a GST regime. The argument had been that India's indirect tax regime is complex, distorted, and has cascading effects due to which there was no significance in buoyancy of tax collection. VAT was supposed to be the efficient tax, based on input credits, which would help to make its administration effective and would lead to increase in tax buoyancy which would translate into a higher indirect tax–GDP ratio (Gurumurthy 1993). The stringent efficiency conditions required a single optimal rate of tax with the assumption of indivisible and homogeneous goods.

More than a decade after its implementation, there is not a single study in India which has till date found a significant, unambiguous and clear structural break in tax buoyancy after the introduction of VAT. In Bihar, on the contrary, we found that except for three tax circles which showed a marginal increase in tax buoyancy, all tax circles showed a decline in tax buoyancy in the five-year period after introduction of VAT (Das Gupta and Sarkar 2011).

The debates around GST have primarily been focused upon the optimal revenue neutral rate (RNR). It has been agreed upon that the states will be compensated for loss of revenue on the basis of calculation of a RNR of GST for all states. These studies are based on data sets (mainly PROWESS) in which the tax base is imputed in the estimate of shares of "sin goods" and hence relies on assumptions. The lack of rigour in these calculations is alarming.

For a rigorous assessment, circle-wise commodity sales and tax collected needs to be available for all tax circles in every state. There has not been any effort by those who are providing technical expertise on GST to study the actual circle-wise commodity base of the VAT regimes implemented in various states based on constructing this data set despite tax officials of state governments having such data on their fingertips after computerisation.

Our study of circle-wise and commodity-wise tax collections from Bihar between 2007 and 2011 shows that around 45% of the total growth in tax collection after implementation of the revised rates of VAT in 2005–06 are accounted for by petroleum products, coal and country liquor, and electricity duties. Thus, commodities which will be exempt from GST together account for around 50% of the VAT base in Bihar (Das Gupta and Sarkar 2011). Thus, half of Bihar's commodity consumption base will be outside the ambit of GST.

The various studies which have calculated the RNR for states using imputations and have informed the debate on GST through these calculations have taken a maximum of 30–35% as the average share of commodities which will be exempted from GST. Thus, the actual tax base assumed in all calculations of RNR for states (even those that have assumed a higher share of exempted goods in calculation of the tax base), are under-projections, and fails to take on board the structure of the narrow commodity tax base of low-income states.

The GST debate has also abstracted away from the issues of intra-state disparity in its assumption of a uniform tax spread within the state in the projection of its potential gains. It completely ignores the structural constraints of intra-state disparities with concentration of taxable transactions in commercial hubs. Patna accounts for 86% of the total VAT collected in Bihar. Such issues of spread are not just confined to low-income states like Bihar.

Large share of indirect taxes in states like Andhra Pradesh and Maharashtra are accounted for by Hyderabad and Mumbai (Das Gupta 2016b).

The GST rationale in developed countries is based on the relative homogeneity of consumption rather than a common market after decades of social democratic universal provisioning. Without such a minimum level of basic consumption being achieved, the shift to a GST regime is simply a leap of blind faith based on flawed economic reasoning. It has sold a false binary between production and consumption to low-income states. A middle/high-income state is likely to be a middle/high production state and a high consumption state depending on the composition of economic sectors. A low-income state will both be a low-production and low-consumption state with a relatively large agrarian base. The only way to ascertain this is to study existing commodity-wise indirect tax regimes in every state.

Thus, the tax reforms initiated under the rubric of fiscal federalism after 1991 have failed to take into account the macrostructural limits and contradictions of a low-income economy with a high degree of informality of transactions with large monopolies and oligopolies controlling at the very least close to 40% of assets and investments (Das Gupta 2016a). The political economy of fiscal federalism in India of the last two decades rests on the contradictions generated by the infirmities of the sound finance paradigm along with a concerted undermining of federal provisions. Though the academic justification of this process stems from the collective blinkers of techno-managerialism, the political drive is in keeping with the agenda since 1991 of erosion of the relative autonomy of the state to turn it into a facilitator of a macroeconomic expansion process in which the wage-surplus distribution becomes more and more favourable to capital.

Notes

1. In 2012–13, the official data categorised six types of assesses as compared to five for all the other years up to 1999–2000. The additional category was defined as AOP/BOI (association of persons/body of individuals), the Effective Tax Rate for which stood at 24.51%. AOP/BOI was included in

"others" in earlier years. The "others" category in 2012–13 includes trusts, cooperative society, limited liability partnerships, local authorities and artificial juridical person.

2. Kerala Joint Family Abolition Act (1976), Andhra Pradesh Amendment Act (1986).

References

Academic Foundation (2003): *Reports on India's Tax Reforms*, New Delhi.

Ahluwalia, M.S. (2016): "The 1991 Reforms: How Home-Grown Were They?," *Economic & Political Weekly*, Vol 51, No 29, pp 39–46.

Bhattacharya, J. (2002): "The Fiscal Deficit," *Macroscan*, viewed on 19 October 2016, http:// www.macroscan.org/eco/aug02/eco170802Fiscal_Deficit.htm.

Byres, T.J. (1997): "State, Class and Development Planning in India," *The State, Development Planning and Liberalisation in India*, T.J. Byres (ed), New Delhi: Oxford University Press.

Das Gupta, C. (2010): "Unravelling Bihar's 'Growth Miracle'," *Economic & Political Weekly*, Vol 45, No 52, pp 50–62.

———— (2012): "Growth and Public Finance in Bihar," IDE Discussion Paper No 331, Institute of Developing Economies, Kyoto.

———— (2016a): *State and Capital in Independent India: Institutions and Accumulation*, New Delhi: Cambridge University Press.

———— (2016b): "The Flawed Premises of GST in India," *Governance Now*, 16–31 August.

Das Gupta, C. and P. Sarkar (2011): *Setting Tax Targets: An Experiment for Government of Bihar*, International Growth Centre (IGC), Bihar.

Ghosh, P.P. and C. Das Gupta (2009): "Political Implications of Inter-state Disparity," *Economic & Political Weekly*, Vol 44, Nos 26–27, pp 185–91.

Government of India (2007): *Report of the Expert Group on Agricultural Indebtedness*, Ministry of Finance, New Delhi.

Gurumurthy, S. (1993): "Value Added Tax and Fiscal Federalism: A Possible Model of VAT in a Federal Economy," *Economic & Political Weekly*, Vol 28, No 22, pp 1108–20.

Krishna, K.L. (2004): "Patterns and Determinants of Economic Growth in Indian States," Working Paper No 144, Indian Council for Research on International Economic Relations, New Delhi.

Mazumdar, S. (2006): "Business Groups and Concentration in the Private Corporate Sector in India," unpublished PhD thesis, Jawaharlal Nehru University, New Delhi.

——— (2014a): "Union Budget 2014–15 and the Myth of UPA's 'Populism,'" *Vikalp*, 3 March, viewed on 2 February 2016, http://www.vikalp.ind.in/2014/03/union-budget-2014-15-and-myth-of-upas.html.

——— (2014b): "Globalisation and Growth: The Indian Case in Perspective," *Market, Regulations and Finance: Global Meltdown and the Indian Economy*, Ratan Khasnabis and Indrani Chakraborty (eds), Springer, pp 213–30.

Muralidharan, T., G.D.B. Paul and A.B. Murti (2014): "Should Real Wages of Workers Go Up in Indian Manufacturing?," *Economic & Political Weekly*, Vol 49, No 30, pp 153–62.

Patnaik, P. (2006): "What Is Wrong with Sound Finance?" *Economic & Political Weekly*, Vol 41, Nos 43–44, pp 4560–64.

——— (2016): "Economic Liberalisation and the Working Poor," *Economic & Political Weekly*, Vol 51, No 29, pp 47–51.

Patnaik, U. (2007): "Neoliberalism and Rural Poverty in India," *Economic & Political Weekly*, Vol 42, No 30, pp 3132–50.

Ramakumar, R. (2014): "Economic Reforms and Agricultural Policy in India," paper presented at the Tenth Anniversary Conference of the Foundation for Agrarian Studies, Kochi, 9–12 January.

Rao, M. Govinda and P.R. Jena (2005): "Balancing Stability, Equity and Efficiency," *Economic & Political Weekly*, Vol 40, No 31, pp 3405–12.

Rao, M. Govinda (2007): "Fiscal Adjustment: Rhetoric and Reality," *Economic & Political Weekly*, Vol 42, No 14, pp 1252–57.

——— (2015): "Fiscal Federalism: Opportunities and Challenges for Nepal," *Economic & Political Weekly*, Vol 50, No 10, pp 30–35.

Rao, K. (2015): "Corporate Taxes and Exemptions: What Does the Proposed Agenda Mean?," *Economic & Political Weekly*, Vol 50, No 12, pp 27–29.

Reddy, D.N. and S. Mishra (2008): "Crisis in Agriculture and Rural Distress in Post-Reform India," *India Development Report 2008*, R Radhakrishna (ed), New Delhi: Oxford University Press, pp 40–53.

Saxena, R. (2012): "Is India a Case of Asymmetrical Federalism?," *Economic & Political Weekly*, Vol 47, No 2, pp 70–75.

Sood, A., P. Nath and S. Ghosh (2014): "Deregulating Capital, Regulating Labour: The Dynamics in the Manufacturing Sector in India," *Economic & Political Weekly*, Vol 49, Nos 26–27, pp 58–68.

Sood, A. (2016): "Politics of Growth: Script and Postscript," *Economic & Political Weekly*, Vol 51, No 29, pp 56–60.

Toye, J. (1981): *Public Expenditure and Indian Development Policy, 1960–1970*, Cambridge: Cambridge University Press.

Economic Reforms and Manufacturing Sector Growth

Need for Reconfiguring the Industrialisation Model

R. Nagaraj*

Manufacturing output grew 7–8% annually since 1991, with a marked improvement in the variety and quality of goods produced. Yet, its share in gross domestic product has practically stagnated, with a sharp rise in import intensity. Liberal (or market-friendly) policies were expected to boost labour intensive exports and industrial growth. Why did the manufacturing sector fail to realise these goals? It is widely believed that India needs to "complete" the reform agenda to realise its potential. Critically examining such a view, it is suggested that the long-term constraints on industrialisation perhaps lie in poor agricultural productivity and inadequate public infrastructure. Further, there is a need to re-imagine the role of the development state to realise goals, as the experience of all successful industrialising nations suggests.

৪৯৬৪

Over a quarter century of market-oriented (or liberal, or free market) reforms (1991–2016), the manufacturing (or industrial) sector has grown annually between 7% and 8% on a trend basis (depending upon the data series chosen) (Figure 1, p 169).[1] The growth rate after the reforms is

* I sincerely thank Dennis Rajakumar for providing me with concorded time series Annual Survey of Industries data for the paper.

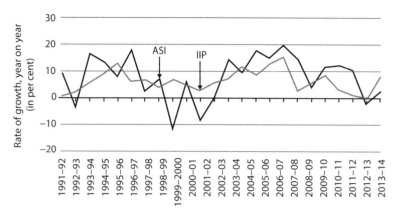

Figure 1   Manufacturing Sector Growth Rate—by ASI and IIP
Source: CSO and RBI's *Handbook of Statistics on Indian Economy*.

higher than in the preceding quarter century, but it is roughly the same as in the 1980s, when the early reforms were initiated. India's share in global merchandise trade has moved up from nearly 0.5% in 2000 to 1.5% by 2015, and the share of services exports rose from 1% to 3% during the same period (Figure 2, p 169).

Industrial production has diversified with perceptible improvements in the quality and variety of goods produced with growing domestic competition. Yet, the manufacturing (or industrial) sector's share has stagnated

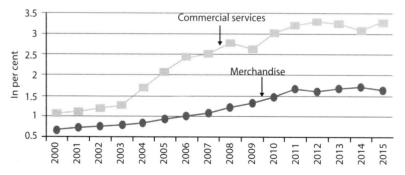

Figure 2   India's Share in Global Trade
Source: Veeramani (2016).

at about 14–15% (26–27%) of gross domestic product (GDP) after the reforms (Figure 3, p 170). Though India has avoided deindustrialisation—defined as a decline in the manufacturing (industrial) sector's share in GDP, or share in workforce—it stares at a quarter century of stagnation, in contrast to many Asian economies that have moved up the technology ladder with a rising share of manufacturing in domestic output and global trade (Rodrik 2015).

However, over a longer period, Indian industry has regressed. The telling evidence of it is a comparison with China. Around 1950, both the large Asian giants were roughly at the same level of industrialisation (or lack of it); if anything, India had an edge (Raj 2006; Kumar 1988). By 2010, however, China became world's second largest manufacturing nation, and India ranked 10th, producing one-third or one-fourth of China's industrial output (at the current market exchange rate) (Figure 4, p 171).

The reforms were built on the initial success in delicensing and import liberalisation (that is, a switch from quotas to tariffs) in the 1980s. However, deepening of the reforms since the 1990s—as part of the broader stabilisation and structural adjustment programme—meant a clear departure from the state-led domestic-oriented, capital goods-focused, "heavy" industrialisation strategy, towards a market-friendly regime, as advocated

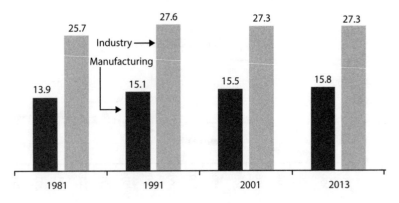

Figure 3   Share of Manufacturing and Industry in GDP (in per cent)
Source: National Accounts Statistics, various issues.

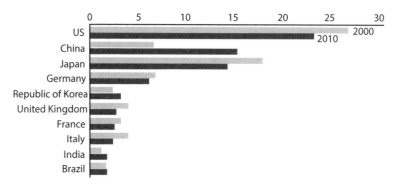

Figure 4   Shares of the World's Top 10 Manufacturing Nations in 2000 and 2010 (in per cent)
Source: UNIDO's *International Yearbook of Industrial Statistics, 2012.*

by most mainstream economists and development agencies, such as the World Bank (as evident in its official publication, *The East Asian Miracle*, 1993). The reforms were initially underwritten by structural adjustment loans from the Bretton Woods institutions, conditional upon implementation of the policy changes (as against World Bank's predominant interest in project finance). Though perhaps modest, these loans signalled to global capital markets and international business the Bretton Woods institutions' endorsement of the shift in India's economic policy.

Jagdish Bhagwati, the most ardent and long-standing critic of India's planning, succinctly summarised what the reforms really meant, when he said:

The main elements of India's policy framework that stifled efficiency and growth until the 1970s, and somewhat less so during the 1980s as limited reforms began to be attempted, and whose surgical removal is, for the most part, the objective of the substantial reforms begun in mid-1991, are easily defined. I would divide them into three major groups:

(1) Extensive bureaucratic controls over production, investment and trade;
(2) Inward-looking trade and foreign investment policies;
(3) A substantial public sector, going well beyond the conventional confines of public utilities and infrastructure. (Bhagwati 1993: 46)

In other words, to put it more graphically using Bhagwati's picturesque imagery, the reforms meant making a bonfire of industrial investment and output controls, or ending the much criticised permit–licence raj. However, in practice, the speed and scope of the reforms was gradual—slow by international standards, but pretty rapid by domestic yardsticks—and they were undertaken by trial and error, regardless of the political dispensation at the helm.

The reforms, though initially centred on industry and trade, culminated in encompassing financial globalisation in the last decade, when India got enmeshed in the global economic cycles of boom and bust.[2] The public sector was rolled back even within the "conventional confines of utili-ties and infrastructure" by allowing private and foreign capital in these indus-tries. India surely rode the boom during its "dream run" for five years from 2003 to 2008, to clock an unprecedented annual economic growth of about 9%, to be counted as among the world's fastest growing large economies (Nagaraj 2013). If China came to be known as the world's factory, India was reckoned, albeit briefly, as its back office. After the global financial crisis, as with the rest of world, India's boom went bust, with industrial deceleration, rising import dependence, and growing short-term capital inflows (or, simply, hot money) financing the balance of payments deficit.

After a quarter century of market-oriented reforms, why did India fail to emulate (or catch up with) the Asian economies to cement its reputation as a successful industrial nation with rising manufactured exports? Perhaps, with booming services exports, India dreamt of skipping the industri-alisation stage to be counted as the world's back office, leveraging its large "educated" English-speaking workforce, and ignoring outsourcing services' narrow employment base domestically, and even the slender market seg-ment it was tied to in the financial services sector in the United States (US).

We are now back to the drawing board, trying to configure how to rein-dustrialise, given India's persistent economic backwardness (with half of its workforce still engaged in low productive agriculture, and over two-thirds of the population still living in villages) with bleak export prospects, and fickle capital inflows financing its external deficit.

This is not a new question, however. The "Make in India" campaign seeking to raise the manufacturing sector's domestic output to 25% (Invest India nd), or, the previous regime's National Manufacturing Policy, 2011, aimed at raising the manufacturing sector's share in GDP to 25% by 2022 (Ministry of Commerce and Industry 2011) are the official efforts to grapple with the question. But, the real challenge apparently is to translate these lofty goals to into actionable policies with suitable instruments. While working out the specifics of such a strategy is beyond the scope of the study, it hopes to lay out a broad framework of analysis for such an initiative.

This paper critically reviews industrial performance and policy after the reforms in 1991, and seeks to address the question of how to get over the stagnation.

Industrial Trends

Over the entire period of reforms (1991–2014), the manufacturing sector grew at an annual trend growth rate of 7.7% or 7.2% as per the Annual Survey of Industries (ASI) and Index of Industrial Production (IIP), respectively (Figure 1). Evidently, the ASI recorded much wider yearly fluctuations than the IIP, which would show wide differences in the growth rates over shorter periods.[3]

From Figure 1, it is evident that the 25-year period can be subdivided into three distinct phases: 1992–96, 1997–2003 and 2003–14 (Figure 5, p 174). The first phase represents the initial euphoria of reforms, with booming output and investment in the anticipation of a virtuous cycle of faster growth and exports. However, with the expectations of a boost in demand not being realised, industrial growth decelerated. It coincided with the Asian financial crisis, bust of the dot-com bubble, and freezing of credit markets in the US in the early 2000s.[4]

The period from 2003 to 2014 represents, as mentioned earlier, the recent debt-led cycle of boom and bust, perhaps best illustrated by the trends in India's and global exports (Figure 6, p 174) (Nagaraj 2013). After the global financial crash in 2008–09, fiscal and monetary stimulus domestically and

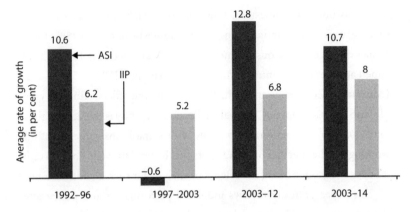

Figure 5   Manufacturing Sector Growth as per ASI and IIP
Source: CSO and RBI's *Handbook of Statistics on Indian Economy*.

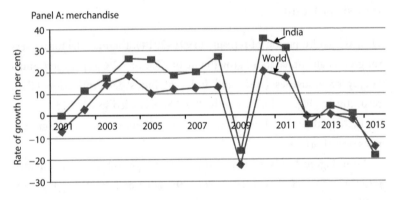

Figure 6   Annual Merchandise Export Growth Rate for India and the World
Source: Veeramani (2016).

capital inflows on account of quantitative easing (QE) in the advanced economies sustained economic growth until 2011–12 (as also in many emerging
market economies), giving rise to a short-lived euphoria of emerging market
economies (EMEs) getting "delinked" from the advanced economies.

The industrial growth scenario after 2014 remains hazy on account of
unreliable data. While the IIP shows marginal improvement, the new series
of the National Accounts Statistics (NAS) reports a distinct upturn—a

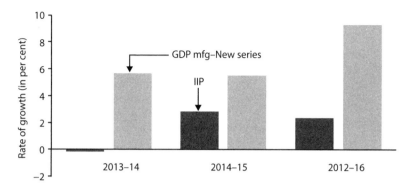

Figure 7   Manufacturing Growth Rate as per IIP and New GDP Series
Source: National Accounts Statistics, various issues, and RBI's *Handbook of Statistics on Indian Economy*.

widely contested statistic (Nagaraj 2015) (Figure 7, p 175). The turn-around in industrial and domestic output growth rates are not supported by the trends in (i) credit growth and (ii) capacity utilisation in industry (Figure 8, p 175 and Figure 9, p 176).[5]

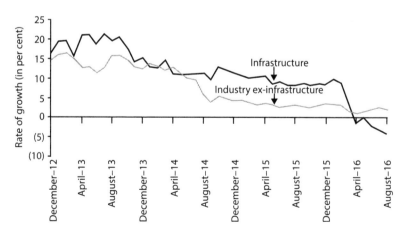

Figure 8   Quarterly Credit Growth to Infrastructure and Industry, 2012–16
Source: CEIC, RBI, Kotak Economic Research.

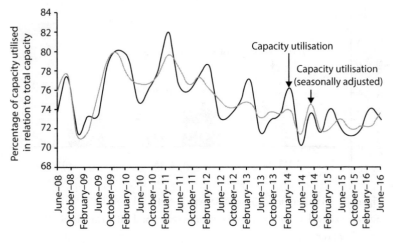

Figure 9 Capacity Utilisation in Industry, 2008–16
Source: CEIC, RBI, Kotak Economic Research.

Performance during the Boom and Bust

From 1991 to 2003, industrial performance was not particularly impressive. After the initial boom until 1996, there was a nine-year period of deceleration, when the output growth was buffeted by many shocks, such as the Asian financial crisis. However, the following cycle of boom and bust (2003–14) was significant in many respects. Five years of India's dream run (2003–04 to 2007–08) were surely led by outsourcing services exports, but manufacturing growth matched the boom with a 10% annual growth rate. This was made possible by a steep rise in domestic savings, investment, and capital inflows, boosting the capital formation rate to close to 40% of GDP at the peak of the boom in 2008 (Figure 10, p 177).

The growth rate recovered after the financial crisis in 2008–09, but at a slower rate of 7.3% per year in the following four years until 2011–12, and decelerated rapidly thereafter. Table 1 provides the average of annual growth rates from 2004–05 to 2013–14, as per the IIP, for use-based industrial categories. In this period, consumer durable goods and capital goods (with each weighing about 8% in the IIP) grew close to 10% per year, while consumer non-durable goods (with a weight of 21%) grew the slowest at 4.2% per year.

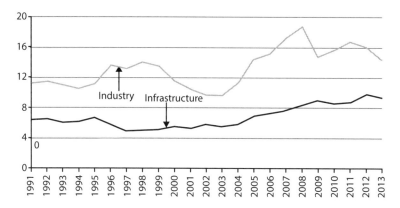

Figure 10   Fixed Investment as Percentage of GDP
Source: National Accounts Statistics, various issues.

Table 1   Growth Rates by IIP's Use-based Industrial Classification, 2005–14

Use-based Industrial Output	Weights	Average of Annual Growth Rates (in per cent)
Basic goods	45.68	5.2
Capital goods	8.83	9.7
Intermediate goods	15.69	4.3
Consumer goods	29.81	5.9
Consumer durables	8.46	9.8
Consumer non-durables	21.35	4.2
Index of Industrial Production (general)	100	5.7

Source: RBI's *Handbook of Statistics on Indian Economy*.
Note: Weights are in relation to the general index of IIP (= 100)

This was also the time when foreign firms and brand names came to dominate many markets, especially consumer durables and capital goods. The import to domestic output ratio went up quite sharply in most industries (Chaudhuri 2013). However, if indirect imports are included, the ratio would go up further.[6]

In the 2000s, two significant policies were initiated for industrialisation, namely, special economic zones (SEZs) and unfreezing of the land market for private industrial and infrastructure investment. Until then, export processing zones were set up by the public sector, and land acquisition for infrastructure was their exclusive domain. When these activities were thrown open to private and foreign capital, the results were dramatic. The land market quickly got commercialised, with easy access to domestic and international capital, and with property development acquiring primacy over industrial use of land (Levien 2012).

In practice, these policies—meant for promoting industrial exports and infrastructure—quickly became a means of acquiring scarce land, often with state support, from gullible farmers who sold their land cheap or were evicted with the state's connivance, giving rise to the term, "predatory growth" (Bhaduri 2008). This resulted in widespread political and social agitations against such policies, contributing little by way of industrial output.

Competing Explanations for the Trends

How does one understand the foregoing account of industrial performance? Many would agree that industry underperformed, but the reasons proffered for it could vary considerably.[7] By no stretch of imagination could state policy constrain industrial decision-making any longer. With India's tariff getting reduced, and with numerous bilateral trade and investment treaties, India's openness became comparable to its Asian peers. Crucially, if the much derided permit–licence raj had held up industrial growth during the planning era, then why did industrial output and exports not zoom after the reforms?

Protagonists of reforms, however, would contend that the reforms have not gone far enough or the agenda remains incomplete—with restrictions remaining on foreign direct investment (FDI) (especially in retail trade), labour market regulation (in the ability to hire and fire at will), full convertibility of capital, etc. These arguments seem questionable. There is no clear theoretically valid and empirically sound association between pro-market reforms and growth (Rodrik 2011). There is perhaps room for critically examining what has been the outcome of the liberalisation carried out thus far.

What has India's open-door policy for FDI led to? In the last decade, the most significant variety of FDI inflow has been private equity (PE), venture capital (VC), and hedge funds (HF), which are, by definition, loosely regulated alternative investment funds that are part of shadow banking. They are not even considered as FDI by the United Nations Conference on Trade and Development definition since they are not for the long-term. Quantitatively, the most important of these sources is PE funds, which, by definition, acquire existing assets and sell these after three–five years in the stock market after restructuring. These are hardly the kind of foreign capital that India needs for getting technology and acquiring industrial capability.[8] Table 2 (p 180) provides information on PE and VC inflows into India since 2005 and an illustrative list of projects in which they have invested during 2015. Economic implications of PE investment are that it is financing of domestic consumption using foreign debt, not productive investment.[9]

The labour market rigidity hypothesis is seriously contested; careful reviews of the literature find little support for the widely held proposition (Kannan and Raveendran 2009; Teitelbaum 2013; Sood et al 2014). That the labour market rigidity argument holds little water now can be gauged by the recent news report that Larsen & Toubro, India's largest machinery and construction firm (turnover $16 billion) reportedly laid off 14,000 work-ers (11.2% of its workforce of 1.22 lakh workers) during July–September 2016 (Prasad 2016). It amply demonstrates that the "hire and fire" policy effectively rules the organised labour market today.

Arguably, the retrenched workers are temporary or contract workers who are not protected by labour laws, which are the bone of contention. But, the fact that such a large enterprise employs non-permanent workers in such large numbers only goes to show how the seemingly rigid laws do not apply to a growing segment of organised workers and that the laws

Table 2   PE Inflow since 2005 and Illustrative List of Their Investments in 2015

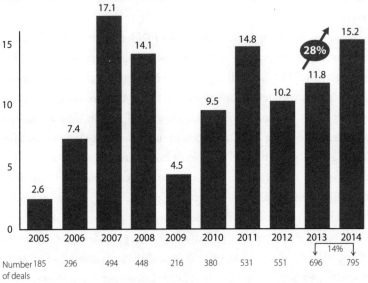

Annual PE and VC investment in India
$20B

Year	Number of deals
2005	185
2006	296
2007	494
2008	448
2009	216
2010	380
2011	531
2012	551
2013	696
2014	795

Top Deals in 2014		
Company	**Fund(s)**	**Values (SM)**
Flipkart	Naspers, Tiger Global Mgmt, Accel Partners, Morgan Stanley Investment Mgmt, DST Advisors, GIC, Sofina, Iconiq Capital	1,000
Flipkart	Qatar Investment Authority, DST advisor Greenoaks Ventures, GIC, Iconiq Capital, Tiger Global, Steadview Capital, T Rowe Price, Baillie Gifford & Co.	700
Snapdeal.com	Black Rock, Tybourne Capital Mgmt, Temasek, Soft. Bank, PI Opportunities Fund I, Myriad Asset Mgmt.	636
Unitech Corporate Parks	Brookfield	581
Kotak Mahindra Bank	Canada Pension Plan Investment Board (CPPIB)	376

(Cont'd)

Table 2   *(Cont'd)*

Company	Fund(s)	Values (SM)
	Top Deals in 2014	
Shriram Capital	Piramal Enterprises	334
L&T IDPL	CDPQ, CPPIB, State General Reserve Fund (SGRF)	323
Jaiprakash Power ventures	IDFC Private Equity, PSP Investments	316
Sutherland Global Services	TPG Capital	300
Minces	CX Partners, Others	260
	Total	4,826

Source: India Private Equity Report, 2015, Bain & Company.

really have no teeth. Hence, the contention that labour laws are holding up flexible and efficient use of labour simply does not hold water.

Currently, policymakers are using the World Bank's "Ease of Doing Business" (EDB) as a measure of hurdles faced by entrepreneurs, and are busy trying to improve India's global ranking to attract more foreign investment. This dubious measure, both conceptually and empirically, hardly explains the foreign investment inflows in developing countries, as evident from a World Bank research paper quoted below:

> The World Bank's Ease of Doing Business reports have been ranking countries since 2006. However, do improvements in rankings generate greater foreign direct investment inflows? ... The paper shows this relationship is significant for the average country. However, when the sample is restricted to developing countries, the results suggest an improved ranking has, on average, an insignificant (albeit positive) influence on foreign direct investment inflows. ... Finally, the paper demonstrates that, on average, countries that undertake large-scale reforms relative to other countries do not necessarily attract greater foreign direct investment inflows. This analysis may have important ramifications for developing country governments wanting to improve their Doing Business Rankings in the hope of attracting foreign direct investment inflows. (Jayasuriya 2011)

If the foregoing arguments are reasonable and evidence credible, then we should look elsewhere for the reasons of the industrial stagnation. The answer perhaps lies with the structuralist economic arguments and the long-term constraints, such as less than satisfactory or poor agriculture performance after the reforms (Figure 11, p 182). Moreover, despite gradual improvements, land productivity in agriculture continues to be a modest fraction of the global average (Figure 12, p 182). Further, lack of adequate

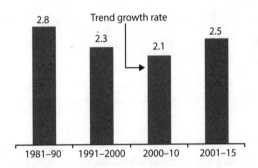

Figure 11 Agriculture Growth Rates, 1981–2015 (in per cent)
Source: *EPW* Research Foundation, India Times Series data.

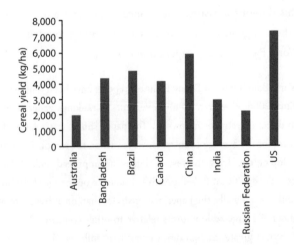

Figure 12 Average Cereal Yields in Selected Countries, 2013
Source: *Economic Survey*, 2015.

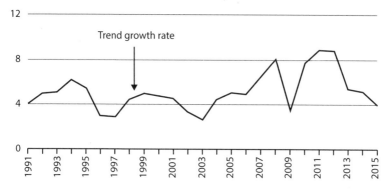

Figure 13   Installed Capacity, Annual Growth (in per cent)
Source: *Economic Survey* various issues.

public infrastructure investment (as capacity creation for power generation by proxy) seems to be holding back industrial growth (Figure 13, p 183).

At the moment, in the aftermath of the global financial crisis, Indian industry is suffering from excess capacity in major industries like steel, coal and machinery, as investment rates and exports have fallen. Fixed capital formation ratio, for instance, has fallen by almost 10 percentage points, from close to 40% of GDP in 2008. As the private corporate sector is mired in debt, and the banking sector is left holding non-performing assets, there is little option but to revive public investment to boost investment and domestic output (Nagaraj 2014).

Need for Reconfiguring Development State

While the foregoing arguments for removing the structural constraints on industrial growth still hold, it is perhaps an opportune moment to revisit the role of state support for industrialisation. Admittedly, state intervention during the planning era (1950–80) had many shortcomings (too widely acknowledged to bear repetition), and many aspects of it may have outlived their utility. Yet, perhaps, the rush to open up markets after 1991 (under stressed macroeconomic conditions) seems to have hurt long-term industrial and trade prospects.[10] So, there seems to be a need to rebalance the equation between the state and the market keeping in view the strategic considerations.[11]

The basic arguments for industrial policy come from Nicholas Kaldor's stylised fact that faster manufacturing sector growth propels the rest of the economy following Verdoon's law of positive externalities. In a somewhat similar vein is Paul Krugman's (1995) hypothesis of economies of locational agglomeration giving rise to positive externalities. Finally, the arguments of market failures due to information imperfections, and state intervention solving the coordination problem offer credible reasons for having an industrial policy Suzumura (1997). Moreover, the comparative Asian experience (starting with Japan to a contemporary account of China and Vietnam) offers powerful empirical arguments for industrial policy.

Three aspects of industrial and investment policies that seem to need careful attention are: (i) long-term finance, (ii) domestic research and development (R&D) efforts, and (iii) bilateral investment and trade treaties. India seems to have a disadvantage vis-à-vis its trading partners, especially with respect to China in all these policies. As part of financial liberalisation, India turned its development financial institutions (DFIs)— such as IDBI (the Industrial Development Bank of India) and ICICI (Industrial Credit and Investment Corporation of India)—into commercial banks, resulting in shortening of loan maturity, thus constraining capital-intensive manufacturing and infrastructure financing. The domestic debt market was expected to fill the vacuum, and that has not happened (as in most industrialising countries). In response, large firms were allowed to borrow internationally even for investments in the non-traded goods sector, leading to currency and maturity mismatches, thus raising potential financial instability.

China, which is still not officially granted the status of a market economy, is known to use cheap credit (including trade credit) as an instrument for penetrating international markets, especially in project exports. Commercial sources often suggest that Indian firms are perhaps unable to match the Chinese firms' commercial terms, despite producing goods of comparable quality and variety. This is not new. Historically, finance is widely used as an instrument of trade policy.

If the above speculation is correct, then there is a case for revisiting national development or investment banks for supply of long-term, low-cost credit for industrial capital formation. Such a case has acquired greater urgency in the context of the continuation of the global financial crisis, and the need for public investment to pull the depressed economies out of the present crisis (Skidelsky and Martin 2011; Turner 2015).

Another setback after the industrial reforms has been the decline in domestic industrial R&D. The licences to import technology and capital in the pre-reform era were conditional upon setting up domestic R&D centres (sweetened with fiscal concessions) to promote indigenous know how. After the reforms, firms no longer needed to make such efforts, and foreign firms had no reason to invest in R&D in India that could potentially compete with their parent firms' global interests. The net result: stagnation in R&D efforts, best illustrated again with a Chinese comparison. In 1996, both China and India spent the same share of their GDP on R&D, at 0.6%. However, by 2011, the ratio for China had tripled to 1.8% of GDP, whereas for India the ratio had marginally moved up to 0.8% (Figure 14, p 185). Interestingly, despite its liberal FDI policy, China did not take its eyes off the strategic significance of R&D, whereas India

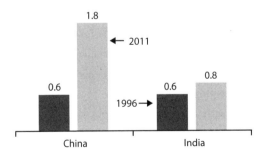

Figure 14   R&D Expenditure as Percentage of GDP in China and India
Source: World Bank's World Development Indicators.

perhaps lost its focus in the free market rhetoric (Mani and Nabar 2016; Mani 2016).

At the height of the financial opening-up in the last decade, India signed a large number of bilateral free trade and investment agreements, whose outcome for industry appears to be questionable (Dhar et al 2012). In particular, the treaty with Thailand, a large base of the Japanese automotive industry, seems to have hurt Indian automotive firms', enabling the duty-free entry of goods.[12] If the observation is correct, then there is perhaps merit in reviewing such agreements.

This is not to argue for unconditional protectionism or unalloyed faith in the state's capacity to promote industrialisation, but to seek for a more reasoned, rule-based support for industry. This should not be seen as a plea for putting the clock back; such a view would be a historical. What is needed, perhaps, is the redefining and reconfiguring of the boundaries of state and market in view of the changed ground realities, comparative experiences, and the renewed analytical arguments for suitable state intervention.

Conclusions

Liberal economic reforms or the market-friendly policy framework constructed over the last quarter century has not served the manufacturing sector well, despite faster economic growth, and output diversification. The goal of rapid industrialising to catch up with Asian peers, in an open trade and capital regime employing abundant labour for labour-intensive exports, did not materialise. There has been undeniable improvement in domestic competition with the rise in the quality and variety of goods produced and exported. Yet, the share of manufacturing in GDP has stagnated, and its share in merchandise exports declined, and import content in domestic consumption shot up.

An eroding industrial base has found political expression in the current political dispensation's slogan, "Make in India," or in the previous regime's National Manufacturing Policy, 2011, albeit these ideas are yet to get translated into workable policies and suitable instruments for implementation.

The easy starting point of it would be to try producing domestically what is being imported. The sharp rise in imports during the recent years clearly shows the potential to indigenise production quickly.

Ruling dispensations, regardless of their political colour and candour, have argued for "finishing" or "completing" the liberal economic reforms agenda, including institutional reforms, to reap their virtuous outcomes. However, after a quarter century of persuasion, such an advocacy rings hollow as it does not have support either in theory or in comparative experience. Worldwide rethinking on the virtues of unbridled globalisation of trade and investment after the global financial crisis is a testament to limits of such arguments, in the current stage of political democracy.

The policymakers' single-minded focus on improving India's ranking in the World Bank's Ease of Doing Business index (mainly by whittling down protective measures for the working poor) seems seriously misplaced as the index has no analytical basis or empirical support. Further, easing of entry of foreign capital even into defence production is completely misplaced when most of the FDI inflow is from private equity firms, which specialise in flipping assets for quick returns, not digging their heels for long-term growth of shared gains.

Unalloyed faith in liberal reforms seems passé (Ostry et al 2016). As Dani Rodrik (2016) said recently,

> The new model of globalisation stood priorities on their head, effetively putting democracy to work for the global economy, instead of the other way around. The elimination of barriers to trade and finance became an end in itself, rather than a means toward more fundamental economic and social goals. Societies were asked to subject domestic economies to the whims of global financial markets; sign investment treaties that created special rights for foreign companies; and reduce corporate and top income taxes to attract footloose corporations.

With global economic recession continuing after eight years of the financial crisis, and its political fallout in terms of Brexit, or ultra nationalism in the US, and the proposed scrapping of the Trans-Pacific Partnership by the US seem clear signals of the current limits to globalism. Considering the current global political and economic uncertainties, it would be prudent to pause and reflect on the liberal model. There is perhaps a need to revitalise the idea of the development state for retaking the initiatives for industrialisation.

Such a vision should not be misconstrued as a plea for a reversal to uncritical infant industry protection or complete delinking from international trade and capital flows. Surely, with rising agriculture productivity and structural transformation, industrial growth will have to turn increasingly to exports for sustaining domestic growth. Yet, for a large economy like India—to paraphrase Arthur Lewis—exports will have to be the efficient lubricant for the large domestic economy, especially to meet energy import needs. It calls for strategic integration with the global economy and reinventing industrial policy keeping in view the long-term national goals.

The structuralist economic view of India's long-term constraints, as low agriculture productivity (compared to the global average), poor public infrastructure and extreme energy import dependence, seem to hold considerable value to this date. So, at a macroeconomic level, such a view would call for state intervention to step up domestic savings and public investment, and insulate the domestic economy from shortterm volatility emanating from the global economy.

We probably need to identify industries and products in which imports are succeeding on account of easy credit, and those which require productivity improvement. There is apparently a need for reconfiguring a strategy for capital goods development (in items like information and communications technology hardware or in solar energy), in which India has become seriously import-dependent, undermining the strategic national interests. This is not, however, a plea for blanket import substitution, and export pessimism, but for infusing technological dynamism to recapture the domestic market and the dynamic comparative advantage in trade. Capital and technology import should be accompanied with commitments for R&D investment.

There is a need to reimagine the role of domestic financial institutions to provide long-term credit for capital intensive industries, infrastructure and exports; along the lines advocated (separately) by Robert Skidelsky and Adair Turner in the current global context. These measures necessarily have fiscal counterparts, which need to be addressed by revisiting fiscal rules.

Similarly, domestic R&D, expenditure which has barely inched up during the reforms as a share of the GDP—compared to China, which tripled the ratio—needs to be seriously viewed and corrected if our present political dispensation is serious of realising its dream of techno-nationalism.

Notes

1. Unless otherwise mentioned, all figures are at constant prices.
2. This is different from the earlier experience of the 1980s when India's annual economic growth (as also that of China) accelerated to around 5.5%, while much of the global economy got mired in the debt crisis—known as the lost decade of development—after Mexico defaulted on its international payments.
3. The index of industrial production (IIP) is a leading indicator of physical output with minimum lag, whereas the annual survey of industries (ASI) is largely based on the annual census of production accounts of large factories, with data available with a two-year lag. Usually, the ASI output growth estimates are higher than the IIP-based estimates. The gap between the two output series tends to diverge after about five years from the base year of the IIP.
4. For a detailed analytical account of this phase, see Nagaraj (2003).
5. Considering the uncertain data quality, we would restrict the analysis up to 2014.
6. For a detailed economic analysis of this period, see Nagaraj (2013).
7. For the details of the arguments reported in this section, see Nagaraj (2011) for a critical review of industrial performance until the boom of 2008.
8. The surge in initial public offerings (IPO) in 2016 seems to be a case in point. Indian companies have mobilised close to $3 billion (Rs 19,379 crore) during January–September 2016, the highest since 2007. Yet, it does not seem to be for augmenting fixed capital formation, but for enabling PEs, which invested during the boom in the last decade to cash out their profits, or dilute promoters' equity holding to pay off PE investors, see Aarati Krishnan (2016).
9. As official data on FDI inflows are not available by type of institution, we have relied on nonofficial sources.

10. For a careful account of how the changes in the policy-affected industrial growth and capability, see Chaudhuri (2013, 2015).

11. China's entry into the World Trade Organization (WTO) seems instructive. It carefully negotiated its terms of entry, timed the entry well to take advantage of the global market for its labour-intensive goods at an undervalued exchange rate, and defended the rate for well over a decade to flood the world with its cheap manufacturing. In the process, China, strategically, was able to convert its surplus labour into trade surplus, to gain immense advantage in global financial markets.

12. "Industry has been ruined by FTAs," says Baba Kalyani, Chairman of Bharat Forge, and Kalyani group of companies with a turnover of $2.5 billion, specialising in automotive forging, supplying to major OE manufacturers worldwide. He said in an interview, "Industry has been ruined by FTAs … because of the FTA, due to which companies come and set up plants here, they don't manufacture anything, they just assemble" (Bhagat 2014).

References

Bhaduri, Amit (2008): "Predatory Growth," *Economic & Political Weekly*, Vol 43, No 16, pp 10–14.

Bhagat, Rasheeda (2014): "Industry Has Been Ruined by FTAs," *Business Line*, 10 February.

Bhagwati, Jagdish (1993): *India in Transition: Freeing the Economy*, Oxford: Clarendon Press.

Chaudhuri, Sudip (2013): "Manufacturing Trade Deficit and Industrial Policy in India," *Economic & Political Weekly*, Vol 48, No 8, pp 41–50.

——— (2015): "Import Liberalisation and Premature Deindustrialisation in India," *Economic & Political Weekly*, Vol 50, No 43, pp 60–69.

Dhar, Biswajit, Reji Joseph and T.C. James (2012): "India's Bilateral Investment Agreements: Time to Review," *Economic & Political Weekly*, Vol 47, No 52, pp 113–22.

Invest India (nd): "National Manufacturing: Make In India," viewed on 2 December 2016, http:// www.makeinindia.com/policy/national-manufacturing.

Jayasuriya, Dinuk (2011): "Improvements in the World Bank's Ease of Doing Business Rankings: Do they Translate into Greater Foreign Direct Investment Inflows?," Policy Research Working Paper No WPS5787, September, World Bank, Washington DC.

Kannan, K.P. and G. Raveendran (2009): "Growth Sans Employment: A Quarter Century of Jobless Growth in India's Organised Manufacturing," *Economic & Political Weekly*, Vol 44, No 10, pp 80–91.

Krishnan, Aarati (2016): "Why This Time isn't Different," *Business Line*, 26 October.

Krugman, Paul (1995): *Development, Geography and Economic Theory*, Cambridge, MA: MIT Press.

Kumar, Dharma (1988): *Colonialism, Property and the State*, New Delhi: Oxford University Press.

Levien, Michael (2012): "The Land Question: Special Economic Zones and the Political Economy of Dispossession in India," *Journal of Peasant Studies*, Vol 39, Nos 3–4, pp 933–69.

Mani, Sunil (2016): "New IPR Policy 2016: Not Based on Evidence," *Economic & Political Weekly*, Vol 51, No 38, pp 28–32.

Mani, Sunil and Janak Nabar (2016): "Is the Government Justified in Reducing R&D Tax Incentives?," *Economic & Political Weekly*, Vol 51, No 30, pp 22–25.

Ministry of Commerce & Industry (2011): "National Manufacturing Policy," press note no 2, 4 November, Government of India, New Delhi, viewed on 2 December 2016, http://dipp.nic.in/english/policies/national_manufacturing_policy_25october2011.pdf.

Nagaraj, R. (2003): "Industrial Policy and Performance since 1980: Which Way Now?," *Economic & Political Weekly*, Vol 38, No 35, pp 3707–15.

——— (2011): "Industrial Performance, 1991–2008: A Review," *India Development Report, 2011*, D M.

Nachane (ed), Mumbai/Delhi: Indira Gandhi Institute of Development Research/ Oxford University Press.

——— (2013): "India's Dream Run, 2003–08: Understanding the Boom and Its Aftermath," *Economic & Political Weekly*, Vol 48, No 20, pp 39–51.

——— (2014): "Economic Challenges to the New Government: A Policy Proposal," *Economic & Political Weekly*, Vol 49, No 21, pp 35–41.

——— (2015): "Seeds of Doubt on New GDP Numbers: Private Corporate Sector Overestimated?," *Economic & Political Weekly*, Vol 50, No 13, pp 14–17.

Ostry, Jonathan D., Prakash Loungani and Davide Furceri (2016): "Neoliberalism: Oversold?," *Finance and Development*, June, International Monetary Fund, viewed on 30 December 2016, https://www.imf.org/external/pubs/ft/fandd/2016/06/pdf/ostry.pdf

Prasad, Rachita (2016): "In One of India's Biggestever Layoffs, L&T Sheds 14,000 Employees from Its Workforce," *Economic Times*, 23 November.

Raj, K.N. (2006): "The Indian and Chinese Plans: Similarities and Differences," *Inclusive Growth: K N Raj on Economic Development*, Ashoka Mody (ed), Hyderabad: Orient Longman.

Rodrik, Dani (2011): *The Globalisation Paradox: Democracy and the Future of the World Economy*, New York: W W Norton & Company.

————— (2015): "Premature Deindustrialisation," paper no 107, Economics Working Papers, January, School of Social Science, Institute for Advanced Study, Princeton.

————— (2016): "Put Globalisation to Work for Democracies," *New York Times*, 17 September, viewed on 20 December 2016, http://www.nytimes.com/2016/09/18/opinion/sunday/put-globalisation-to-work-for-democracies.html

Skidelsky, Robert and Felix Martin (2011): "For a National Investment Bank," *New York Review of Books*, 28 April.

Sood, Atul, Paaritosh Nath and Sangeeta Ghosh (2014): "Deregulating Capital, Regulating Labour: The Dynamics in the Manufacturing Sector in India," *Economic & Political Weekly*, Vol 49, Nos 26–27, pp 58–68.

Suzumura, Kotaro (1997): "Industrial Policy in Developing Market Economies," *Development Strategy and Management of the Market Economy*, Volume 1, Edmond Malinvaud et al (eds), Oxford: Clarendon Press for the United Nations.

Teitelbaum, Emmanuel (2013): "Labour Regulation, Trade Unions, and Unemployment," *Routledge Handbook of Indian Politics*, Atul Kohli and Prerna Singh (eds), Abingdon: Routledge.

Turner, Adair (2015): *Between Debt and the Devil: Money, Credit and Fixing Global Finance*, Princeton: Princeton University Press.

Veeramani, C. (2016): "Inter-linkages between Exports and Employment in India," Occasional Paper No 179, November, Export–Import Bank of India, Mumbai.

World Bank (1993): *The East Asian Miracle: Economic Growth and Public Policy*, New York: Oxford University Press.

Economic Reforms and Agricultural Growth in India

Shantanu De Roy

It was argued that economic liberalisation would ensure a favourable shift in the terms of trade for agriculture in India, enabling producers to plough back surplus from cultivation to make long-term improvements on land, and raise agricultural productivity and growth rate. Contrary to expectations, there was no improvement in the terms of trade for agriculture after the reforms. The decline in capital formation in agriculture, inadequate expenditure on irrigation and extension services in rural areas, and a dearth of cheap institutional credit, resulted in a slowdown of agricultural growth and heightened livelihood insecurity for a substantial proportion of those dependent on agriculture.

৽৽৽

I t was argued that the initiation of reforms, liberalisation of external trade and corresponding price incentives would lead to enhanced investment, availability of crucial inputs and increased output in agriculture. Moreover, it was expected that a shift in the terms of trade in favour of agriculture will improve agricultural exports and increase growth rate (Ahluwalia 1994). Favourable terms of trade were expected to have a positive impact in terms of raising agricultural production and private investment in India (Misra 1998: 2105–2109). These expectations notwithstanding, policy measures adopted following the initiation of economic reforms did not lead to increased rate of agricultural growth.

Economic liberalisation entails a set of measures that are inimical to petty production in general, and agriculture in particular. In that sense, these policies have a distinct class bias against petty producers and the poor. These policy pursuits resulted in a reduction of public investment in rural infrastructure, including irrigation, agricultural research and extension services and a decline in the supply of rural credit to small and poor cultivators, and the pursuit of agricultural trade liberalisation. In this paper, I have analysed how each of these policies have affected the agriculture sector in India.

Growth Rate of Agriculture

High growth of the agricultural sector is crucial for overall development of economy. In India, its importance is heightened with a substantial section of the population dependent on agriculture for employment. As per the National Sample Survey Office (NSSO), about 59% of male workers and 75% of women workers were dependent on agriculture in 2011–12 (NSSO 2014: 14). High agricultural growth is important to reduce rural poverty. It was argued that doubling of the rate of agricultural growth from 2% to 4% along with 9% rate of growth of the economy will reduce income disparities between agricultural and non-agricultural sectors (Planning Commission 2006). In this context, it will be worthwhile to analyse growth rates of agricultural sector, and evaluate its performance in the context of the overall economy, after the initiation of the reforms in 1991–92.

Table 1 shows that growth rate of gross domestic product (GDP) of agriculture has declined since the initiation of economic reforms in India. However, during this period, growth rates of GDP have been increasing except for the two years between 2010–11 and 2013–14. Table 1 shows an increasing divergence between growth rates of GDP of agriculture and economy between 1990–91 and 2009–10, thereby indicating the declining importance of agriculture in the growth trajectory of India.

Declining contribution of agriculture is also reflected in terms of a steady decline in the share of agriculture in overall GDP. Table 2 shows

Table 1 Growth Rates of GDP of Agriculture Sector and GDP of the Economy, 1981–82 to 2013–14 (in per cent)

Periods	Growth Rate of Agriculture	GDP Growth Rate
1981–82 to 1989–90	2.9	4.7
1990–91 to 1999–00	2.8	5.3
2000–01 to 2009–10	2.4	6.8
2010–11 to 2013–14	2.1	3.7

Source: Handbook of Statistics, Reserve Bank of India, various years.

Table 2 Share of Output from Agriculture in GDP, 1981–82 to 2013–14 (in per cent)

Year	Share
1981–82	29.6
1989–90	25.2
1994–95	23.5
1999–00	19.6
2004–05	16
2009–10	12.3
2013–14	11.8

Source: Same as Table 1.

that the share of agricultural output in GDP had declined by half between 1989–90 and 2013–14. This decline had started in 1980s; however it was sharper in the 1990s and in the new millennium since 2000. The share of agricultural output in GDP had declined by 4.4 percentage points in the 1980s, the corresponding figures in 1990s and post 2000 were 5.6 and 7.3 percentage points respectively. This shows that the agricultural sector is losing its importance as an income generating activity at a faster pace with the onset of reforms in India. Expectations regarding performance of the agriculture sector as highlighted in the Approach Paper of Eleventh Plan (Planning Commission 2006) have not been realised.

Table 3 shows that the growth rates of production and yield of most of the major crops have declined in the years following the initiation of economic

Table 3 Growth Rate of Area, Production and Yield of Major Crops, 1981–82 to 2014–15 (in per cent)

Crops	1981–82 to 1989–90			1990–91 to 1999–00			2000–01 to 2009–10			2010–11 to 2014–15		
	Area	Production	Yield	Area	Production	Yield	Area	Production	Yield	Area	Production	Yield
Food grains	-0.2	2.8	3.02	-0.37	1.75	2.13	0.02	1.03	1.01	-0.75	0.66	1.4
Rice	0.39	3.66	3.25	0.56	1.9	1.33	-0.64	0.47	1.12	0.46	1.77	1.31
Wheat	0.66	3.23	2.55	1.3	3.31	1.99	1.01	1.49	0.47	1.27	0.47	-0.7
Coarse cereals	-1.31	1.25	2.58	-2.1	-0.75	1.4	-0.88	0.77	1.67	-3.15	-0.77	2.46
Total cereals	-0.2	2.95	3.15	-0.12	1.94	2.05	-0.26	0.9	1.19	-0.26	0.8	1.07
Pulses	-0.2	1.24	1.43	-1.53	-0.6	0.94	1.35	2.85	1.47	-2.63	-0.12	1.5
Oilseeds	2.1	3.81	1.67	0.05	1.07	1.02	1.32	3.04	1.69	-1.12	-3.85	-2.76
Groundnut	1.78	1.29	-0.49	-1.88	-3.51	-1.64	-1.78	-1.6	0.14	-4.35	-4.5	-0.16
Rapeseed and mustard	1.36	6.31	4.9	0.42	1	0.6	2.24	4.66	2.38	-3.45	-5.06	-1.67
Soyabean	18.73	20	0.87	9.28	10.54	1.15	4.25	6.55	2.22	2.93	-3.73	-6.47
Cotton	-0.52	4.2	4.75	1.59	1.6	0	1.73	9.7	7.8	3.07	1.46	-1.6
Sugarcane	0.84	2.14	1.31	1.35	2.19	0.82	-0.33	-0.12	0.2	1.04	0.97	-0.06

Source: Computed from the Handbook of Statistics, Reserve Bank of India, various years.

reforms as compared to the 1980s. Exceptions to this general trend were observed for pulses and cotton (2000–01 to 2009–10) for which growth rates of production and yield have increased, and sugarcane and wheat (1990–91 to 1999–00) whose production increased marginally as compared to 1980s.

Growth in production of foodgrains between 1981–82 and 2014–15 was largely due to growth rate of yield. In the period under study, highest growth rates in yield of foodgrains were in the 1980s, the second phase of green revolution. Since 1990s, growth in production of foodgrains was mainly driven by rice and wheat. Increase in growth rate of production of wheat, more pronounced since 2000–01, was largely due to expansion in area under cultivation. The decline in area under coarse cereals in all the sub-periods between 1981–82 and 2014–15, has been sharper with the onset of reforms. It can be argued that increase in the acreage under wheat and rice cultivation has taken place at the expense of coarse cereals. Decline in area under cultivation of coarse cereals did not translate into a steep decline in production due to growth registered in yield rate in all the sub-periods. According to Dev and Pandey (2013: 82), growth in yield rate of coarse cereals can largely be attributed to adoption of new seed technology.

There was a sharp rise in the production of oilseeds in the late 1980s and early 1990s due to quantitative restrictions on imports and technological modernisation programme of the government as part of Technological Mission on Oilseeds. Due to an increase in imports as part of trade liberalisation measures, there was a sharp decline in the area under cultivation and production of oilseeds. This can be seen from Table 3 where expansion in area under cultivation and growth rate of output of oilseeds had declined drastically in 1990s as compared to the preceding decade. With the re-introduction of import duties on imports of oilseeds in 2001, and more favourable prices in the domestic market, there was an increase in the area and production, post 2000 (Ramachandran 2011). Import duty on crude edible oil was eliminated in 2010–11, from a high of 75% in 2004. This adversely affected domestic oilseeds producers and Table 3 shows the decline in area, production and yield of different varieties of oilseeds between 2010–11 and 2014–15 (Sharma 2013).

Of all major crops studied in Table 3, cotton has registered the highest rate of growth in the post-reform period, specifically between 2000–01 and 2009–10. Trends in cotton production show that increases in yield were the main factors for growth of output in the 1980s and in the 2000s; increases in area under cultivation were mainly responsible for the growth of output in other periods. Sharp increases in the yield rate between 2000–01 and 2009–10 was due to the adoption of Bt cotton technology in cotton growing areas in India. However, growth of yield rate and production of cotton declined between 2010–11 and 2014–15. It was argued that high costs and risks associated with Bt cotton technology, particularly for subsistence farmers in low yield areas made cotton cultivation unviable. Also, increased use of pesticides even with the adoption of Bt cotton meant that pests (like bollworm) that were not major threats in Indian varieties of cotton, started to have an adverse impact on the yield rate of cotton (Gutierrez et al 2015).

Non-price Factors Affecting Agricultural Growth

Capital Formation in Agriculture

Capital formation is necessary for improving long-term growth potential in agriculture. Figure 1 shows that share of agriculture and allied activities in gross capital formation in the economy was increasing in the mid-1960s, and this trend continued till the late 1970s. Higher growth rates of agriculture witnessed in 1980s were due to the lagged impact of increases in the share of agriculture and allied sector in gross capital formation during the late 1960s and 1970s (Tables 1 and 3). However, since 1980s, the share has shown a declining trend. There was a mild recovery during late 1990s till 2001–02, and then the share declined again. Declining trend since 1990s implies that there has been lesser investment in agriculture as compared to the non-agriculture sector.

Chand and Kumar (2004) argued that public capital formation has a long-term beneficial impact on agriculture as compared to subsidies whose impact is short-term. They estimated that a rupee spent on public sector

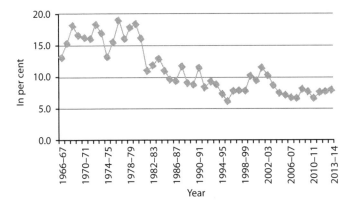

Figure 1   Share of Agriculture and Allied Sectors in Gross Capital Formation
(1966–67 to 2013–14) (in per cent)
Source: Planning Commission of India and Agricultural Statistics at a Glance
(2015).

capital formation contributes to GDP growth in agriculture by Rs 35.21 over
a period of 58 years. They argued that diverting 1% of resources from subsidies to public investment raises output by more than 2%, and is highly desirable in ensuring growth of agriculture GDP (2004: 5611–5616). The trend of
aggregate capital formation in agriculture since 1981–82 is shown in Table 4.

Table 4 shows that aggregate capital formation remained stagnant
in the 1980s. Private and public capital formations moved in divergent
directions. Decline in public capital formation continued well into the
1990s, and it was only in 2004–05 that public investment exceeded
the levels attained in 1981–82. Private investment was increasing at a
faster rate than public investment in the 1990s, and it was instrumental
in raising total investment during this decade. Private and public investments had registered increases from 2004–05 to 2012–13, though the
former increased at a faster rate than the latter. While public investment
doubled, there was almost eight-fold increase in private investment over
the three decades between 1981–82 and 2012–13. The share of public
capital formation in total capital formation in agriculture had gone down
from 52% in 1981–82 to 21% in 2012–13.

Table 4 Capital Formation in Agriculture (1981–82 to 2013–14) (Rs crore, 1999–2000 prices)

Year	Public Investment	Private Investment	Total
1981–82	12,723	11,549	24,272
1982–83	12,665	13,467	26,132
1983–84	12,962	14,816	27,778
1984–85	12,488	12,938	25,426
1985–86	11,248	12,960	24,208
1986–87	10,667	13,051	23,719
1987–88	10,981	17,816	28,797
1988–89	10,302	15,564	25,866
1989–90	8,909	17,132	26,041
1990–91	8,938	29,116	38,054
1991–92	7,901	16,634	24,535
1992–93	8,167	22,862	31,030
1993–94	8,907	19,230	28,137
1994–95	9,706	17,183	26,890
1995–96	9,560	17,777	27,336
1996–97	9,225	20,589	29,814
1997–98	7,812	24,692	32,504
1998–99	7,949	24,956	32,905
1999–00	8,668	41,483	50,151
2000–01	8,085	37,395	45,480
2001–02	9,712	47,266	56,978
2002–03	8,734	46,934	55,668
2003–04	10,805	42,737	53,542
2004–05	16,187	38,309	54,496
2005–06	19,940	42,629	62,569
2006–07	22,987	44,167	67,154
2007–08	23,257	52,745	76,002
2008–09	20,572	68,137	88,709
2009–10	22,693	70,640	93,333
2010–11	19,854	72,181	92,035
2011–12	21,184	86,958	1,08,142
2012–13	23,886	88,371	1,12,257
2013–14	23,191	72,446	95,637

Source: Planning Commission of India and Agricultural Statistics at Glance (2014).

It has been argued that the agricultural sector will have a long-term adverse impact in growth rates with declining importance of public capital formation (Chand and Kumar 2004). There is a difference in the nature of public and private capital formation and contribution in the production processes, in which the former is mainly in the nature of public goods such as irrigation projects and road networks. These will not be provided by private capital. Thus, in terms of contribution to the production process, decline in public capital formation till 2004–05, is not adequately compensated by an increase in private investment in agriculture (Balakrishnan et al 2008).

In India, irrigation accounts for 90% of gross capital formation in agriculture. Table 5 shows productivity of irrigation for foodgrains in Indian agriculture. It was argued that increase in the irrigated area under foodgrains was largely responsible for increase in foodgrains output, and hence growth of foodgrains output with respect to growth of irrigation is a good measure of changes in the productivity of irrigation water (Rao 2002).

Table 5 shows that productivity of irrigation was highest in the 1980s. It was a period when green revolution was broad-based, with the inclusion of rice growing regions in eastern India. Growth rate of irrigated area increased marginally in the 1990s as compared to 1980s; growth rate of output of foodgrains declined during this period. Decline in

Table 5   Productivity of Irrigation for Foodgrains in Indian Agriculture
(Growth Rates in per cent)

Year	1981–82 to 1989–90	1990–91 to 1999–2000	2000–01 to 2009–10	2010–11 to 2012–13
Growth rate of gross irrigated area	2.07	2.28	1.11	1.36
Growth rate of output of foodgrains	2.8	1.75	1.03	0.66
Productivity of irrigation	0.73	−0.53	−0.08	−0.7

Source: Same as Table 3.

productivity of irrigation in the 1990s was due to a loss of momentum in the development of yield-increasing technologies such as cultivation of drought-resistant crops. This loss of momentum is directly related to the decline in public expenditure on research. Also, the political economy of irrigation from groundwater sources had a significant role in reducing productivity of irrigation in the 1990s. As Rao noted that, "there was a sharp decline in agricultural growth in east UP on account of severe cuts in the supply of power for pumping water, which was diverted to west UP to satisfy the powerful farm lobby" (2002: 1743). From 2000–01, growth rates of gross irrigated area and output declined sharply as compared to the preceding decades.

Although, the fact that assured supply of water is crucial for high agricultural growth is acknowledged in policy circles, the response of the government in terms of allocation of resources for extension of irrigation facilities in India has been inadequate. Table 6 shows the decline in the share of outlays on irrigation in GDP over time from the already low levels of the 1980s. Given the increase in GDP over this period, this means that lesser proportion of the income generated in the economy is ploughed back to enhance facilities of an input crucial for the agricultural growth. The decline in this ratio shows that in terms of allocation on irrigation, the policy pronouncements were not really implemented in practice.

Role of Credit

The policy of social and development banking, initiated with the nationali-sation of commercial banks in the late 1960s, was rolled back on account of financial liberalisation. It was argued that reduced emphasis on prior-ity sector lending with financial liberalisation had led to reduction in the

Table 6   Share of Outlays on Irrigation and Flood Control in GDP (in per cent)

Year	1981–82	1990–91	1995–96	2000–01	2005–06	2011–12	2013–14
Share	1.4	0.7	0.7	0.7	0.8	0.6	0.6

Source: Computed from the *Economic Survey of India*, various years.

availability of credit to small and marginal cultivators and made cultivation more expensive. Credit, particularly from the formal sector, is useful for farmers whose income is tied to the harvest, to smoothen consumption for the entire year. Reduction in bank branches in rural areas and declining credit–deposit ratios led to increased dependence of smaller cultivators on private moneylenders at exploitative conditions. These had made agriculture a loss-making activity and reduced the ability of farmers to reinvest surplus, thereby adversely affecting capital formation in agriculture (Dev 2009).

Figure 2 shows that the share of rural branches in total number of branches increased from 36.3% in 1975 to 58.2% in 1990. It declined from 57.2% in 1994 to 38.6% in 2014. Thus, by 2014, the share of rural branches had declined to a level very similar to that of 1975.

Figures 3 and 4 show the trends in credit–deposit ratio and shares of priority sector and agriculture in total outstanding credit of commercial banks respectively. Both declined in the 1990s as compared to 1980s. Since 2001, however, there has been a turnaround, whereby there were steep increases in these ratios. Ramakumar and Chavan (2007) argued that increase in rural credit since 2001 was largely due to an increase in indirect finance in agriculture and definitional changes that incorporated export-oriented

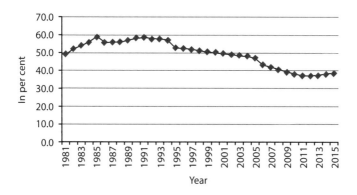

Figure 2 Share of Rural Bank Branches in Total Commercial Branches (1981–2015) (in per cent)
Source: Same as Table 3.

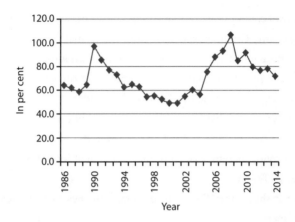

Figure 3   Credit–deposit Ratio of Commercial Banks in Rural Areas (1986–2014) (in per cent)

Source: Same as Table 3.

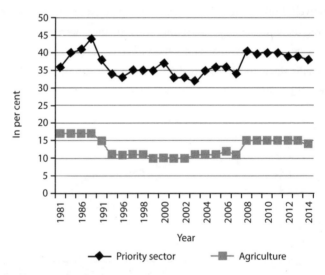

Figure 4   Shares of Priority Sector and Agriculture in Total Outstanding Credit of Commercial Banks (1981–2014) (in per cent)

Source: Same as Table 3.

and capital intensive agriculture under priority sector lending. They also argued that the main beneficiaries of this change were large agri-business companies and big cultivators. The share of the latter in total credit outstanding and loan per account increased substantially between mid-1990s and 2004–05. It can be argued that the revival of rural credit in the new millennium did not improve the performance of agriculture sector as compared to the 1980s, and neither did it benefit an overwhelming number of small and marginal cultivators.

Research and Extension Services

Extension and research are public goods that are prone to market failures, and hence the government has to take a leading role in investment in these activities. Mohan (1974) in a study on the productivity of Indian agriculture across 15 Indian states between 1953 and 1971, argued that states that showed highest productivity gains during this period had higher research intensity as compared to others. He also argued that agricultural research was primarily responsible for the success of green revolution in India. Table 7 reports the estimated marginal internal rates of return (EMIRR) to agricultural research in India from various studies.

Table 7 Estimated Marginal Internal Rates of Return (EMIRR) to Agricultural Research and Extension in India (in per cent)

Category/Study (Research)	Period of Study	EMIRR
Evenson and Jha (1973)	1953–71	40
Kahlon et al (1977)	1960–73	63
Evenson and Mckinsey (1991)	1958–83	65
Rosegrant and Evenson (1992)	1956–87	62
Evenson et al (1999)	1956–87	58
Category/Study (Extension)	**Period**	**EMIRR**
Rosegrant and Evenson (1992)	1956–87	52
Evenson et al (1999)	1956–87	55

Source: Evenson et al. (1999).

Note: This is a modified version of the original table.

Despite these positive impacts, Evenson et al (1999) observed that the share of public spending on agricultural research and extension services in GDP of agriculture in India has been lower than that observed in the 1990s in developed nations (2% to 4%), and the average share in developing nations (0.75%).

Table 8 shows public expenditure on research and extension in agriculture and allied sector as a share of GDP of agriculture and allied activities. It shows that the share of public spending on research and extension in GDP of agriculture and allied activities was low since 1960s, as well as in the subsequent decades. In other words, public spending on agricultural research and extension services did not increase after reforms.

Price Factors Affecting Agricultural Growth

It was expected that with agricultural trade liberalisation, India will emerge as a major exporter of agricultural commodities which will lead to inflows

Table 8   Public Expenditure on Research and Extension in Agriculture and Allied Sector as Share of GDP of Agriculture and Allied Activities (in per cent)

Year	Research and Education	Extension
1960–62	0.21	0.09
1970–72	0.23	0.14
1980–82	0.39	0.11
1989–91	0.41	0.16
1992–94	0.40	0.15
1995–97	0.38	0.14
1998–00	0.44	0.15
2001–03	0.52	0.13
2004–06	0.52	0.13
2009–10	0.30	0.06
2011–12	0.32	0.05

Source: Balakrishnan et al. (2008). Figures for 2009–10 and 2011–12 are computed by the author from Finance Accounts, Comptroller and Auditor General of India.

of scarce foreign exchanges reserves in the economy due to elimination of bias against agriculture after reforms. In view of these arguments, it will be interesting to analyse trends in the movements of terms of trade in agriculture. This is shown in Figure 5.

Figure 5 shows that the terms of trade had started to move in favour of agriculture in the 1980s, and this trend continued till 1994–95. It was stagnant till 1998–99, and worsening mildly till 2008–09, falling further after 2010–11. There was no marked improvement in the terms of trade for agriculture as was expected with the onset of reforms. In fact, in certain phases in the post-reform period, the terms of trade for agricultural producers worsened.

Furthermore, international prices of agricultural commodities are characterised by fluctuations in prices. Table 9 shows that international prices of most of the commodities, except for cotton (Egypt) and sugar, had declined in the 1980s. It recovered briefly till the mid-1990s, although international prices of most of the agricultural commodities in 1995 were lower as compared to 1981. Prices again went down in the late 1990s, and this trend continued till 2005. There was a brief recovery again between 2005 and 2010, after which prices declined. It can be seen that the price of all agricultural commodities in 2015 had gone down compared to 2010.

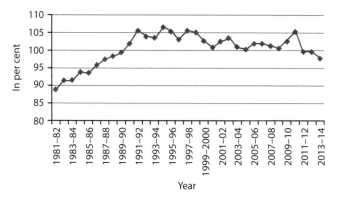

Figure 5 Movements of Terms of Trade in Indian Agriculture (1981–82 to 2013–14)

Source: Price Policy Reports, Commission of Agricultural Costs and Prices.

Table 9   Annual International Prices of Selected Agricultural Commodities (in $, Current Prices), 1991 to 2015

Commodities	Period							
	1981	1986	1991	1995	2000	2005	2010	2015
Wheat US	178	115	129	179	119	158	243	232
Wheat Argentina	191	89	100	167	120	131	253	226
Rice, Thailand	483	210	314	322	204	288	521	380
Sugar (cents/ pound)	9	6	9	13	8	10	21	13
Soyabean, US	288	209	240	259	212	275	450	390
Soyabean oil, The Netherlands	507	343	454	625	338	544	1005	757
Sunflower oil, EU	639	366	474	693	392	677	1074	846
Groundnut oil, The Netherlands	1043	570	895	991	714	1060	1404	1337
Cotton, Egypt, (cents/pound)	155	147	226	NA	109	101	170	NA
Cotton, US, (cents/pound)	89	57	82	104	66	59	103	75

Source: United Nations Conference on Trade and Development (UNCTAD).

Note: Prices of sugar and cotton are in US cents/pound, the rest are in US Dollars/ton.

Ghosh (2010) points out that changes in regulations related to spot and futures commodity trading had given a major boost to speculative activities in commodity markets whereby speculators and financial firms—banks, pension funds, and hedge funds—increasingly entered the market in order to profit from short-term changes in prices. It meant that international prices of primary commodities, with a history of volatility, fluctuate more due to speculative activities of large financial firms to the detriment of a large agrarian population in developing economies like India.

In India, where almost 91% of households are marginal, small and medium farmers who cultivate on less than 2 hectares (5 acres) of land, exposure to fluctuations in international prices through greater participation in trade of agricultural commodities will endanger livelihood security of substantial sections of the population in rural areas. In a survey of eight villages across different states of India between 2005 and 2007, it was observed that a significant proportion of households across villages located in different agro-ecological settings with different irrigation and cropping patterns, had negative incomes mainly due to losses suffered in cultivation of agricultural crops. This shows that income generating capacity in agriculture is under serious threat (Swaminathan and Rawal 2011).

Rao and Charyulu's (2007) study on the basis of surveys between 2001 and 2004 conducted in six villages of Andhra Pradesh and Maharashtra found that except for two villages, incomes from crop production were negative for farmer households. This included large landowners. They argued that in 1975–78, when a similar study was conducted in these villages by the International Crops Research Institute for the Semi-Arid Tropics (ICRISAT), incomes from cultivation of agricultural crops were positive in all study villages. Their study brings out the following: first, there has been an increase in net annual household incomes across the study villages between 1975–78 and 2001–04. Second, the importance of agriculture as an income generating activity has gone down in the latter period. Third, not only has the share of agriculture gone down in the latter period, it has been generating losses for crop producing households in most of the study villages in 2001–04. Fourth, except for only one village, absolute incomes from crop production at constant 2001–04 prices, was higher in 1975–78 compared to 2001–04. Thus, the arguments that economic reforms would eliminate the bias against agriculture, thereby improving livelihood security of the rural population remains largely unfulfilled.

Conclusions

It was argued that with the initiation of reforms in 1991–92, the bias against agriculture will be reduced, there will be shift in the terms of trade in its favour, and price incentives will favour producers to increase production. This would enable the producers to increase the surplus from cultivation of agricultural crops that can be ploughed back to make long-term

improvements on land, undertake purchase of machines and farm imple-
ments that raise productivity of land. However, contrary to this expectation, the actual performance of the agricultural sector was not impressive
in the post-reform period in comparison to the pre-reform period. Growth
rates of the agriculture sector as a whole and across major crops culti-
vated in India has deteriorated, as has the importance of agriculture as an
income generating activity. However, the sector remains the main source
of employment in India. This implies that disparity in income generation
between agriculture and other sectors, particularly services, has increased.

Non-price factors such as capital formation in agriculture (with an
important role for irrigation), rural credit, and research and extension services were not given adequate importance in the post-reform period. Share
of agriculture in gross capital formation started to decline in the 1980s,
with no turnaround in the 1990s, the greatest casualty being public capital
formation in agriculture. A similar pattern is witnessed for irrigation, where
share of outlays in GDP and productivity have declined in the post-reform
period. Trends in rural credit show that there has been a steady decline in
rural branches of commercial banks in line with financial liberalisation initiated after reforms. There was a decline in credit–deposit ratio in the 1990s
as compared to 1980s, adversely affecting supply of credit in rural areas.

The increase in the credit–deposit ratio, as well as the share of priority
sector and share of agriculture in total outstanding credit since 2001 were
largely due to definitional changes benefiting large agri-business corporations and large cultivators. Agricultural research and extension are seen to
have been systematically neglected during the reform period. It needs to be
mentioned here that it was neglected prior to the initiation of reforms as
well; this neglect further accentuated after the 1990s.

Expectations regarding improvements in terms of trade for agriculture
did not materialise after the reforms. Besides, agricultural trade liberalisation has exposed domestic producers to the volatilities of international
prices of agricultural commodities that have turned agriculture into an
unviable occupation. Studies carried out in different parts of India, have
also shown that a significant proportion of households were earning

negative incomes from crop production. Neither there has been any significant movement in the terms of trade in favour of agriculture after reforms, nor have the cultivators gained from more exposure to international markets and prices.

References

Ahluwalia, Montek Singh (1994): "India's Economic Reforms," Planning Commission, http://www.planningcommission.gov.in/hindi/aboutus/speech/spemsa/msa012.pdf.

Balakrishnan, Pulapre, Ramesh Golait and Pankaj Kumar (2008): "Agricultural Growth in India Since 1991," Study No 27, Reserve Bank of India.

Chand, Ramesh and Parmod Kumar (2004): "Determinants of Capital Formation and Agriculture Growth: Some New Explorations," *Economic & Political Weekly*, Vol 39, No 52, pp 5611–5616.

Dev, S. Mahendra and Vijay Laxmi Pandey (2013): "Performance and Key Policy Issues in Indian Agriculture," S Mahendra Dev (ed), *India Development Report 2012–13*, India: Oxford University Press, pp 79–94.

Dev, S. Mahendra (2009): "Structural Reforms and Agriculture: Issues and Policies," *Seminar*, Keynote Paper presented at the 92nd Annual Conference of the Indian Economic Association, Bhubaneswar, Odisha, 27–29 December.

Evenson, R.E. and D. Jha (1973): "The Contribution of Agricultural Research System to Agricultural Production in India," *Indian Journal of Agricultural Economics*, Vol 28, No 4, pp 212–230.

Evenson, Robert Eugene, Carl Pray, and Mark W. Rosegrant (1999): "Agricultural Research and Productivity Growth in India," Report No 109, *International Food Policy Research Institute*.

Evenson, R.E. and J. McKinsey (1991): "Research, Extension, Infrastructure and Productivity Change in Indian Agriculture," R.E. Evenson and C.E. Pray (eds), *Research and Productivity in Asian Agriculture*, Cornell University Press.

Ghosh, Jayati (2010): "The Unnatural Coupling: Food and Global Finance," *Journal of Agrarian Change*, Vol 10, No 1, pp 72–86.

Gutierrez, Andrew Paul, Luigi Ponti, Hans R. Herren, Johann Baumgärtner, and Peter E. Kenmore (2015): "Deconstructing Indian Cotton: Weather, Yields and Suicides," *Environmental Sciences Europe*, Vol 27, No 1, pp 1–17.

Kahlon, A.S., H.K. Bal, P.N. Saxena and D.N. Jha (1977): "Returns to Investment in Agricultural Research in India," T.M. Ardt, D.G. Dalrymple and V.W. Ruttan (eds), *Resource Allocation and Productivity in National and International Agricultural Research*, University of Minnesota Press.

Misra, V.N. (1998): "Economic Reforms, Terms of Trade, Aggregate Supply and Private Investment in Agriculture: Indian Experience," *Economic & Political Weekly*, Vol 33, No 31, pp 2105–2109.

Mohan, Rakesh (1974): "Contribution of Research and Extension to Productivity Change in Indian Agriculture," *Economic & Political Weekly*, Vol 9, No 39, pp A97–A104.

NSSO (2014): "Employment and Unemployment Situation of India: NSS 68th Round," National Sample Survey Office, Ministry of Statistics and Programme Implementation.

Planning Commission (2006): "Towards Faster and More Inclusive Growth: An Approach to the 11th Five Year Plan," Planning Commission of India.

Ramachandran, V.K. (2011): "The State of Agrarian Relations in India Today," *Marxist*, Vol 27, No 1–2, pp 51–89.

Ramakumar, R. and Pallavi Chavan (2007): "Revival of Agricultural Credit in the 2000s: An Explanation," *Economic & Political Weekly*, Vol 42, No 52, pp 57–63.

Rao, C.H. Hanumantha (2002): "Sustainable Use of Water for Irrigation in Indian Agriculture," *Economic & Political Weekly*, Vol 37, No 18, pp 1742–1745.

Rao, K.P.C. and D. Kumara Charyulu (2007): "Changes in Agriculture and Village Economies," International Crops Research Institute for the Semi-Arid Tropics, Research Bulletin 21.

Rosegrant, M.W. and R.E. Evenson (1992): "Agricultural Productivity and Sources of Growth in South Asia," *American Journal of Agricultural Economics*, Vol 74, pp 757–791.

Sharma, Devender (2013): "How India Destroyed its Oilseeds Revolution and Became the World's Second Biggest Importer of Edible Oils," http://devinder-sharma.blogspot.in/2013/02/how-india-destroyed-its-oilseeds.html.

Swaminathan, Madhura and Vikas Rawal (2011): "Is India Really a Country of Low Income Inequality? Observations From Eight Villages," *Review of Agrarian Studies*, Vol 1, No 1, pp 1–22.

No Room for Complacency

Can We Afford Build-up of External Liabilities

A.V. Rajwade

Tracing the major changes in the monetary and exchange rate policy post 1991, it is argued that an exchange rate policy with an external account targeting approach is required to arrest the build-up of net external liabilities.

༄༅

Over the 25 years since the balance of payments crisis of 1991, major changes in monetary and exchange rate policies, and reforms in financial markets have been instituted. From a macroeconomic perspective, perhaps the most important were the changes in the external sector; structurally, equally significant were reforms in the stocks, bonds and derivatives markets. That there was need for both is undoubted: as for the first, the crisis itself emphasised the importance; as for the second, the need for changes in market practices was highlighted by the so-called "Securities Scam," which became headline news in April 1992, a little after the balance of payments crisis.

External Account

For a long time, all transactions in foreign exchange and/or with non-residents were governed by the Foreign Exchange Regulation Act (FERA).

The provisions made any violation a criminal offence. There were a plethora of controls on imports; most imports needed a licence; gold imports were banned (though gold continued to be smuggled in); there were product-specific import duties, sometimes very high; exports, once again, attracted product-specific cash (and other) subsidies. Much of the regulatory framework was changed after the crisis; the rupee became convertible for all current account transactions (including gold imports); while many restrictions remained in place for capital account transactions, portfolio investment by non-residents was allowed beginning 1992 and the capital account gradually liberalised.

In due course, FERA was replaced by the Foreign Exchange Management Act (FEMA), and the Reserve Bank of India Act was amended to authorise the central bank to permit and regulate derivatives trading.

There were major changes in the exchange rate policy, which are covered in some detail, later in this article.

Monetary and Interest Rate Policies

While the basic objective of monetary policy has always been inflation control through manipulation of money supply and interest rates by the central bank, until June 1992, all interest rates were prescribed by the Reserve Bank of India (RBI). The type of deposit facility which a bank could offer, period of deposits, interest payable on different types of deposits, interest rates on loans and advances, were all subject to RBI regulations and directives: commercial banks had no discretion to change them. Government bonds were issued at coupons fixed by the RBI, and sold at par. Coupons were generally lower than what voluntary investors would have demanded, in order to keep the cost of government borrowing low. There was a captive market in the form of commercial banks which were subject to very high statutory liquidity reserve requirements which were prescribed by the central bank: in other words, banks had to invest a given proportion of their net demand and time liabilities in government securities. (At one time, the statutory liquidity ratio [SLR] requirements were as high as 38.5%.) There was also a ceiling on the interbank call money rates. In this regime of interest rate repression, banks were naturally anxious to increase income.

When even the sky-high SLR was insufficient to meet the government's borrowing requirements, the RBI used to purchase these securities in the primary market: in other words, there was automatic monetisation of government deficit. This apart, the government was also using a system of so-called ad hoc treasury bills, which too were purchased by the central bank. The result of tightly regulated and uneconomic interest rates was that the secondary market in government securities was not very liquid.

The Market Infrastructure

Government securities used to be held in the form of entries in the so-called "subsidiary general ledger" (SGL) maintained by the Reserve Bank. The SGL accounts were maintained not bank-wise but individual issue-wise. Again, when a trade took place, there were often delays in the corresponding entries being made in the SGL account: the result was that it was very difficult for banks to reconcile their books with the entries in the SGL account.

A few years before 1992, public sector undertakings had started issuing bonds in the market. There was often a delay of a year or longer between the issue and the buyers getting bond certificates: the only document of ownership the subscriber would have in the interim was a letter of allotment. This system was not very different from that in the stock market. Again, the letters of allotment could not be readily split into tradeable lots.

Apart from corporate bonds, another instrument which became popular with commercial banks for investment purposes was the unit of the Unit Trust of India's US 64 mutual fund scheme, after dividends on US 64 were made tax-free. The problem in trading in US 64, however, was that every transfer required the payment of a stamp duty.

Interbank repos in government securities also became established as banks used these to finance shortfalls in cash reserves through repos of SLR securities held in excess of statutory reserve requirements. The counterparty was a bank with surplus cash reserves, on which it otherwise earned no return. By being counterparty to repos it earned income on the surplus. Such transactions were particularly large on "reporting Fridays," the days on which banks had to meet the stipulated SLR and cash reserves. Repos were also being done with nonbank clients in order to give them returns higher than the regulated bank deposit interest rates.

As the repo transactions increased in volume, and given the operational weaknesses of the RBI's SGL system, bank receipts (BRs) came to be used in support of repos, in preference to actual sale/purchase entries in the RBI's subsidiary general ledgers. The BRs were extinguished on completion of the repo's second leg.

In the secondary market, government and corporate bonds were not traded on the floor of an exchange but in an over-the-counter (OTC) market in which brokers played an intermediary role. One major weakness of the system was that once a deal was done, the broker would issue a sale/purchase note, without disclosing the counterparty's identity. In other words, unlike in the interbank foreign exchange market, no contracts were exchanged between the principals, i.e., the buyer and the seller: the broker's note was the only document evidencing that a trade had taken place.

The broker's commission was often not separately disclosed in the deal slip but was included in the price or had to be otherwise settled. Where the brokerage was included in the price this meant that the price quoted to the counterparty to a transaction was different. In this case the buyer bank would issue a cheque in favour of the seller bank, which included the broker's commission/margin. Brokers preferred to have accounts with banks which adopted a practice of crediting cheques in their favour to the broker's account—and preferred them as buyers. In some cases such credits were given to broker accounts on the basis of instructions of the issuer of the cheque to that effect. Finally, settlement of securities transactions and physical delivery of cheques, securities SGL forms/BRs, etc., between counterparties was often allowed to be effected by the brokers.

In short, while practices varied from bank to bank, brokers aware of the laxity in systems/procedures were in a position to take advantage by abusing them.

The "Securities Scam"

The system weaknesses allowed some unscrupulous brokers to divert the funds generated by ostensible sale of government securities to the stock market to finance their speculative transactions. The market boomed: the index went up from 950 at the beginning of 1991 to 4500 by April 1992–at a time when the economy was in the midst of a balance of payments crisis!

The bubble burst in April 1992 when the Times of India reported a huge overdraft in the account of a broker with State Bank of India, and that SBI was unable to reconcile its holdings of government securities with the entries in the SGL of the RBI. The stock market crashed and many banks, both Indian and foreign, incurred large losses in what came to be called the "Securities Scam".

The scam was investigated by both the RBI, and considering its scale, also by a Parliamentary Committee. Clearly, major reforms were needed in both the interest rate policy of the RBI and the systems and procedures in the government securities market.

The Reforms

In June 1992, the coupons on new issues were raised to near-market levels, and primary issues were sold in "auctions".

The system of Primary Dealers (PDs) was introduced in India in 1995, with the objective of developing underwriting and market making capabilities in the primary and secondary markets in G-Secs. PDs are also an effective conduit for the central bank's open market operations.

On the market infrastructure side, the major reforms included the introduction of trading on a Negotiated Dealing System with an order matching procedure. Later this was converted to an electronic platform (NDS-OM). The RBI's SGL was also computerized. The formation of the Clearing Corporation of India Ltd. in 2001 to clear and guarantee settlements of interbank foreign exchange and securities trades was the next step.

Another major reform was the introduction of the Market Stabilisation Scheme (MSS) in 2004 to finance sterilization of increase in money supply resulting from RBI's purchases of dollars in the market in pursuance of its exchange rate policy. Traditionally, sterilization was done by sale of government securities from RBI's holdings purchased from its open market operations. When intervention reached levels which, in effect, exhausted RBI's stock, MSS was introduced: in substance it created government securities, not to finance fiscal deficits but for sterilisation purposes, holding the funds in a special account with RBI.

In 2006, the Fiscal Responsibility and Budget Management Act came into force. It prohibited monetising of primary issues. (To be sure, the RBI can still influence yields through its open market operations).

Historically, RBI used the Wholesale Price Index as the measure of inflation. In the last few years, it has started using the Consumer Price Index (CPI) and has been mandated a target range of 4% +/− 2%. A Monetary Policy Committee with three nominees each of the Government and the RBI has been formed to decide the monetary policy and interest rates. In the event of a tie in the members' views, the Governor has a casting vote.

The Stock Market

The Securities and Exchange Board of India (SEBI) was established in 1988. (Before 1988, securities market regulation was in the hands of the Controller of Capital Issues, in the Ministry of Finance). It was given statutory powers after the crisis through the SEBI Act, 1992. It regulates not only stock exchanges but also mutual funds; in 2015, the Forward Markets Commission, which was the regulator for commodity trading (both spot and futures), was merged with SEBI.

The Bombay Stock Exchange (BSE) is the oldest stock market in Asia and was the largest in India until the National Stock Exchange (NSE) started operations in 1994. One reason for the rapid growth of NSE was that, from the start, it was based on electronic trading, and guaranteed settlements of trades even as the BSE stuck to the age "open outcry" system of trading. It was only the rise of NSE that forced major reforms in BSE.

Exchanges offering trading and guaranteed settlements in commodity trades both spot and in futures, were also established.

Today, the Indian securities market, in terms of its trading, clearing and settlement systems, is comparable to any global market. All traded stocks and corporate bonds are issued and held in dematerialised form.

While the first mutual fund in India, the Unit Trust of India, was established in 1963, it was only in the 1980s that a few other public sector entities were allowed to set up mutual funds. Private sector funds were allowed only after the crisis of 1991. Today, the Indian investor is served by a large number of mutual funds promoted by entities in both the public and private sectors. They offer investment opportunities in stocks, bonds, money market instruments, etc.

Derivatives Market

Historically, the only "derivatives" in the Indian markets were (a) the so-called "Badla" on BSE, in effect, a mechanism to postpone delivery to the next settlement, and (b) the forward contract in the foreign exchange market. The trading of stock index futures started on NSE in 2000, followed by index options in the next year. Other derivatives followed in later years, including futures and options in individual stocks and currencies.

In the foreign exchange market, cross currency options (i.e., not involving the rupee) were allowed in 1994: authorized dealers would buy them in the global market to sell them to clients in India. This was followed by foreign currency interest rate derivatives, INR swaps (1997) and interest rate derivatives (1999). USD/INR options were introduced in 2003, and "structured products" a couple of years later.

Exchange Rate Policy

India was a founder member of the International Monetary Fund. During the fixed exchange rate era, the intervention currency of the Reserve Bank was the British pound; the RBI ensured maintenance of the exchange rate parity by selling and buying pounds against rupees at fixed rates. After the

collapse of the fixed exchange rate system in 1971 also, the RBI continued to maintain the parity with the pound, with some minor changes; the
exchange rates against other currencies were determined through their
cross rates against the pound.

This link with the pound continued until September 1975. By then,
in recognition of the fact that India's trade had substantially diversified in
terms of both currencies and destinations and that, therefore, the link with
the pound was no longer very logical, the rupee's exchange rate was linked
to a basket of currencies. The composition of this basket was kept secret
and the pound continued as the intervention currency. Its exchange rate
against the rupee was so fixed by the RBI daily, and sometimes changed
intra-day, as to ensure that the value of the (secret) basket of currencies
remained within a band of $+/- 2.25\%$ (later $+/- 5\%$) in rupee terms.

The purchasing power parity theory of exchange rates suggests that, to
remain competitive in the global markets, the nominal exchange rate needs
to change to compensate for inflation differentials: this was not possible with
fixed parities. In the early 1980s, the RBI undertook the first ever study of the
real effective exchange rate of the rupee (Joshi 1984). The principal conclu-
sions of the study were that the real effective rate (RER) of the rupee depreci-
ated by 11.5% between 1971 and 1975 and by a further 17% between 1975
and 1979 (perhaps due to the pound's fall in global markets). From 1979 to
1983, however, it showed a sharp 15% appreciation (Rajwade 2010: 7).

There were obvious limitations to the results of the study, given the
product-specific, and very high, import duties which were part of the full
cost of imports, and export subsidies. In any case, it seems the RBI started
to depreciate the rupee in nominal terms beginning late 1983. This policy
continued up to June 1991.

July 1991 to March 1993

In the first week of July 1991, a two-step devaluation of the rupee was engi-
neered; the subsidies for exports were discontinued; and the intervention
currency changed to the US dollar.

The next major change was the introduction of a liberalised exchange rate management system (LERMS) in March 1992. This introduced a dual exchange rate: out of the receipts of foreign exchange from exports, 60% could be sold in the market at the market rate and the balance had to be surrendered to the Reserve Bank at the official rate. The foreign currency purchased by the RBI through this mechanism was sold to importers of oil (and a few other products) at the official rate.

The market rate was determined by demand and supply and, as can be expected, the rupee was at a discount in the market, as compared to the official rate. In March 1993, this system was abolished and a single market-determined rate is since applicable for all transactions. In practice, the RBI influences the rate by buying/selling dollars in the market.

The capital account was also liberalized allowing foreign portfolio investment in the equity market.

After March 1993

Since the introduction of the market-determined exchange rate in 1993, the central bank has consistently maintained that it does not "target" any specific rate or level; and it intervenes in the market only to smoothen volatility. However, the measure of volatility has never been defined in terms of periodicity of changes or the measurement quantum—absolute numbers or their natural logarithms, etc.

The IMF's *Annual Report on Exchange Arrangements and Exchange Restrictions 2014* currently describes our arrangement as being of "type"— "floating regime (market determined rates)", and in the (sub)category "floating," that is, not "free floating".

I have tried to analyse the actual real effective exchange rate (REER) from 1993 from published data (see Table 1, 1993–94 to 2005–06, and Table 2, 2004–05 to 2015–16): the former table is based on the wholesale price index as the measure of inflation, and the latter uses the consumer price index. (I could not get data for the whole period with a single measure of inflation.) The two measures can differ significantly, both directionally

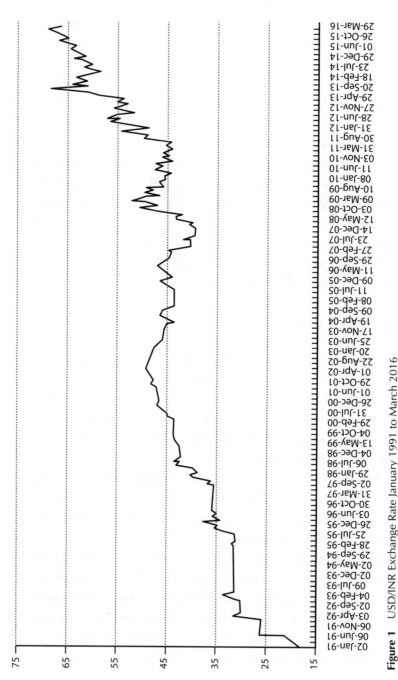

Figure 1 USD/INR Exchange Rate January 1991 to March 2016

Source: Internal Database, A.V. Rajwade and Co. Pvt. Ltd.

Table 1   Real Effective Exchange Rate Trade Weighted
(36 Currency)

Financial Year	WPI-based REER
1993–94	100.0
1994–95	104.3
1995–96	98.2
1996–97	96.8
1997–98	100.8
1998–99	93.0
1999–00	96.0
2000–01	100.1
2001–02	100.9
2002–03	98.2
2003–04	99.6
2004–05	100.1
2005–06	107.6

Base Year: 1993–94.

Table 2   Real Effective Exchange Rate Trade Weighted
(36 Currency)

Financial Year	CPI-based REER
2004–05	100.0
2005–06	102.4
2006–07	100.8
2007–08	109.2
2008–09	99.7
2009–10	103.9
2010–11	112.7
2011–12	110.3
2012–13	105.6
2013–14	103.3
2014–15	108.9
2015–16	112.1

Base Year: 2004–05.

and quantitatively, particularly when the CPI and WPI gap widens as it has in recent years—and it is not clear which REER (36 country, 6 country, WPI or CPI, etc.) is more closely correlated to our trade performance. This apart, the weight assigned to each currency is based on the bilateral trade with that country. This methodology suffers from one major limitation: it does not reflect competition in third countries. For example, Bangladesh may be our major competitor in garment exports in global markets and therefore the taka's exchange rate important for our competitiveness. However, if the bilateral trade with that country is negligible, it may not get any weight in our basket. I have often wondered whether an invoicing currency based REER may be a better measure of competitiveness. Again, commodity prices, the oil price for example, do not depend on the producer country's exchange rate—but on demand/supply of the commodity in global markets.

Subject to these limitations, the data in Tables 1 and 2 suggest that for the first 15 years or so after the introduction of the floating rate, the rupee was fairly stable in REER terms, but has been more volatile in the last seven/eight years, with greater tolerance of rupee appreciation. (Volatility in 2007–08 and 2008–09 was influenced by the global financial crisis of 2008).

This apart, we need to look at the impact of the exchange rate policy on our external account, on both flow (current account) and stock (International Investment Position) bases.

The External Account

Table 3 summarises the data on both flow and stock bases from 2000–01.

It will be seen that we recorded a surplus on current account in the early years of this century, and the deficits, on both trade and current account in other years, were modest until 2006–07. Reserves were built up to $ 200 bn by the end of fiscal 2006–07, and further to $ 310 bn by the end of the next year. In broad terms, the policy seems to have been to intervene in the market to the extent necessary to maintain the rupee at a targeted level,

Table 3 External Account (in USD bn)

Financial Year	Trade Deficit	Current Account Balance	Current Account Balance net of Remittances	Reserves	Net Investment Position
2000–01	−12.5	−2.7	−15.5	42.3	N.A.
2001–02	−11.6	3.4	−12.0	54.1	N.A.
2002–03	−10.7	6.3	−10.0	76.1	N.A.
2003–04	−13.7	14.1	−7.5	113.0	N.A.
2004–05	−33.7	−2.5	−23.0	141.4	−41.8
2005–06	−51.9	−9.9	−34.4	151.6	−47.9
2006–07	−61.8	−9.6	−39.4	199.2	−61.4
2007–08	−91.5	−15.7	−57.4	309.7	−51.2
2008–09	−119.5	−27.9	−72.5	252.0	−66.6
2009–10	−118.2	−38.2	−90.0	279.1	−158.4
2010–11	−127.3	−48.1	−101.2	304.8	−218.9
2011–12	−189.8	−78.2	−141.6	294.4	−249.5
2012–13	−195.7	−88.2	−152.5	292.1	−307.3
2013–14	−147.6	−32.4	−97.9	304.2	−331.6
2014–15	−144.9	−26.8	−93.1	341.7	−363.0
2015–16*	−105.6	−21.9	−70.0	359.80	−362

Note: *upto/as on December.

and sterilise the resultant money supply by selling government securities. At one time (February 2004), when the Reserve Bank exhausted the stock of securities in its books, it formulated a Market Stabilisation Scheme to create artificial short-dated securities for sterilization purposes.

The general policy focus of intervention and sterilization continued in 2007–08, but the capital inflows were so large that the rupee appreciated sharply in the second half of the year. It fell in 2008–09 after the financial crisis and capital outflows, has moved erratically since then, but with a strong bias towards appreciation. Overall, one wonders whether, in recent years, the exchange rate policy is being used partly to control inflation. There are countries which use floating exchange rates as part of the "inflation-targeting framework", though India has not been so described in the IMF Report (IMF 2014).

The External Account after 2007–08

The appreciation of the rupee seems to have been an important factor in the sharp increase in India's merchandise trade deficit in recent years, from $ 61.8 bn in 2007–08 to a high of almost $ 200 bn in 2012–13. It fell by around $ 50 bn in the next year (2013–14) partly because of lower imports and a fall in the international gold price. In the next year, the oil price dropped from $ 110 in June to $ 50 by December 2014, and further in 2015–16. Oil is our single largest import, but the sharp fall in oil price has not led to an improvement in the trade balance over the last two years: it is perhaps not coincidental that the REER index has moved from 103.3 in 2013–14 to 112.1 in 2015–16.

In short, the REER data suggests that, over the last seven years or so, while the volatility has been controlled, the level has been determined more by capital flows, with little weight being given to the need to encourage manufacturing in general and the tradeable goods sector in particular. The result has been that the contribution of manufacturing to GDP has been stagnant for a long time. Most other fast growing Asian economies had substantially increased the contribution of manufacturing to GDP, in particular China.

Broadly speaking, the current account balance can be looked at from three different perspectives: (a) gap between savings and investments; (b) output loss on the external account; and (c) its impact on the international investment position.

Savings–Investment Gap

It is sometimes argued that the current account balance is determined by the savings/investment gap in an economy, and that exchange rate has little to do with it. This is a debatable proposition: savings/investment are not a given, but are influenced by the exchange rate. For example, an appreciated currency increases consumption particularly of imported goods and services; reduces corporate profitability particularly in the tradeables sector; all these reduce savings—personal, corporate and government. Thus the exchange rate not only directly impacts the competitiveness of the tradeables sector in both global and domestic markets, but indirectly also the savings in the economy.

Output Loss

It is often argued that a current account deficit of 1–1.5% is "sustainable". The reason why the deficit is reported in GDP terms is that it represents a corresponding deficit of domestic output: indeed, this could well be the reason why the convention came into being. The other side is that for this we need to look at the current account deficit net of "secondary income", principally private remittances which are not "earnings" of the domestic economy. In our case, this is as high as 3.5/4% of GDP; in other words, the output loss on the external account is as high as 5% of GDP!

Another problem in the conventional way of reporting the deficit, in absolute terms or as a percentage of GDP, is that it does not highlight the number as a percentage of the income. For example, the deficit of $24.5 bn (net of secondary income) in Q2 of fiscal 2015–16, is the difference between credits of $ 110.2 and debits of $ 134.7 bn: this is almost a quarter of our earnings.

International Investment Position

This quarterly report was introduced a few years back and, to my mind, is particularly relevant for looking at the vulnerability of an economy to capital outflows (see Table 3). Over the last 7-odd years the net negative index of industrial production (IIP) has gone up seven times from $ 50 bn to $ 350 bn, despite the record high level of reserves, thanks to persistent deficits on the current account, and their easy financeability so far through build-up of liabilities.

The "record" level of reserves suggests to some that we have a "bullet proof" balance sheet on the external account. But the "quality", as distinct from the "quantity", of the reserves gives a different picture: they are not built out of "retained earnings" (or current account surpluses) but by a build-up of external liabilities. Out of the latter, something like $ 80 bn consists of debt maturing within a year, and another $ 220 bn (end-September 2015) of portfolio capital which can go out when circumstances change. It is worth emphasizing that this level of liabilities is despite the "subsidy" of a few hundred billion dollars over the last seven years, in the form of private remittances.

An Exchange Rate Targeting Approach?

We have recently adopted an inflation target as the single point agenda of the central bank. This may well bias policymakers towards an overvalued rupee to keep the cost of imports and hence inflation down. The question is how long we can afford a further build-up of net external liabilities, with all its implications. Do we need an external account target approach—a current account balance, *net of secondary income,* of +/− x% of GDP? And, an exchange rate policy to meet this target?

Remember that the proximate cause of the 1991 crisis was a sharp rise in oil prices following Iraq's invasion of Kuwait—after the build-up of external liabilities over many years. By definition, "Minsky Moments"[1] can never be predicted!

Note

1. "Minsky moment" refers to "the point at which excess debt sparks a financial crisis". According to the economist Hyman Minsky, who studied this phenomenon, "such moments arise naturally when a long period of stability and complacency eventually leads to the buildup of excess debt and overleveraging". (John Mauldin, 'The Market Is Headed For A 'Minsky Moment'—It Can Happen Quickly, Too', Forbes, 20 June 2017, available at https://www.forbes.

com/sites/johnmauldin/2017/06/20/the-market-is-headed-for-a-minsky-moment-it-can-happen-quickly-too/#759cb7a5dd38 [accessed on 4 July 2017]).

References

IMF (2014): *Annual Report on Exchange Arrangements and Exchange Restrictions 2014*, International Monetary Fund, Washington, October.

Joshi, Vijay (1984): "The Nominal and Real Effective Exchange Rate of the Indian Rupee 1971–83," Occasional Papers, Reserve Bank of India, June.

Rajwade, A.V. (2010): *Cash and Derivatives Markets in Foreign Exchange*, New Delhi: Tata McGraw-Hill.

A-Meri-India

A Note from the Land of Frustrated Aspirants

Aseem Shrivastava

Indian economy and society are facing a tumultuous start to the 21st century. Statistics may show record-breaking growth rates since 1991. Yet, the truth is that formal employment, especially in the corporate sector, has been stagnant, leading to mounting demands for caste-based reservation for government jobs. India is now, effectively, an outpost of global finance. We have preyed on our own culture and ecology, while the economy we chose to import hides our torn social fabric. Beneath the glitter that our politicians wish to plug is the ugly truth: cultural colonisation is at a historic peak, while we march confidently towards ecocide.

ஐஒஓஐ

Winning is not everything. It is the only thing.
                    —Vice Lombardi, American football coach (Dure [2015])

I expect either the United States singly or a combination of the United States and the British Commonwealth to re-establish and rejuvenate the foreign domination of India.

                    —Nirad C. Chaudhuri (1997: 58)

In the race that is "New India," everyone can come first at the same time.

How many Virat Kohlis can the Indian cricket team accommodate at most, at a time? The right answer: as many young, ambitious male cricketers as there are in India. This is the elementary takeaway for our youth from prime-time television. Do not let a trivial number like 11 stop you from reaching for the sky.

Picture a scene still very familiar from one of India's rural roads. A train is expected to pass through a level crossing. Both sides of the level crossing are now packed with vehicles. The spaces on either side of the track resemble rival armies in battle formation. As soon as the train is in sight, almost in unison (as if responding to a battle call) engines are revved up. As soon as the train has passed, the barriers are lifted and the road reopens. Thus begins the war-of-way, an expected chaos wherein drivers from either side of the road try to outdo each other in making the crossing first.

Something like the chaos of this rail crossing is what appears to be happening to Indian economy and society in this tumultuous start to the 21st century. Possibly over a few hundred million working people, mostly young and restless, are vying for jobs that are not even appearing in the tens of millions. However, such is the despairing fever of "aspirational India" that each of the hopefuls has been led to believe that they are among the "chosen ones" who will "one day" make the cut. Mass youth frustration is written deep into the script of the Indian reform-era economy, with tectonic implications for politics and society. If these are discussed at all in the media, euphemisms are deployed.

"Amerindia," or "A-Meri-India," is the name I have given to the country we now live in, given that our children and grandchildren are even more subject to American rule (via global corporate-controlled markets and cultural invasion) than our foreparents ever were subject to during British rule. Ironically, during the decades since independence, psychological colonisation has only intensified (especially during 1985–91), instead of getting attenuated, with time.

Some data from the Government of India's *Economic Survey* will illustrate the point about frustrated aspirations with stark clarity. The taxpaying formal (organised) sector, home to the most coveted jobs in the economy, accounts for well under 7% of all jobs; a fact of enduring obstinacy remarkable in itself. Over 93% of jobs are in "informal" occupations like construction, domestic work, street-hawking, and farming. Despite record-breaking growth rates since 1991, especially since 2003, formal employment in India's organised sector has been resiliently stagnant, rising imperceptibly from 26.7 million in 1991 to just under 30 million after almost a quarter century of growth.

If we account for the fact that government and public sector jobs have declined (due to mechanisation and divestment) from 19 million to just under 18 million, it turns out that the private corporate sector has generated a net increase of formal employment for about 4 million workers. This has happened over a period during which the total workforce has increased by over 200 million! Even if we charitably assume that chain-multiplier effects generated by growth in the organised sector have implications for employment in the unorganised sector, and make a liberal assumption that 10 jobs in the unorganised economy result for every job generated in the organised mainstream economy, the sum total of the contribution made by the private corporate sector to the generation of jobs across the country over a period of 25 years is 44 million; well under a quarter of the asking rate (Ministry of Finance 2016).[1]

It Pays To Be 'Backward'

Few have even discussed at length the fundamental difference between jobs and livelihoods. Nor is there an attempt to relate the failure of the private sector to generate jobs to the rising demand for reservations in public sector and government jobs around the country. Most analyses have stayed shy of pointing to the impossibility of aspirations (a word that entered public "development" discourse only in the 21st century, thanks to the marketing divisions of the megacorps) and of seeing the critical importance of the phenomenon of land-based caste power getting overtaken in rural India by lower landless castes who gain a measure of social mobility through market opportunities or, more commonly, through government jobs reserved for them.

For all the hoopla made about the imperative for economic growth in order to generate jobs, the data reveals that most of the growth has been job-destroying (millions have been laid off over the years since 1991), just like it has been in China and much of the rest of the world. Given rapidly automating technology, the outlook for the future, both short- and long-term, is equally bleak (ILO 2016).

The drying up of jobs in the mainstream corporate-led economy means that there is suddenly far greater demand for government positions and for caste-based reservations for such jobs. When I met Bihar Chief Minister Nitish Kumar on the eve of the assembly elections in November 2015, he told me that, on average, some 2–3 lakh people apply for 2,000 positions in the Bihar government. (He took some satisfaction in the fact that in Gujarat the ratio of applicants to jobs is two to three times higher!)

In Uttar Pradesh, stories have been recorded of the struggle for government jobs for sweepers, wherein many college graduates have been known to apply. Again, the ratio of applicants to the number of jobs was in the range of 100:1. Local Dalits were so disconcerted by this that they asked for reservation of sweeper jobs for themselves.

There is an incentive for every caste, no matter how high up in the traditional hierarchy, to get classified as "backward" in order to secure preference in reservations. The Jat agitation in Haryana has already taken many lives. The same is true of the Patidar *andolan* in Gujarat. Kapus in Andhra Pradesh, Marathas in Maharashtra, Gujjars in Rajasthan, and Ahoms in Assam are all also asking for the same thing: quotas for their community.

These landowning OBCs (or those belonging to the "Other Backward Classes") have been traditionally powerful in rural India. They have derived benefits from the fact that the government abolished agricultural and land taxation after independence. They have also taken advantage of free or highly subsidised electricity, fertilisers and canal irrigation.

However, economic growth in the reform era has generated a new middle class that has reduced the hold of the traditional landowning castes. Many Patidars, Kapus and others have seized the opportunities of the new economy and done well for themselves. But, many more have been left behind, surpassed by an aspirant class that often includes lower castes who have taken advantage of reservations in education and jobs. Sweepers employed by the government may be from the lower castes, but they are earning more than many of the landowning castes above them in the traditional hierarchy.

India's political leaders and policymakers have been arguing for years that farmers should leave agriculture since there is no money in it, and move to more "productive" occupations. (The money magically reappears in agriculture, of course, when global agribusiness corporations enter it.) Under the tutelage of international financial institutions, the economics of agriculture has been rendered adverse over a period of time to induce farmers to quit farming. This has made way for food multinationals and facilitated land acquisition for real estate, infrastructure, mining and industry. Should we be surprised then that in the last two decades the country has witnessed the fact that 3.5 lakh people who chose to stick to agriculture committed suicide?[2]

The promise being made to the millions, especially the youth leaving farming households, is of industrial and service jobs in the cities, of a place in the metropolitan economy of the country, and of global lifestyles. This promise is far from being met. However, it exists as a real fantasy in the minds of millions of young Indians.

It was a young and desperate India that voted for a man desperate to become Prime Minister of the country two years ago. The flood tide of support from urban and urbanising youth, which was crucial in bringing Narendra Modi and the Bharatiya Janata Party (BJP) to office, is more than likely to turn against him in 2019, unless he achieves the impossible and in fact delivers the promised jobs.

The data is not on his side.

India 2041

Let us conduct a thought experiment and examine what would have to become true if every Indian finance minister's dream for India (and it is fundamentally the same development dream for all of them: an Indian edition of the American dream) were to be realised in the next quarter century;

as many years into the future as it has taken for India to get here from the 1991 reforms. The dream is for India to become a fully "developed" powerful modern nation.

To spell it out precisely, not only would poverty have become a thing of the distant past by 2041, and prosperity and well-being the general norm, some 75–80% of India's population of 1.6 billion, which is to say some 1.2–1.28 billion people (the entire population of India at the moment) will find itself living in cities. Finance ministers in both Congress-led United Progressive Alliance as well as BJP-led National Democratic Alliance governments have shared this hope.[3]

What would this mean in concrete terms? In urban and metropolitan India, it would mean that a miraculous 200 million additional jobs will be created in the next quarter century, at the rate of 25 million new jobs every year. As pointed out earlier, we are already an order of magnitude behind the asking rate of job creation for the rapidly growing workforce since 1991. It would also mean that our cities are suddenly able to provide the enormous infrastructure—of clean air and water, sanitation and power, roads and communication, housing and security—for some 800 million more people! Smart cities, anyone?

In the countryside, such a vision entails equally heroic achievements. If over three-quarters of India is to be urban by 2041, and villagers have been dissuaded from agriculture, it will be a profound epistemic break from the past, the like of which has never happened in India's history: a whole generation of young Indians would have been reared without any knowledge of manual agriculture. This has the widest imaginable implications. Consider just a few:

(a) It would mean that agriculture would be virtually fully mechanised, as in the "developed" world. To fire the threshers, combine harvesters, and other agricultural machinery would make gargantuan demands on energy resources. Even if only half the energy is drawn from fossil fuels (itself a heroic ask), it would make the most severe demands on the world's remaining oil and coal reserves, in an era dominated by peak oil, and approaching "peak coal". Where will these fossil fuels come from? A good fraction will have to be imported with increasingly scarce foreign exchange reserves, provided countries are still as willing to sell these fuels.

(b) It could be argued that India, now a wealthy country, will import food. Again, the scarcity of foreign exchange might be the operative constraint. It is worth keeping in view that India's exports have been declining steadily for a year and a half at the time of writing, and we have had only two years of trade surplus during the last four decades! One must also reckon with the prospect of bartering away the foundations of our food security to nations who will presumably sell us food or the fuel to grow it.

Even if India finds the foreign exchange in 2041, will there be countries left on earth willing and able to supply food for, possibly, over half a billion people? Is there an agro-ecological substitute for the Indo–Gangetic plains on earth?

(c) Finally, one would have to consider the fact that this level of fossil-fuel-driven agriculture would make extraordinary demands on climate space precisely in an era when the latter will be shrinking virtually exponentially. Compared to early developers, India's industrialisation is taking place in vastly altered conditions, inhibiting modernisation. The shortfall of resources (both inputs as well as pollution and climate space, saturation of global markets (in terms of effective demand), industrial automation/robotisation, limited but precise skill requirements in 21st century industry and services (making many in the aspirant class effectively unemployable, as is the refrain from so many corporations), and the political constraint of a democracy are only the tip of the iceberg.

So far as we have been able to ascertain, India is the only instance in all of history of a country of significant size trying to industrialise, modernise and urbanise under conditions of universal adult franchise, making the forcible movement of large human populations very difficult. Suffice it to say that the only adjective such a "developmentalist" vision merits is "absurd". Will capitalism and development be the next victims of the interrogation done by Indian democracy?[4]

Haves, Have-nots, Have-lots

> It would be folly to assume that an Indian Rockefeller would be better than the American Rockefeller. Impoverished India can become free, but it will be hard for any India made rich through immorality to regain its freedom ... money renders a man helpless.
>
> —Mahatma Gandhi (2010: 89)

One reason India is in such a sorry ecological, cultural, economic and political mess today is because of our near-total intellectual failure to grasp the big picture of things as they have been unfolding for a generation. Today, a drive from the airport of any major Indian city to the city centre is likely to reveal the open secret of the Indian "developmental" vision to an attentive observer. This is what one may justly call "the developer's view" of development. Unlikely to ever meet the pages of a development textbook, such a vision is all about luxury living in every conceivable dimension. Billboards advertise homes in apartment complexes with tag lines free of irony, like: "an epitome of beauty, serenity and colonial charm," "Venice in Greater Noida," "Golf and live in paradise," and so on.

By no means are these idle fantasies. For three-dimensional proof one only need be familiar with some of the quite ordinarily luxurious new homes in Palm Meadows in Bengaluru or Cleo County in Noida.

Behind these "developments" are some of the most powerful and politically influential people in the country: property dealers, land speculators, realtors, builders, developers; the men whose Audis, BMWs and Jaguars race on our city streets. Often such people double up as politicians themselves, representing their constituencies in state assemblies and Parliament. India is the haven of political entrepreneurship in the 21st century.

It is this model of "development"—which structurally excludes the vast majority of Indians, and which entirely reinforces and is founded on colonial premises—that will increasingly be questioned by the frustrated aspirants to "New India". The haves (even more than the have-nots who have been beaten into the earth) are seeking their share of the creamy pie which, so far, has been restricted preponderantly to the have-lots.[5]

Marching towards Ecocide?

If the reigning plank of policies persists for another generation, the eco-logical dismemberment of the subcontinent is a foregone conclusion; the floods, fires, and droughts of recent summers being early warning signals of times to come. It is necessary to state that the agro-ecological basis of this civilisation is now in mortal peril. In a little-noticed tract on the Visva-Bharati University, written almost a century ago, Rabindranath Tagore (2004: 75–76) wrote:

> [B]efore Asia is in a position to co-operate with the culture of Europe, she must base her own structure on a synthesis of all the different cultures which she has. When, taking her stand on such a culture, she turns toward the West, she will take, with a confident sense of mental freedom, her own view of truth, from her own vantage-ground, and open a new vista of thought to the world. *Otherwise, she will allow her priceless inheritance to crumble into dust, and, trying to replace it clumsily with feeble imitations of the West, make herself superfluous, cheap and ludicrous. If she thus loses her individuality and her specific power to exist, will it in the least help the rest of the world?* Will not her terrible bankruptcy involve also the Western mind? If the whole world grows at last into an exaggerated West, then such an illimitable parody of the modern age will die, crushed beneath its own absurdity [emphasis added].

I believe it is extremely important to invoke such writers of unim-peachable integrity as Nirad Chandra Chaudhuri, Mahatma Gandhi and Rabindranath Tagore, who will hold us to vital values in the recession nowadays. It scarcely bears mention that the timely warning issued by them went, and still goes, remarkably unheeded by their countrymen, especially its so-called educated elites. We have now created a country that has more

"Americans" living in it than are to be found in the land they take inspiration from.

In trying to meet the impossible promise of letting a million new people enter, mentally, the globalised metropolitan economy every month from the ranks of aspirational India—selling them the sky itself in order to carry on with a vaingloriously triumphant business-as-usual attitude—our leaders are not only showing a dismal absence of imagination (especially indigenous imagination), they are in fact radically transforming Indian society and culture for the worse. Mimicking the patterns of the "mother country," we have now before us a winner-takes-all economy, led by young and virile role models like Virat Kohli and Kangana Ranaut; the erotic innuendos never coincidental in a world cognitively dominated by the messaging of 24/7/365 aggressive marketing. Society and culture are but forms of collateral damage to such an invasive economy.

Much violence is to come on account of this culturally corrosive historical process unfolding before us, threatening the constitutional polity of the country like never before. India was never more psychologically colonised than it is today. Even as a thoroughly specious and vainglorious variety of corporate "nationalism" is on show, people's patriotic credentials are under unprecedented scrutiny by those who continue to betray the heritage of the land through systematic persistence and reinforcement of the policies of their predecessors, claiming monopoly on the legacy of India's cultures.[6]

Never was the country ruled more by non-resident Indians (NRIs) and resident non-Indians (RNIs) than it is today. For, make no mistake, Modi's rapidly digitising India is but an upgraded version of the dream of one of his predecessors; a comparison with whom, given his political rhetoric, would surely embarrass him. Let us remind ourselves that we now live in Rajiv Gandhi's utopia. Did he not, after his electoral victory by a record margin in 1985, deploy the slogan that he would be "taking India into the 21st century" on the wings of information technology? He would be surely delighted to learn today that information technology now rules the fantasy-filled Indian imagination, as it does the imagination of few other cultures or polities.

This is an era of nested eras. Long periods of history that began decades, sometimes centuries, ago are converging into a climax in these turbulent decades of the 21st century. In this "longue durée" perspective, the following dates are critical: 1492 (Columbian voyage to "India"), 1600 (founding of the East India Company), 1757 (the decisive Battle of Plassey and the beginning of Company rule in Bengal), 1857 (the inauguration of British Crown rule in India), 1947 (formal Indian independence), 1985–91 (the birth of A-Meri-India/Amerindia, following Rajiv Gandhi's tech-push and the International Monetary Fund-led reforms beginning June 1991).

India is now a proud outpost of global finance, preying faster every day on its own culture and ecology, even as the imported economy (true to former British Prime Minister Margaret Thatcher's dismissal of the very notion of society) has all but eclipsed human society itself, apart from failing to redeem the jobs promise.

One can only hope and pray that the cultural confidence of our civilisation will revive, as Tagore had hoped, soon enough to not only protect India from the worst socio-ecological damages of breakneck globalisation, but also play the role of the world's ecological pioneer, instead of the "superpower" it has somehow come to believe it is destined to become one day (swallowing perhaps a canard started by Wall Street). India has now become an embarrassing case of voluntary colonialism. It is for India to bring this to a final end and recover the authentic currents of its ancient civilisation.[7]

Notes

1. For a detailed analysis of the data on lay-offs and retrenchments, see Aseem Shrivastava and Ashish Kothari (2014), Chapters 2 and 3.
2. For a detailed analysis, see Shrivastava and Kothari (2014), Chapters 6 and 7.
3. See, for instance, Congress Finance Minister P. Chidambaram's view as expressed in an interview (Ray and Chaudhury 2008). Needless to add, the National Democratic Alliance's Finance Minister Arun Jaitley does not believe in a different vision of India's future.

4. A populist, modernising, "developing" democracy finds itself unable to articulate in the public domain that the developmentalist project, certainly as currently conceived, is in fact an impossibility. A senior retired professor from the University of Delhi, a brilliant maverick, is said to have opined that if someone had a good theory, they should bring it to India, and we would test it out for them. We did a pretty thorough job on socialism. We are busy these days doing an equally impressive interrogation of democracy. It remains for development (read capitalism) to pass what one might call—with qualified pride—"The Indian test". Needless to add, the odds are well-stacked against the theory, for all the reasons discussed above.

5. See Chapters 6 and 7 of Shrivastava and Kothari (2014), for an analysis of India's internal colonialism.

6. For an elaboration of the oxymoronic concept of "corporate nationalism," please see Shrivastava and Kothari (2014), Chapter 11.

7. For an alternative vision for India's economy/ecology, interested readers are directed to see Shrivastava and Kothari (2014), Part II, and also await the publication of my paper with Elango Rangasamy "Localization and Regionalization of Economies: A Preliminary Sketch for an Ecological Imperative" in a forthcoming volume titled *Alternatives,* edited by Ashish Kothari and K.J. Joy.

References

Chaudhuri, Nirad C. (1997): *Three Horsemen of the New Apocalypse,* New Delhi: Oxford University Press.

Dure, Beau (2015): "Winning Isn't Everything; It's the Only Thing. Right?," *Guardian,* 24 September, viewed on 7 July 2016, https://www.theguardian.com/sport/2015/sep/24/winning-everything-sports.

Gandhi, M.K. (2010): *Hind Swaraj: A Critical Edition,* Suresh Sharma and Tridip Suhrud (eds), New Delhi: Orient BlackSwan.

ILO (2016): *World Employment Social Outlook: Trends 2016,* Geneva: International Labour Organization.

Ministry of Finance (2016): *Economic Survey 2015–16,* Statistical Appendix, Government of India, New Delhi, viewed on 7 July 2016, http://indiabudget.nic.in/survey.asp.

Ray, Shantanu Guha and Shoma Chaudhury (2008): "My Vision Is To Get 85% of India Into Cities," interview with P Chidambaram, *Tehelka*, 31 May, viewed on 7 July 2016, http://archive.tehelka.com /story_main39.asp?filename=Ne310508cover_ story.asp.

Shrivastava, Aseem and Ashish Kothari (2014): *Churning the Earth: The Making of Global India*, New Delhi: Penguin Viking.

Tagore, Rabindranath (2004): "An Eastern University," *Rabindranath Tagore Selected Essays*, Delhi: Rupa & Co, pp 72–94.

About the Contributors

Montek S. Ahluwalia is former deputy chairman of the (erstwhile) Planning Commission and former secretary, Ministry of Finance, Government of India.

Pulapre Balakrishnan teaches at the Ashoka University, Sonepat, India and is senior fellow, Indian Institute of Management, Kozhikode, India.

Anjan Chakrabarti teaches at the Department of Economics, University of Calcutta, India.

Chirashree Das Gupta teaches at the Centre for the Study of Law and Governance, Jawaharlal Nehru University, New Delhi, India.

Shantanu De Roy teaches at the Department of Policy Studies, TERI University, New Delhi, India.

Rajiv Kumar is with the Centre for Policy Research and is also founder director, Pahle India Foundation.

Surajit Mazumdar teaches at the Centre for Economic Studies and Planning, Jawaharlal Nehru University, New Delhi, India.

R. Nagaraj is with the Indira Gandhi Institute of Development Research, Mumbai, India.

Deepak Nayyar is professor emeritus at the Centre for Economic Studies and Planning, Jawaharlal Nehru University, New Delhi, India, and Chairman, Sameeksha Trust, which owns the *Economic & Political Weekly*.

T. Sabri Öncü is an economist from Istanbul, Turkey, currently based in the US.

Prabhat Patnaik is professor emeritus at the Centre for Economic Studies and Planning, Jawaharlal Nehru University, New Delhi, India.

A.V. Rajwade is a currency risk management consultant and financial journalist based in Mumbai, India.

Aseem Shrivastava is a writer and economist based in Delhi, India.

Atul Sood is with the Centre for the Study of Regional Development, Jawaharlal Nehru University, New Delhi, India.